FEAR IN A HANDFUL OF DUST:

Horror as a Way of Life

Other books by Gary A. Braunbeck

Collections:
Things Left Behind
Escaping Purgatory: Fables in Words and Pictures
  (co-authored with Alan M. Clark)
Sorties, Cathexes, and Personal Effects
Graveyard People: The Collected Cedar Hill Stories, Volume 1
From Beneath These Fields of Blood
A Little Orange Book of Odd Stories
x3

Novels:
The Indifference of Heaven
In Hollow Houses
This Flesh Unknown
Isaac Asimov's I-BOTS: Time Was
  (co-written with Steve Perry)

Non-Fiction:
Fear in a Handful of Dust: Horror as a Way of Life

FEAR IN A HANDFUL OF DUST:

Horror as a Way of Life

GARY A. BRAUNBECK

BETANCOURT & COMPANY

Doylestown, Pennsylvania

FEAR IN A HANDFUL OF DUST:
Horror as a Way of Life
An original publication of
Betancourt & Company, Publishers
P.O. Box 301
Holicong, PA 18928-0301
www.wildsidepress.com

FIRST EDITION

Dedication

I would like to thank Alan Rodgers, Crispin Burnham, William Simmons, the gang at Gorezone, and most especially Ron Horsley and Lucy Snyder for their faith, friendship, support, and for going above and beyond the call of duty on my behalf.

This book is dedicated to all of you, with respect and affection.

Except for Ron.

Just to be a pain.

"... I will show you something different from either
Your shadow at morning striding behind you
Or your shadow at evening rising to meet you;
I will show you fear in a handful of dust."
— T.S. Eliot
"The Burial of the Dead"
from *The Wastelands* (1922)

FADE IN: CRAMPED APARTMENT OFFICE — NIGHT

Sitting at the desk is a HORROR WRITER. 40-ish, with way too much gray hair in his beard. He is hunched over his computer keyboard in a position that health guides insist in no uncertain terms is uncomfortable, even dangerous, but he doesn't seem to notice. CAMERA TRACKS in slowly, and we see his hands madly typing away in a self-taught two-finger method that you can just tell has served him well over the years. CAMERA PAUSES on his face, which is wearing a PERPETUAL BEMUSED SCOWL that we will come to know and dread and find endlessly irritating.

HORROR WRITER stops his typing, runs a hand through his hair (which also has too much gray, but what the hell, he figures he's earned it so screw those "Just For Men" hair coloring ads). He looks around the office as if the word he's searching for has skulked off to hide in a corner just to annoy the living shit out of him.

<u>WRITER</u>
(in VOICE-OVER)
I should have done something noble with my life,
like becoming a cesspool cleaner or a CPA ... but,
no, I have to be a goddamn writer.

If this was the opening scene to a movie I was writing, half the effing audience would be home by now. I dunno, maybe it's like everyone says — I'm too hard on myself. Still . . . how in the hell do you make yourself seem interesting to readers who've seen this type of thing a hundred times before. Stephen King nailed it with *Danse Macabre,* but I'm not trying to write another book like that. That would be silly. Stupid. Suicidal. Very hard. Difficult, even. And, besides, he's got that whole "I'm big enough to tie knots in your spine" thing going for him.

He looks around a bit more, can't find where the word is hiding, then sighs loudly, reached for his smokes, remembers that he can't smoke inside, and stares at the screen.

WRITER
I'll bet Stephen King can smoke in *his* office. Lucky bastard.

He looks over to his bookshelves, which contain several books by Stephen King, as well as William Goldman, Carson McCullers, John O'Hara, Eudora Welty, Raymond Carver, Harlan Ellison, M.R. James, Kobo Abe, Ed Gorman, John Cheever, T.C. Boyle, Russell Banks, and about a hundred other writers. He STARES at the King books. His upper lip twitches on the left side.

WRITER
How come we all have to walk in your shadow?

STEPHEN KING BOOKS
That is not our fault, and speaking from the heart, we are sick and tired of always being shat upon and pointed at and blamed for every little thing that goes wrong in other writers' careers. "Oh, if only they didn't pay *so much money* to Stephen King for his books! If only they would recognize that some of *us* are deserving of hefty advances! If only they would recognize that some of us are *just* as brilliant!" Jesus!

What a bunch of whiny, self-pitying, self-indulgent, greedy little resentful toads you are sometimes!

WRITER
I was unaware that you could talk.

BOOKS
Oooh, listen to him, why don't you? "I was unaware . . ." What a shock that is to us! See how we tremble at this revelation? And yet you seem to be taking it so well.

WRTER
It's late and I'm stuck for a good opening; nothing would unnerve me right now.

BOOKS
We could do an interpretive dance number. We've been rehearsing.

WRITER
That's all right.

BOOKS
No, seriously, we've been rehearsing like nobody's business. We can do other things besides take up space on the bestseller lists and raze entire forests. We have an identity outside of the guy who wrote us. Make some room over there and we'll show you a Bob Fosse routine that'll have you —

WRITER
— no, really, you don't need to do this —

BOOKS
— but we insist! We do. You'll never regret this, we swear it! On your deathbed when your grandchildren ask you what was the high point of your life, you'll say it was without a doubt the night *Firestarter* did the forbidden dance with *Hearts In Atlantis* while *On Writing* got all jiggy with *Misery* and —

HORROR WRITER grabs a STRONG BAD DOLL and
THROWS it at *Different Seasons,* hurting that book's feelings and causing it to weep quietly, but with great dignity.

HORROR WRITER mutters an apology to the books,
then turns back toward his computer.

WRITER
(V.O. con't)

I wonder if King ever has his books offer to dance for
him. Nah . . . for him they probably mount a full-
scale production of *La Traviata* . . . or the Broadway
version of *Carrie.*

He shakes his head.

BOOKS

Excuse us, not to be a bother —

WRITER

Too late.

BOOKS

— but we have what we think is a fairly solid if arguably uninspired idea for your opening.

WRITER

This makes me despair. Sincerely. Regardless of what I
do, this will be thought of as just another rip-off of
Danse Macabre.

DANSE MACABRE
(from bookshelf)

Did I *ask* to be dragged into the middle of this? No, I
did not. I was up here, minding my own business,
and bothering who? *No one.* And yet now, suddenly,
here I am at the heart of a controversy, and I gotta
tell you guys, it is tiresome. Leave me out of this, I'm
begging you. Besides, I've seen your dance routine

and trust me, you're better off up here on the shelf.

BOOKS
You always did have a superiority complex.

DANSE MACABRE
Not listening. See? This is me, not listening.

WRITER
(to himself)
I have *got* to start taking my medication again.

BOOKS
Look, this is a book about horror films and horror literature, right?

WRITER
Sort of . . .

BOOKS
"Sort of?" What decisiveness, what direction, what well thought-out structure. It is so very important to have a definite goal in mind. No wonder you have two-way conversations with inanimate objects.

STRONG BAD DOLL
(from floor)
Holy crap! This is really a not-at-all comfortable position I'm in down here, guys —

WRITER and BOOKS
Shut up!

STRONG BAD DOLL
. . . you really ought to call an exterminator to come and kill that stupid crap-for-crap bug up your —

WRITER
(to BOOKS)
— you were saying. . . ?

BOOKS
Since it's a book — okay, okay, a *sort-of* book — about horror movies and horror literature, why not start with something that combines the two?

WRITER
Gimme a 'frinstance.

BOOKS
Start things off like a really pedestrian, self-conscious screenplay. You can open with a shot of the office and this pathetic middle-aged dweeb banging away at his keyboard, then have something truly ridiculous happen to show just how pedestrian it all is, then work your way back around to the dweeb at the computer and move into the book that way. See? Both film and the printed word combine to save your sorry ass.

WRITER
That's a good idea. I think I'll go with that. Yeah — that's a *really* good idea.

BOOKS
That's why we're bestsellers and you're . . . well . . . *not.*

WRITER
Watch the tone and the 'tude.

STRONG BAD DOLL
Uh, I can't seem to breathe, not that anyone cares. . . .

HORROR WRITER leans in toward his computer screen, aware that *Danse Macabre* will always be looking over his shoulder. He is oblivious to the hideous death screams of the DOLL and the self-satisfied smirk of the BOOKS, who really do seem quite pleased with themselves.

DISSOLVE THRU TO:
THE COMPUTER SCREEN,
which reads:

Establishing Shot:
It Was Already Broke When I Got Here

I've eked out what I euphemistically refer to as my living writing fiction for the last sixteen years. I've published somewhere in the neighborhood of two hundred short stories, five novels, half a dozen collections, a handful of not-bad poetry, dozens of film columns and book reviews, and have seen my work nominated for some lovely awards and translated into five languages. I'm forty-three, divorced, on anti-depressants, and am on my third attempt in as many months to quit smoking; I like to watch movies, listen to music, read everything I can lay hands on . . . and write stories — *God,* how I love to write stories. I have no hobbies of which to speak because a full 85% of my time is spent on work, making me one of the most single-minded, hyper-focused, evangelically monomaniacal little writin' pricks you'd never want to meet. I have a terrific agent by the name of Richard Curtis, more grey hair than I'd like, twenty pounds I need to lose, and a cat named Monte who will eat anything that doesn't run away from him in time. A lot of my work has been classified as horror, and I'm good with that, because I think horror is — or, rather, *can be* — a noble field in which to toil. But there remain a number of dilemmas (not as many as it had back in the 80s, thank the Fates) still facing the field as we begin a new but you-bet-your-ass-*cautious* resurgence of the you-should-pardon-the-word genre.

What you hold in your hands both is and isn't a book of film and fiction writing commentaries; yes, you'll find several reviews and (hopefully intelligent) analyses in here, but a format like that can quickly grow wearisome and repetitive — any schmuck with desktop-publishing capabilities can churn out a book of reviews and opinion pieces about the same books and movies we've all seen discussed a thousand times before — so I've decided to take it a couple of steps . . . well, let's say *sideways*: one's reaction to horror movies and literature is a highly subjective and personal thing, emphasis on the latter term. Consider this to be a thinly-disguised autobiography by means of reflections about movies, books, and writing. It's not enough for someone to simply say, "I liked it," or "I really hated it"; those are not opinions in and of themselves, they are *prefaces* to opinions. To qualify as *actual* opinions, they must be followed by reasons why, and in order for you to understand the reasons *why*, you have to understand something about the person giving the opinion.

Like it or not (and there are times when I fall more on the "not" side), horror in all its written, recorded, and visual forms is the core of my life. I have loved the darkness ever since I was a little boy of five watching *Zontar: The Thing From Venus, The Lodger, Tarantula, The Creature From the Black Lagoon,* and other movies on Channel 10's *Chiller Theater* on Friday nights, along with my dad, who always smelled of machine grease, Old Spice, and factory foulness from his day's labor at a manufacturing plant that would eventually screw him up one side and down the other and toss him away like a rusty machine part.

My parents — though not great readers themselves — always bought books for me, encouraged me to read, and always watched scary movies with me. You'll hear more about them as we go on.

But we need to begin where this will all end: in the darkness, in a seat on the aisle, watching phantom images flicker across the screen as the observers gathered there become an audience and metamorphose temporarily into what the late Jim Morrison dubbed, ". . . quiet vampires": film spectators.

Now, from among these quiet vampires, let's pick someone . . .

. . . ah, there, middle row, right-hand section; we can all guess as to his story, but I think I might have a little inside information; so let me tell it:

There's this guy sitting in a second-run movie theater where he's come with a minivan full of friends to see Rob Zombie's *House of a Thousand Corpses,* it's about sixty minutes into the thing, and he's suddenly asking the following question to a God he's not sure pays any attention to humankind, assuming that He/She/It/Them is even there: *Why in the hell am I liking this movie?*

Make no mistakes about it: *Corpses* is an exercise in sadistic, inhuman, grotesque brutality, it hates all of its characters, and a good argument can be made that it has nothing but contempt for its target audience (who stayed away in droves during its initial run in theaters) — but, unlike, say, the *Scream* films, it doesn't attempt to disguise its contempt for its audience with a lot of overly-clever visual gimmicks, trendy film-geek references, and smartass asides. *Corpses* is up-front about it, as if Zombie was saying, "Okay, you sick, twisted things, this is what you want, so here it is, right in your face and up your nose and down your throats. Gag on it." It fails as an out-and-out horror film, it fails as a black comedy, and it fails in its core intent to be an affectionate *homage* to the psycho-horror films of the 1970's such as *The Texas Chainsaw Massacre* and *Last House On the Left.*

But for all the levels on which it fails — and they are legion — there is a raw, primal, kinetic energy to the movie that gets under your skin, no matter how much you don't want that to happen.

All while giving you the finger from first shot to last.

In an odd sort of way, you have to respect a movie this arrogant and condescending. Yeah, it's garbage, but it's *ingenious* garbage that, for about one minute halfway through the movie, actually achieves a moment of genuine sick brilliance: one of the family of psychos which our unlucky quartet of boys and girls has encountered forces a sheriff's deputy to kneel at gunpoint, then holds the gun in front of the deputy's face while the camera does this slow, slow, *slow* pull-back to a distant overhead shot; it takes the camera almost fifty seconds to pull back and then remain still, and while this is happening there's nothing going on — no movement, no dialogue, no music, no sound, *nothing.* Absolute silence. And then, once the camera has stopped moving, this silence and stillness continues for almost another *twenty seconds* before the psycho pulls the trigger and kills the deputy.

Here's the thing: we *know* the second that deputy drops his gun and kneels down that he's toast, burnt on both sides. We *know* this, we've seen too many horror movies *not* to know this, and so this unbearable, nerve-wracking, agitating silence is nothing but Zombie's way of drawing out the dread of the moment; he knows that we know what's coming, but he also knows that suspense and dread are not created by hyperactive editing (which he's utilized to alarming effect thus far) but by that most precious and misunderstood element available to storytellers and filmmakers both: hesitation. There is more outright terror in a held breath than in a million deafening screams, and with this single shot, Zombie shows the audience that he knows this — and since Zombie possesses this understanding and skill as a director, you can't help but wonder why he decided to squander it for most of *Corpses* 93-minute running time (which feels more like two-and-a-half hours by the time the credits roll).

As far as this guy watching from his seat on the aisle is concerned, Rob Zombie — for all the lambasting he's taken from critics and audiences alike — knows *precisely* what's he's doing every step of the way.

House of a Thousand Corpses contains almost *everything* this guy in the audience despises about the modern horror genre — the only element missing from it is that of a heterosexual couple being snuffed immediately following sex.

In short: there was — and remains — no sensible reason for him to like this movie.

But he does.

And the guy has now counted thirteen people who have walked out on the movie so far — something he himself should have done a while back.

He's sitting there and all around him people are leaving, yet he watches the screen, fascinated, and suddenly finds himself thinking about, of all things, the A-word: art.

Here's some background on this guy: over the last eighteen months he has buried his father, his grandmother, and his mother — who he had to order taken off life-support and then spend three terrible hours watching her life grind to its end in a series of sputtering little agonies (he still has nightmares filled with her heartbroken, angry, accusing eyes); he has recently moved to a new city; he has gone through an emotionally devastating divorce which was completely his fault; he has undergone a fairly serious surgery to repair nerve damage in his right hand; and he has had a suicidal meltdown that landed him in The Bin for a while where they kept him doped to the gills and under constant observation.

Ain't exactly been a banner time for him up until now, and he knows that the last thing he needs is to be sitting here watching a vicious, mean-spirited, gleefully sadistic, inhumanly brutal so-called movie that is the most crystalline encapsulation he's ever seen of everything he hates about the horror field.

Yet he's not moving.

People are running for the exits all around him, and this silently pleases him, even makes him feel some hope for the human race —

— yet sitting there he remains. A movie that would offend his mother, that would make his father's often-pessimistic view of the world darken thirty shades of onyx, a movie that he himself knows has absolutely nothing to recommend giving it any more time that he'll never, ever, *ever* get back (*I'm going to be dead soon enough,* he keeps thinking) . . . and his ass stays glued to the seat.

There is a contradiction here that needs exploring, and that's something else we're going to do along the way; after all, how many of you have continued reading a horror novel or story that you know is sub-par, or stayed in your seat during a horror movie that even the medically brain-dead could recognize as being bad?

For this guy — and guess who it is? — that number is easily more than he cares to count.

But he knows he's not alone in this; thousands of you share his interest in, fascination with, and love of, the darkness.

Admit it; you're right there with me in that movie theater; you've been with me there before, and you'll be there with me again. And again. And again.

Don't point fingers and accuse me of being elitist, biased, unpleasant, acerbic, grim, arrogant, depressing, untoward, discourteous, and generally no fun at parties; I already *know* I'm all of these, thanks so much. And you'd better damn well not accuse me of being part of the problems which I intend to discuss here; horror movies and horror fiction existed long before I first put pen to paper, as did their problems, so if anything said herein and onward strikes a nerve with you, don't try to put the blame on me, folks: it was already broke when I got here.

HORROR WRITER leans back, looks at the screen, and nods.

BOOKS

See there? What'd we tell you?

WRITER

Okay, you were right. Thank you.

BOOKS

Always listen to us, pal, we're never wrong.

WRITER

I have two words for you . . .

DANSE MACABRE
(to itself)

This oughtta be good . . .

WRITER

. . . "Maximum Overdrive."

THE BOOKS are silent for a moment, but we can HEAR *Danse Macabre* chuckling uncontrollably.

BOOKS

That was a cheap shot. You should be nicer to us.

WRITER

It's late and I'm tired. Sue me.

BOOKS

You really shouldn't criticize a movie until you've tried making one yourself.

WRITER

Easy for you to say.

BOOKS
(pouting)
Yeah, well, *still* . . . that was pretty low, even for a horror writer.

WRITER
(to himself)
Is it just me, or has the doll been awfully quiet. . . ?

BOOKS

What now, oh follower-in-our-creator's-shadow?

WRITER

Well, I think we've taken this opening bit about as far as we can without trying readers' patience, so . . .

He places his hands on the keyboard. The STRONG BAD DOLL's legs twitch for a moment, then are still. CAMERA MOVES to the screen and we SEE:

CUT SHARP TO:

Part One:

A View from the Aisle Seat

"Film spectators are quiet vampires."
— Jim Morrison, *The Lords*

I

Small (and Not-So) Beginnings; Second Chances; and Lots of Things Which Dance

"Life is material — you just have to live long enough to see how to use it."
— William Goldman, *The Color of Light*

This is how the majority of this book is going to unfold: things are going to jump and skitter and bounce around like pieces of a jigsaw puzzle caught in the wind but, believe me, it'll all come together in the end — or as Jim Morrison once wrote: "The subjects says, 'I see first lots of thing which dance . . . then everything becomes gradually connected.'"

Structure and reading experience dictate this is the place to start with some appropriate anecdote about the first time I was ever really scared by a horror movie or nearly jumped out of my shorts when a sudden sound startled me from the story I was reading, some humorous moment of epiphany where All Was Revealed, but the truth is my "revelation" (a word I find more than a bit overly-dramatic, so we'll use "discovery" from here on, thanks for enduring this parenthetical pause) did not come about from reading a book or seeing a movie but, rather, because of two incidents in my life that occurred five years apart; the first was solitary and quiet, while the second . . . wasn't.

The first came about because of music. Specifically the music of The Who; even more specifically the album *Quadrophenia*; and even *more* specifically, the second song on Side 4 (this was, after all, back in the glory days of holy vinyl).

By its musical structure alone, *Quadrophenia* opened my eyes and my intellect to the endless possibilities offered by the metaphor; add to that its compelling and challenging narrative structure, and you've got something that, to my mind, qualifies as a masterpiece.

Quadrophenia centers on a young kid in 1960s England named Jimmy. Jimmy comes from a hard-luck, working class family. He wants to be popular among his friends. He also wants to be a good son, a good worker, and a great lover. In the midst of trying to be all things to everyone, he realizes that he presents four very distinctive personalities to the world over the course of his days: the tough guy, the romantic, the crazy fun friend, and the troubled son. All of these separate personalities are represented by a distinct musical theme, and each personality encompasses only one aspect of the real Jimmy; none of them represent who he is in his heart. On top of all this, he's saddled with having a deeper insight into the human spirit than most people think a person of his station is capable. He admits that even he doesn't know who he really is. Being a confused angry young man with rampaging hormones, it doesn't take long before certain aspects of his other personalities start bleeding over into the parts of his life where they don't belong.

There's much, much more to *Quadrophenia's* story, but that's the spine of it.

Okay, Christmas Eve, 1972. I was 12 years old. I had been in the hospital for over a week with pneumonia and had been released the previous morning. My dad was at work and his shift didn't end until eight p.m., and my mom and my little sister (age 4) were doing the visiting rounds with friends and relatives but had promised me they'd be back before seven. I'm lying there in bed, feeling like I'm gonna bite the big one any second, and there's nothing to do — a phrase not used in the existentialist, Vladamir and Estragon, *Waiting For Godot* manner, no; what I mean is: I was bored out of my skull. I was also so weak I couldn't draw a conclusion, let alone move.

Now, it was a tradition at the Braunbeck home that everyone got to open one present on Christmas Eve, and I knew which one I was going to unwrap. However, I was convinced that I wasn't going to live to see the morning (I was having trouble breathing and every inch of my body, inside and out, felt like it was boiling away), but I somehow rallied and stumbled downstairs in a medicated haze and stole one of my presents from under the tree. I knew it was the *Quadrophenia* album and I was damned if I was going to die without listening to it. I took it back up to my room, put it on my record player, lay down (*collapsed*, actually) and listened to it all the way through, sides 1–4.

This sounds like a ham-fisted cliché, but the thing changed my life. On side 4 of the album there's an instrumental piece called "The Rock" which remains for me one of the most amazing and moving pieces of music — and that's music, period, not just rock music — that I've ever heard.

In *Tommy*, the central character's epiphany is conveyed through words and music; but in *Quadrophenia*, it is conveyed solely through music. "The Rock" starts off by repeating each of the four themes separately, then, one by one, begins overlapping them until the four themes blend seamlessly into one, creating a fifth, unique, defining theme as Jimmy finally realizes who he really is.

That was a revelation — ahem . . . uh, er . . . *discovery* — for the 12-year-old me. Pete Townshend and The Who had pulled an incredible musical sleight-of-hand, created a musical Rubik's Cube that I hadn't even realized existed until the puzzle was completed.

I knew then that I wanted to someday create a piece or body of work that did what Townshend had done with *Quadrophenia's* music; present you with a group of seemingly disparate pieces/themes that in the end converged into a unified whole that was not only rewarding in and of itself (as "The Rock" most definitely is), but also enriched the sum of its parts.

"The Rock" is a perfect metaphor for what we as human beings strive toward during every moment between that first slap on the ass and the last handful of soil tossed on the lid of the coffin; call it the psychological equivalent of string theory or whatever you will: we strive to bring the various Selves together to form the whole that is uniquely 'me' or 'you', all the while treasuring the journey that has led to this time, this breath, this moment.

That's why I admire "The Rock," and that's why *Quadrophenia* — both in its musical and narrative structure — was, is, and ever shall be the prime example of the standard I compare — get this — my *storytelling* abilities to. I don't know if I'll ever create something as structurally and aesthetically overpowering as it is — and God knows it's not something that is always in the forefront of my mind — but, damn, it's been a helluva trip toward my own "Rock" so far.

And part of that trip has always led to either the bookshelf, the movie theater, or the typewriter (then electronic typewriter, then word processor, then computer). For me, all of these things — books, stories, movies, music, etc. — have always been connected in one form or another; I balk at many (but not all) writers who claim that the use of modern technologies and cultural icons in fiction is proof of lazy writing by sloppy, unorganized minds who don't want to bother with the work of refining their descriptive skills. "What of Dickens?" they say. "Dickens did not rely on the use of easily-accessible catch-phrases or film, television, and pop-culture references in order to enrich his work." Yeah, no arguments there . . . but are you trying to tell me that if computers, television, radio, and blockbuster films *had* existed in Dickens' day, he *wouldn't* have employed them in his stories? Are you saying that if television news cameras had existed when Sydney Carton walked to his heroic and noble death at the end of *A Tale of Two Cities*, he wouldn't have delivered his famous "'Tis a far, far better thing I do . . ." speech right into the lens so the whole world might hear his final words? Or that if Ye Olde videotape and VCRs had existed during *Great Expectations*, the tragic Miss Havisham *wouldn't* have sat before a television in her wedding dress watching transferred home movies of herself with the man who jilted her, or even played the song they first danced to on her record or CD player? Okay, you could *try*, but I wouldn't be convinced.

In his book of essays *Who Killed Hollywood?* the redoubtable novelist and screenwriter William Goldman makes a compelling — if somewhat insular — argument about the importance of movies: American culture (Goldman argues) is at the center of world culture, and it is *movies* — not books, not symphonies, not poetry or sculpture or dance or any other art form — that lies at the heart of American culture.

This is an argument that I nether fully nor fully disagree with, but like the majority of Goldman's arguments about movies and culture, it has tremendous merit and so should not be ignored. For the sake of that argument, let's say that Goldman's conclusion is correct, and that movies are what lie at the heart of American culture. As writers, we have one of two choices as to what we can do about this: we can ignore the importance movies play in the day-to-day lives of many people, never referencing them in our fiction, or we can accept that it will always be movies that are at the heart of American culture and proceed accordingly; no, I'm not saying that we should write our novels and stories with an eye toward the eventual movie adaptation, nor am I advocating that our prose should be of the clipped, short-hand, eighth-grade comprehension level that we are told most readers don't like reading above; what I *am* saying is that movies, music, television, DVDs, cell phones, and all the other accouterments that decorate the world have uses beyond those for which they were designed, and if as storytellers we fail to employ them (when and if needed, of course) then we have no one but ourselves to blame if our work is thought to be out of touch. In the end, these things are just *props*, and as any good performer can tell you, if a prop can be employed to enrich your performance, you're a fool not to use it.

If fictional stories in all their forms are supposed to be, as often purported, reflections and reinterpretations of reality, then that reality has to include those things that give structure and recognition to the world around its characters; it doesn't matter a damn whether Havisham pines for her lover while trundling around in her wedding dress during the 1800s or while sitting glued to the Internet searching for some nugget of information about him in 2070; universal human conditions never change, only the props surrounding them. Any writer worth their carbon knows that in order to make a story's characters and circumstances immediate and accessible to readers, there must be points of reference to establish in *which* reality this tale is being set. In the case of horror fiction, it becomes not only necessary but vital that reality be firmly established as soon as possible, because it's going to be chewed to shreds soon enough, especially when the promise of the second chance is dangled in front of a character.

Of all the themes explored in fiction and film, none is so recurrent as that of the second chance. From *Faustus* and "The Devil and Daniel Webster" to *Grand Hotel, A Christmas Carol* and *It's a Wonderful Life* (not to mention numerous episodes of *The Twilight Zone, Darkroom,* and *The Outer Limits),* the Second Chance theme is on of the few timeless subjects that hasn't yet been worn down. It's a grabber every time (at least for me). Who hasn't wished for the chance to somehow right a perceived wrong or undo a past failure? Who doesn't carry around a load of regret because we awaken some mornings feeling that we've wasted time and maybe even our life doing something that makes us miserable? Who hasn't tried to ease that regret by briefly retreating into a wistful daydream where a fresh start and clean slate are readily available? Regret is one of the strongest and most self-destructive emotions human beings possess, and that makes it an excellent tool for writers and filmmakers who want to engage both the intellect and emotions of an audience – and I'll state for the record that it's my belief all horror fiction – be it written or cinematic – at its inception must grapple with such strong emotions to have a chance at lasting impact.

I've never been, as either a reader or a writer, one who responds strongly to outside bogies; I am not moved by a scene of someone struck immobile by a vampire's seductive stare or squirming under a psychopath's knife. There are exceptions to this, of course, but they're few and far between. For me, if you're going to scare or disturb a reader, then you've *got* to get under their skin, and the most effective and affecting way to do this is to hit an emotional nerve. Few external horrors carry much of a threat unless the fear is directly connected to an emotion – and unlike Doug Winter's oft-repeated turn of the phrase, I *don't* consider horror to be an emotion: by itself it's nothing more than a gut reaction – not a genuine emotion – one half of an equation, and only becomes *horrific* when it's *intertwined with* a strong emotion that it can manipulate in order to weaken the character's resolve.

Case in point: *Seconds*, arguably director John Frankenheimer's best film. Based on the excellent novel by David Ely, in it we meet middle-aged bank executive Arthur Hamilton (John Randolph in a masterfully shaded performance) whose life is so miserable he walks as if the earth might open at any moment and swallow him whole. His job drains him of humanity. His marriage is hollow and cold. His self-respect is rattling its last breath. He doesn't know how things came to this. He knows that he was once a decent man but he isn't any longer and he can't understand why. He feels alien to the world around him.

Then one day a stranger in the subway hands him a card with an address written on it; the stranger knows Hamilton's name, and as soon as we see the expression on Hamilton's face, we know that he has some idea why he's been handed this slip of paper.

That night Hamilton is called by a supposedly dead friend. "I have a wonderful new life!" he tells Hamilton. "I'm happy, old buddy, and I want to do the same for you!"

It seems there are these "people" who can give you a new life. A new face. A new voice and identity. They can give you a life where you are successful at the thing you always dreamed of (in Hamilton's case, being a famous artist). It costs a lot, and once the process has begun there is no turning back.

Hamilton, after much soul-searching, decides to go through with it, and embarks on a chilling journey to the secret headquarters where these "people" make arrangements for a new life. (He is taken there in the back of a meat delivery truck – some of the most unnerving black-humored symbolism I've ever encountered.) There he meets with the doctor

(Will Geer, Grandpa Walton himself, who is quietly and absolutely terrifying in the role) who has created this program. The decision made, the work begins, and soon Hamilton is transformed into the younger, more vital Antiochus "Tony" Wilson (played by Rock Hudson), given a new profession, a new home, a new life. Things are idyllic for a while, but eventually Hamilton's conscience and its questions about his old life drive him to return to his widow in an effort to find out where he went wrong.

Frankenheimer always dealt with extremes in his best pictures, and *Seconds* is possibly the most extreme film he ever made. His penchant for lean storytelling and muscular pacing is at its peak here, as is his use of his ought-to-be-patented foreground framing technique. Aided by the starkly dazzling cinematography of James Wong Howe (who won an Oscar for his work on the Paul Newman film *Hud)*, Frankenheimer's forceful, in-your-face style was never better suited to its material (the script, by Lewis John Carlino — who went on to write the stunning Ellen Burstyn film *Resurrection,* as well as write and direct *The Great Santini* — is among the most literate ever written for a horror film).

Born in 1930 in Queens, New York, Frankenheimer wanted to be a professional tennis player; thank the Fates he changed his mind, or film lovers would be all the poorer.

Frankenheimer began his career as an assistant at CBS during the days of live television. His enthusiasm, his intelligence, and his knowledge of the camera quickly earned him a chance to direct. In 1957 he helmed the live broadcast of the Emmy Award-winning *The Comedian,* written by none other than Rod Serling. It starred Mickey Rooney, Edmund O'Brian, Kim Hunter (who many of you might remember from the original — and best — *Planet of the Apes,* co-scripted by Serling), and a surprisingly effective Mel Torme. What distinguished *The Comedian* from other live television dramas of the period was not only its superb script (which remains one of Serling's most angry and poetic) but Frankenheimer's maverick direction. Until *The Comedian,* most directors had been limited to the use of one, sometimes two cameras, but Frankenheimer bullied CBS executives into letting him use three — an unheard-of gamble. Not only did Frankenheimer use three cameras, he used them *simultaneously* during the breathtaking opening sequence, which still stuns today. (*The Comedian* is readily available on home video; if you've never seen this benchmark production in television history, you'd do well to find a copy.)

Frankenheimer would work again with Serling on the 1964 political thriller *Seven Days in May,* starring Burt Lancaster, Kirk Douglas, Martin Balsam, John Houseman (in his first film role), Ava Gardner, and the great Fredric March. Based on the novel by Fletcher Knebel, *Seven Days In May* depicts what happens when a military plot to overthrow the United States government is uncovered one week before the President is scheduled to deliver his State of the Union Address. Though it contains a minimum of action, the film is nonetheless gripping, suspenseful, and, at several points, outright nerve-wracking. It also boasts a famous confrontation scene between Lancaster and March toward the end of the movie which Frankenheimer often said was his personal favorite of all the scenes he had directed. Considering that his career spanned five decades, that's no small recommendation. That confrontation sequence remains on of the most taut, literate, and brilliantly directed sequences I have ever seen.

A lot — a *lot* — has been written and said about the film that put Frankenheimer on the map, *The Manchurian Candidate.* How effective you'll find the film today depends on your personal level of cynicism. *Candidate* — a satire in the truest sense of the word — deliberately sets out to make the viewer uncertain as to whether or not it's supposed to funny. Admittedly, some of the scenes in the film have an aura of comedy about them which I think was intentional, while others — scenes obviously intended to be serious, unintentionally draw chuckles. Laurence Harvey's British accent seems ludicrously out of place for a veteran of the Korean War, especially since he's supposed to be American, but once you get past his voice, you cannot help but admire his rich, complex performance. The final sequence, filmed in Madison Square Garden, remains one of the most beautifully edited and unbearably suspenseful ever put on film. (Many critics and film scholars credit Frankenheimer as having created the template for the modern political thriller; viewing such films as *Candidate, Seven Days in May, Black Sunday,* and the recent HBO film *The Path to War* — which is now Frankenheimer's swan song, and a great one, at that — this accolade seems almost understated.)

In 1966, Frankenheimer turned out a pair of films that could not possibly be more disparate in subject matter and execution; *Seconds* and *Grand Prix.* Frankenheimer did not want to make *Grand Prix,* but was forced to do so after *Seconds* died a miserable death at the box office.

Grand Prix, on the other hand, was a tremendous hit at the box office, and remained Frankenheimer's most financially successful film until 1998's *Ronin.* The script by veteran playwright Robert Alan Arthur (who co-wrote *All That Jazz* with the late Bob Fosse), ultimately focuses too much on the soap-opera level problems of the drivers and their families, but it's when the film gets on the racetrack that Frankenheimer and cinematographer Lionel "Curly" Linden (who did a season as *Night Gallery*'s Director of Photography) blindside you. When faced with the challenge of filming a lengthy race in such a way to make it interesting for film audiences, Frankenheimer decided he wanted to have the camera become part of the actual race, so he and Linden designed a special camera and camera harness that could be attached to the front driver's-side of the car, giving the illusion that the viewer was riding on the hood during the race.

You've seen this same shot about a million times over the years in every car chase that's been filmed. You have John Frankenheimer and Lionel Linden to thank for it. Until *Grand Prix,* no director had ever attempted to film a race or chase in this manner; nowadays, a director would feel like a fool *not* to include at least one such shot in an action film.

The decades of the 70s and 80s were not good ones for Frankenheimer. In addition to a string of box-office disappointments (good films such as *I Walk the Line* and not-so-good ones like *99 and 44/100% Dead* — he never fared well with comedies), Frankenheimer was battling depression and alcoholism which began shortly after the assassination of his close friend, Robert Kennedy.

Most people know the story of how Frankenheimer drove Kennedy to the Ambassador Hotel the night of the senator's murder, but during an interview with Larry King, Frankenheimer offered a chilling post-script to the tale: He had left the podium area (where he'd been standing next to Kennedy) about three minutes before Kennedy's speech was finished in order to get his car, drive it to the front of the building, and be ready to pick up the senator. As he sat there with the car idling, he tuned to the news on the radio in time for a special bulletin: Senator Robert Kennedy had just been shot and killed along with acclaimed movie director John Frankenheimer.

"I heard them announce my death on the radio," he said. "It was horrifying and surreal and made me weep."

It also made him angry. Starting with the 1975 thriller *French Connection II* (a film in many ways the equal of William Friedkin's 1973 multi-Oscar winner, and in some ways even better), Frankenheimer's movies became infused with rage and disillusionment which was often difficult, if not impossible, for both audiences and critics to deal with. Many claimed that he had lost his touch as a director, but nothing was further from the truth. Watch *Black Sunday* and see how much of Bruce Dern's emotionally overwhelming breakdown scene you can look at, or test you mettle with the merciless heroin withdrawal sequence in *French Connection II*; even 1979's box-office disaster *Prophecy* (which is rumored to have been re-edited *without* Frankenheimer's participation or approval, though he bore the brunt of the blame when the film flopped) seethes with rage during its first forty-five minutes. (Many scenes in the film's second half were reportedly re-written and re-shot by a different director, and it shows in the inconsistent, embarrassingly sloppy visual and thematic composition.)

A few other films to mention: *Dead-Bang* — despite an awful script, this film should be seen to prove what a gifted director and solid cast can do with sub-standard material; *The Island of Dr. Moreau* — Frankenheimer came in on this one after the original director was fired and half the cast had quit: considering what a debacle the production was when he inherited it (and his well-publicized difficulties with actor Val Kilmer), it's a wonder this film got made at all, let alone be as watchable as it is; *52 Pick-Up* — without a doubt the best film version of any Elmore Leonard novel, full of rage and cynicism and dark humor, with outstanding performances from the entire cast; and *Ronin,* another film wherein Frankenheimer was handed a paper-thin script (co-written by David Mamet under a pseudonym) but managed to instill the story with an immediacy and intensity that made its two-hour running time fly. Crackling performances, muscular editing, and two stunning car chases which forever raised the bar on that particular action-movie staple *should* have earned Frankenheimer an Oscar nomination for Best Director. (Despite winning a plethora of other awards, Frankenheimer was *never* nominated for an Oscar, not even for *The Manchurian Candidate*; don't try to tell me that Hollywood knows "quality" when it sees it.)

On a much more personal note, as a writer, Frankenheimer's films have had a profound and lasting influence on me; he taught me how to temper anger with dry humor, how to pace a story, how to visualize scenes, and, most of all, how to always give the story the spotlight. I was more saddened than I can possibly express by the death of this great American director on July 7, 2002. I think it might take a while for filmgoers to realize what a brilliant man they've lost, but realize it they will.

As I did while viewing *Seconds* for the umpteenth time, a film that remains a staggering and overlooked achievement, whose biggest surprise, perhaps, is the performance of the late Rock Hudson. In a role originally slated to be played by Laurence Olivier (who the studio decided didn't have Hudson's box-office clout), Hudson displays a depth and power that viewers of *Pillow Talk* would never have thought possible. Hudson's face is a subtle prism of conflicting emotions; every joy, every sorrow, every triumph and regret is there, etched into his expressions like words on a headstone. When something hits at his core, you see it on his face — and not in any heavy-handed, watch-me, watch-me way; Hudson's performance is one of impressive constriction, understatement, and substance, heart-felt and affecting, and (like the superb performance of Tony Curtis in *The Boston Strangler)* a rare glimpse at a good but limited actor's one moment of true and undeniable greatness — which gives this film an added dose of bitter irony when viewed today: had Hudson lived, would he have wanted a second chance to prove his worth as an actor of substance and power? It's a saddening and frightening question — and those two adjectives best serve to describe *Seconds.* It is an emotional film, certainly, but it is an also extremely terrifying one that grabs the viewer by the throat and never lets go, continually tying your gut into knots all the way to its tragic, relentless, and horrifying finale — a sequence that remains, in my opinion, the most terrifying finish to a horror movie ever filmed.

Seconds is available on DVD, and if you rent — or better, buy it — make sure to listen to Frankenheimer's commentary; he not only offers a fascinating glimpse into the visual choices made by himself and Howe, but in addition offers an eloquent and frightening oral history of the Hollywood witch-hunts conducted by Senator Joseph McCarthy. With the exception of Hudson and Frankenheimer, *everyone* who worked on *Seconds* (both in front of and behind the cameras) had been blacklisted. Frankenheimer says several times — almost gleefully — that he purposefully hired the cast and crew *because* they had been blacklisted. His way of spitting in McCarthy's face. Bravo.

In the end, *Seconds* succeeds on every level; as an unflinching psychological study of its central character's disintegration, as a metaphor-rich cautionary fable about valuing what your life has rather than what it doesn't, as a science fiction movie, as a domestic drama, and, most of all — perhaps most importantly of all — as proof that a good horror film doesn't have to rely on cheap shocks, overdone special effects, and buckets of grue in order to disturb the viewer on a primal level.

I find a lot of comfort in watching *Seconds* — a film I've now seen easily thirty times. Disturbing, sad, cynical, angry, and existentialistic (in the dictionary sense of the word) as it is, this is one of the few films that still takes me out of the world while I'm watching it, and leaves me feeling . . . well . . . *stronger* once it's over. It has helped me through some very bad times, and under the worst of circumstances . . .

. . . which brings me to the second incident that put me on the path to being a horror writer.

My father was a WWII veteran, 71st Infantry, Artilleryman. He fought in the battles of Regensburg, Straubing, Reid, Lambach, Weis, and Steyer; he crossed the Rhine, Danube, Isar, Inn, and Enns Rivers; and he helped to liberate the concentration camps of Strubing and Gunskirken Lager. He was a loyal soldier. He was born and raised in Ohio. He never made it past the eighth grade because he had to go to work to help support his ailing mother and three younger siblings after his father abandoned them during the Great Depression (he worked as a paper boy, ten different routes each day).

Near the end of the war, Dad was the sole survivor of a crash in Eberstadt, Austria – just beyond the village of Darmstadt – that killed all the men in his unit; while driving up an icy mountain road, the driver lost control of the truck and drove it over the side of a cliff. The truck plunged, upside-down, over 150 feet before landing in the ice and snow below, killing everyone except the driver and himself. He lay inside the wreckage of the truck for nearly two days, kept from freezing to death only because of the bodies on top of and below him. When at last the wreckage was discovered, it was by an SS unit that had been hiding out in the mountains, and who Dad's unit had been looking for. The first thing this unit did was pull all the bodies from the remains of the truck; the second thing was to defile the bodies; the third was to build a pile with the bodies; and the last thing they did, before they left, was to set that pile on fire. My father – who had been faking being dead the entire time – was right in the middle of that pile, and didn't dare move or speak for fear they'd discover he was alive and . . .

. . . and I'll just leave the rest of that to your imaginations.

The smoke from the fire was spotted by the Darmstadt villagers, who immediately came to the scene and put out the (thankfully) slow-burning fire (snow had begun to fall quite heavily, and while it did not douse the flames, it hindered their spreading a great deal). My father was discovered alive, was taken to Darmstadt where he remained in their small hospital for several months before being transferred to one in Munich upon Germany's surrender.

He had broken nearly every bone in his body. He spent 18 months in a full-body cast. (*18 months.* Can you imagine what it must be like to not be able to move *at all* for a year-and-a-half? My entire life, I don't think I ever saw him once sit still for more than thirty minutes at a time.)

After the war, he never received any kind of therapy to help him deal with it. As a result — and because he came from a generation whose members simply Didn't Talk About Such Things — he suffered from nightmares about the incident. He had a tremendous amount of trouble sleeping, and so took to having a few beers before bedtime to make him sleepy. As the years went on and the sleeplessness persisted, those few beers became a few *more* beers, then a few more beers with a couple of belts of whiskey, and he slipped quietly in full-blown alcoholism.

My father, for all his maddening habits and sometimes hateful fits of temper (especially when he was drunk), was one of the most decent human beings I've ever known. He sent all of his money home during the war so his mother could buy a house — a house that she would not allow him to move into upon his return because she thought of him as an embarrassment. This is the same woman who, when my father was a child, would beat him with the business end of her high-heeled shoes until he passed out from loss of blood. His back, shoulders, chest, and legs were a patchwork of scars she so generously gifted him with out of the goodness of her Christian heart. He had always been treated badly by most of the members of his family (the one member who loved him purely and unconditionally, his sister, Lucille, my Aunt "Boots," now seven years in her grave, God rest her selfless soul), yet he still loved them and sought their approval, especially his mother's. He never got it, and he knew it, and that made him one of the saddest human beings I'd ever seen.

The end of the summer of 1977 was, to put it mildly, not

pleasant. Dad's alcoholism was at its violent peak, his self-respect was non-existent, and he saw no point to his life. He had worked for the Roper corporation for nearly twenty-two years when they decided to close down their Newark plant after the fifth labor strike, one that resulted in the worst riot of its kind in the city's history. Through a couple of (in my opinion) criminally deceptive clauses in the last contract they offered to their employees, most of the line workers were ineligible for full pension benefits — which wound up being beside the point because, somehow, the majority of the pension fund just disappeared, and what my father received as a severance package was $125.00 for every year of employment. Dirt money. Chump change. Money gone before it was got. And, oh, yeah: Kiss retirement before sixty good-bye, pal.

In the summer of 1977 my father had been at his new job at Larson's Manufacturing for a little over five years. He operated a sheet metal press, with lathe work on the side. His body was already showing the wear of a life that had been one struggle after another. He still couldn't sleep for shit. He couldn't concentrate. The mortgage — which should have been paid off with some of his pension money — was still looming over his head, and there was talk of layoffs at the plant.

His drinking that summer was the worst it had ever been. The nightmares were incessant. The pain in his body — from both his war injuries and those sustained from working the factory line for thirty years — was nearly unbearable, and the painkillers prescribed by his doctor barely helped. Add to this his heart and blood-pressure medication — plus a recent diagnosis of Type 2 diabetes — and the man never had a waking moment where he wasn't worried to death about something.

So he drank. A lot. He flew into violent rages that usually left my mother bleeding and me having to take her to the emergency room and lie to the attending physicians about how she came to be in such a state. I intervened as often as I could when Dad went into these rages. I've got some impressive scars to prove it.

In the summer of 1977, when I was 17, I came as close to

hating my father as I ever had before. All I saw was a whining, violent, self-pitying drunk who blamed the world for his failures in life — and who saw his life as a wasted one.

On this day, the Fourth of July, my mother had taken my then-seven-year-old sister Gayle Ann to watch the big parade downtown. I had been out partying with some friends the night before, and had come home at four in the morning to crash on the sofa.

I was awakened sometime around ten-thirty by my father falling on me. Drunk on his ass. He'd gone through all the beer and was putting a good dent in the contents of a whiskey bottle.

"Can't get to sleep," he kept slurring at me. "Can't get to sleep. C'mon, get your ass up and let's go make some breakfast."

I rose, groggy-eyed and cotton-mouthed, from the sofa, went into the kitchen, and — at Dad's request — micro-waved a couple of TV dinners for breakfast.

I sat at one end of the kitchen table, Dad at the other. I began to eat. He started rambling on about the way his mother had treated him and my Aunt "Boots" when they were children; about the war and what had happened to him; about how he was too old and too tired to face another twenty-five years on another line at another plant. (He'd once told me he'd wanted to raise chickens for a living when he was a young man; how he wished he'd been able to do that. It was his dream, and it meant the world to him, and it just broke his heart that he and my mother never had the money to buy a proper farm for raising chickens.)

I remember all of this very clearly because, when he first began to talk, I looked up at him and saw the business end of a *Duetsche Werk* 7.65mm semi-automatic pistol pointed right at my face. I knew this gun well. Dad had taken it from where one of the SS officers who'd discovered the remains of his unit had dropped it in his haste to get away.

He ate very little of his TV dinner. But he drank the whiskey. Even used it to chase down some painkillers, as well as his heart and blood-pressure medicine — none of which were supposed to be taken at the same time, let alone with alcohol.

He began unraveling right in front of me.

And all the time that gun stayed pointed right at my face. He wasn't aware of it. I didn't dare make any sudden moves or loud noises for fear of startling him — his finger was on the trigger and the safety was off and the clip, which he always kept fully loaded, was securely in place.

He began calling me other names — Stan, Wille P., "Slim" — all members of his deceased unit. He began talking about what had happened as if it were happening at that very moment and they were still alive to remember the experience with him. A couple of times he started crying and saying things like, "But I don't have any money for a hotel, Mom!" He began looking around the kitchen, whispering, "Shhh, shut your fuckin' mouth, Stan! Can't you hear 'em?"

It was at that moment that I did what was probably the first genuinely wise thing I had done in my life; very quietly, with as even a tone of voice as I could muster (surprised I could find it in me to speak at all), I said, "Hear who, Frank?"

"Goose-stepping cocksuckers," he snarled, then jumped up from the table, threw his chair aside, and started toward the back porch door. He grabbed my arm on the way past and said, "We gotta get 'em first this time."

He pulled me out onto the back porch and forced me to squat down beside him as he aimed the gun. "The trees," he said. "They came out of the trees."

I remembered him telling me that earlier; how he'd seen the SS unit emerge from the snow-covered trees and move toward the detritus of his unit.

I don't know how long we stayed like that. Once I thought he was going to pass out, but just as I was stupid enough to reach for the gun, his eyes snapped open and he stood up and plowed four rounds into the sole tree in our back yard. The dog next door barked and damn near got its head blown off for the effort.

To counteract the wise thing I had done before, I did something supremely stupid — I tried to pull the gun out of his hand.

"The trees," he kept saying. "The trees."

And plowed off two more shots.

I didn't know it at the time, but one of those shots went through my right shoe and blew off part of my big toe (to this day, even in the worst of summer, I won't wear sandals because of that injury).

Finally, Dad hit me one upside the head with the butt of the gun and ran inside. By the time I staggered back into the house he'd reloaded the clip, pulled out his hunting rifle, and was loading it.

I walked into the living room and said something to him — I don't remember what — but the sound of my voice startled him; he screamed, fell backward, and fired a shot that missed me by a good three or four feet but felt like it had come a helluva lot closer. I dropped to the floor in tears, hating myself for being so scared.

Dad crawled over to me and said that it was gonna be okay, we'd keep an eye on the trees, Mom would be proud of him because he got a medal and everything. (He received a Purple Heart and several other medals that left my grandmother notably underwhelmed. They now hang in a display case over my bed.)

Dad rose up, pistol in one hand and rifle in the other, and walked out onto the front porch. By now a couple of our neighbors had figured out that something untoward was happening at the Braunbeck house and decided to come outside for a look.

One of them, a guy named Jess, walked right up to Dad and asked, "What'cha doin' there, Frank?"

Dad started to say something, then turned and looked at me, then turned back to Jess. Somewhere in there a shred of reason had returned to him. "Just showing Gary my guns. Boy don't know nothing about hunting . . . or sports . . . anything interesting." Then he gave me a quick look over his shoulder — one filled with disappointment and a level of embarrassment that bordered on disgust.

Now, I'd always known that I wasn't the kind of son he wished he'd had — I was more interested in theater and books and music and movies than I was in sports or cars or hunting or any of the other bullshit activities by which your value as a man is supposedly measured, especially in a hard-core blue-collar town like Newark — so this in itself was no revelation to me . . . but this was the first time that I realized that my father didn't much like me. Oh, he loved me, I knew that, I just wasn't the type of guy he'd choose for a friend.

I began shaking, feeling like a worthless piece-of-shit failure who was a supreme disappointment to his parent.

Much the same way, I imagine, Dad felt whenever in the company of his mother.

"Well, what say we get you back inside?" said Jess. "Can't stand all this excitement this early in the day."

Dad laughed, and turned to go back in the house, looking as if the madness had passed.

But did not let go of the gun or the rifle.

Jess and I sat him down at the kitchen table and I started pouring coffee down his throat. (Know what you get when you give coffee to a drunk? A wide-awake drunk. I didn't know that then. Important lesson. Teach your children well.)

He began to calm down. Jess said he'd see Dad later, and then left (because he'd called the police before coming over, as I was soon to discover).

We sat at the table for a few minutes, neither of us saying a word. Dad began to drift off again. I took the gun and the rifle from him, setting them down on a chair in the front room. I came back into the kitchen to find him swallowing a handful of pills.

"You already took your medicine."

"Shut your mouth, boy. I don't need any shit from the likes of you."

The likes of you. Twenty-six years later, that one still stings.

He rubbed his eyes, dazed and drained. I don't know that I've ever seen such loneliness on a human being's face.

I got him to his feet and started leading him through the front room toward the stairs. I noticed that my right foot felt really wet, like I was walking in thick mud. I looked down and saw a hole in my shoe. Every time I took a step, something dark squittered up through the hole and ran down the sides, leaving a little spatter-path on the carpeting. Mom was going to kill me, ruining her carpeting like this.

I had Dad on the second or third step leading to the upstairs and his bedroom when there was this loud *crack!* from behind, followed by an equally loud crash.

I turned around just in time to see the police officer who'd kicked open our front door come barreling in, decked out in full riot gear, wielding a pump-action shotgun.

Dad — who was still mumbling to himself — didn't seem to notice.

I propped him up against the wall of the first landing and went back down. My intention was to tell the officer that everything was all right now, that Dad was calm, that it was all over. But as I came off the last stair, the first genuine wave of pain from my foot registered with my brain and I lost my balance. I fell against the chair where the pistol and rifle lay. The officer evidently thought I was making a grab for a weapon, because before I knew what had happened, he slammed the butt of the shotgun into my chest, then shoved the business end right into my face as soon as I hit the floor.

It ain't like in the movies, folks; your first instinct isn't to deliver a Dirty Harry- or Bruce Willis-type smartass remark, one proving that you're made of steel and mere guns hold no fear for you: find yourself staring into the business end of a pump-action shotgun, and you'll know *exactly* what Nietzsche was talking about when he spoke of staring into the abyss.

The rest of it happened like this:

Dad came flying down the stairs and threw himself into the first officer. The shotgun discharged into the floor about a foot to the left of my head (I have a twenty-two percent hearing loss in my left ear as a result). Dad started screaming about filthy Nazi cocksuckers. By this time three other police officers were in the house, and all three of them did every-thing they could — aside from shooting him — to pull Dad off the first officer; they knocked him down; one of them pulled out his pistol and pointed it at Dad but couldn't get a clear shot because of the struggle; another one managed to get his club loose and clobbered Dad pretty good with it; then both officers fell back. One of them had what looked like a broken jaw. The other officer helped him outside where an ambulance waited. The third officer — the one who could not get a shot at Dad — radioed the rest of the outside units about the size of his dick and how his girlfriend was going to be glad it hadn't been shot off or something like that. I wasn't really listening.

I crawled toward the kitchen, pushing Dad's pistol and rifle in front of me. Don't ask me what the hell I thought I was doing, I couldn't tell you. Even now.

Two or three other officers came inside the house. They stood around Dad, looking down at him. I couldn't hear what was being said, but their tones told me everything I needed to know: 1) They were talking to him as if he were just another drunken example of the poor, ignorant, mean-spirited white trash they had to deal with every day, and, 2) They weren't very happy that Dad had hurt one of their own.

Sometime in there Dad was pulled to his feet. The officers laughed at him. Someone slapped on the handcuffs.

The circle of police officers parted. One of them noticed me on the floor in the kitchen and said something to the others.

I looked up and saw Dad looking back at me.

This is the part that I don't often talk about, because whenever I do, someone inevitably tells me that I must have imagined it, that I was in shock, that something like this *couldn't possibly* have occurred, blah-blah-blah, dozy-doe.

I was not then, nor have I ever been, one to "see things," to "imagine things," to "hallucinate things."

I have never used this next incident in any story, nor will I ever, because no one would believe it.

I was on the floor, looking straight into Dad's face, and he into mine.

I was scared, I was in pain, and one of the officers had entered the kitchen and knelt down beside me, his voice ever so calm and patient as he tried to get me to hand over the guns.

The officer standing by the kitchen doorway looked at Dad, then looked at me, then shook his head and laughed.

I couldn't help what I did next; I laughed, too.

Then saw it register on Dad's face.

His son was laughing at him. Because these cops thought

he was pathetic. Because he was an embarrassment. Because he was a failure whose life didn't amount to shit. Because he didn't matter.

I stifled the near-hysterical laugh as soon as it escaped me, but the damage was done.

Dad spluttered out one sob, just one, thick and heavy with humiliation.

Then his face turned into an expressionless slab of granite. And *he* laughed.

Just once.

Then snapped the chain holding the handcuffs together.

Just like that. Laugh. Snap. Like that chain was no more than a slightly thick stick.

I don't care if you believe that or not. I have copies of the police reports, and at least three of them mention being surprised that Dad was able to ". . . free himself of the restraints."

Before any of them had time to realize what had just happened, Dad slammed his elbow into the nearest officer's face and took his gun. The others started to turn toward the movement, a few drawing their weapons. Two of them jumped on Dad and he began to spin. That's all I saw before panic really got hold of me and I crawled and pushed for all I was worth.

Two shots were fired. One went into the wall over the kitchen entryway. The other one got me somewhere between my lower back and the middle of my thighs. (All right, I'll just say it — I got shot in the ass.) I remember being surprised that it didn't hurt more. A few moments later, it registered and then hurt like hell and then made me angry. I rolled over onto my back and saw an officer pointing a gun at me. I offered up the pistol. It probably wasn't the thing to do, raising a gun toward a policeman in the middle of a situation like this, because he fired at me. This third shot is the one I'll always remember: I *felt* that son-of-a-bitch whiz by my temple.

At least two officers lay unconscious on the floor as others came inside, one of them leading an attack dog. Dad threw the gun in his hand. It hit the officer standing over me in the back of the head. Dad screamed: "You don't hurt my boy!

Nobody hurts my boy! Not my Jeff!" At least, that's what it *sounded* like to me. (Jeff, had he lived, would have been my twin brother, but an accident at birth left him dead and me as the consolation prize. He now pops up as an alter-ego in some of my stories. I spell his name Geoff. Perhaps you remember him from a story in *Things Left Behind* called "Searching For Survivors," a story also known as "Safe." The big event in that story took place on the Fourth of July, and it wasn't until recently — believe it or not — that I actually made the connection.)

I tried to get up to stop Dad from making it even worse, but he'd come up behind the officer and yanked him off the floor. The officer pushed back against Dad and kicked out his legs. The toe of his boot got me right in the jaw. I lost three of my back teeth.

I resumed my crawling and bawling, pushing the guns along in front of me. Dad somehow managed to bulldoze his way through the officers clotting up the front room and threw the one he was holding through the front window. One of them screamed like I'd never heard anyone — man, woman, child, beast — scream before or since. It is a sound I never want to hear again.

I was so terrified at this point I was barely able to keep moving.

Then it got worse.

As soon as the officer came crashing through the window, shots were fired into the house from outside. It looked like everyone hit the floor, searching around for weapons.

I thought Dad had been shot; he hadn't, but I didn't know that at the time. I called out to him and he shouted for me to get the hell out. The attack dog was barking and snarling.

Two windows exploded then — one in the front of the house, the other behind me in the kitchen. Tear gas. I remember choking and throwing up on myself. I remember Dad yelling for me to help him. I remember shadow-shape figures moving through the smoke looking like something out of a science fiction movie because of the masks they wore.

I managed to make it down to the basement, guns and all. I didn't so much crawl down the steps as tumble face-first on my belly. I sat there in the semi-darkness and cried like a baby while above I heard the sounds of Dad being wrestled to the ground by what sounded like an army. I looked up only once, and saw another police dog being led by the small window that looked out from the basement onto the little sidewalk that ran parallel to the house. When I looked back down I saw that my hand was bleeding from where three of my fingernails had been crushed; the skin underneath them was swollen and dark purple. How it happened, I don't know.

(For those of you who are interested in final tallies, I ended this day with two cracked ribs, three crushed fingernails, a broken collar bone, a dislocated shoulder, cuts on my head, arms, and chest that garnered a total of twenty-six stitches, a badly sprained left arm, powder burns on my temple, and two "official" gunshot wounds. I remember all this when I *think* I'm having a bad day now.)

I stayed down there for several minutes, until I heard the last of the officers leave the house. I pulled myself and the guns back upstairs and peeked out through the remains of the front window.

This is the important part, pay attention.

There were three ambulances and seven police cruisers parked out front, visibar lights flashing to beat the band. Neighbors lined the street on both sides the length of the entire block. The police officers could have put Dad in any one of six nearby cruisers — there was one right in front of the fucking house! — but they chose, instead, to walk him almost all the way down the block, parading him past the neighbors, to a cruiser that sat at the far end of the street. Dad was in a second set of handcuffs. He was sobbing. He had thrown up on himself. Vomit dribbled from his chin. He kept apologizing to every neighbor he was dragged past.

The worst of it, though, was that my Dad's pants had started to fall down in the back, revealing what some people laughingly refer to as a "workman's crack."

He was completely, totally, and utterly disgraced.

The two officers who were hauling him up the street were putting on quite the show, jerking him around and holding onto this beaten, weary, sad man as if he were still a threat. I hope they felt brave. I hope they felt proud of themselves, turning my father into a one-man freak show.

That moment is forever frozen in my memory, and I knew right then it was important for me to memorize everything I was feeling — the anger, the sick-making sadness, the horror, the pain, the helplessness, the sudden, mystifying, overwhelming love I felt toward this man who once wanted to be chicken farmer but spent his life on the factory line, instead.

I wanted to mark this moment, and to remember it.

And the anger.

And the anger.

And the anger.

God, yes — the anger.

I stumbled over to the sofa and fell onto it. I could still hear the neighbors and the police all milling about, talking, some laughing, a few people crying. They didn't exist for me. All that composed my world at that moment was physical pain, humiliation, and anger.

I stared at my dim reflection in the television screen. The television was off. I didn't want it to be off, I wanted it to be on. To keep my company. So I turned it on —

— and guess what movie was playing?

Way ahead of me, aren't you?

Seconds was at the scene where Will Geer, after listening to John Randolph's heartbreaking recitation of the things in his life which matter (". . . my boat . . . friends at the club . . ." etc.), smiles sadly as says, "So this is what happens to the dreams of youth."

I lost it. The look on Randolph's face at that moment was so much like that on Dad's right before I started leading him up the stairs, I might as well have been looking at a black-and-white photograph of fifteen minutes earlier.

I looked away from the screen just in time to see the two police officers finally — *finally* — finish shoving Dad into the back of the cruiser.

So this is what happens to the dreams of youth.

I wiped my eyes and looked back at the screen and, for a minute or so longer — until people remembered there had been a teenaged boy in the house when all the shooting started, and so started wandering into the house — for just a minute or so, I was pulled out of this world I really didn't want to be in right at this moment and was, instead, immersed in the story on the screen in front of me. Undoubtedly a large part of it was shock — everything within and without had gone numb — but a part of it was also because I *wanted* to be pulled out of the world, and I honestly don't know if anything but *Seconds* could have done it right then.

And while I stared at the movie, I found myself humming, very quietly, a part of "The Rock" to myself, and somewhere in there I began thinking of each individual incident that had happened — to Dad during the war, to the police, to myself, to the Randolph character in the movie, all of it — as being an isolated musical theme that was trying to overlap with the others in order to create a cumulative, distinct, and final theme; I was grasping at straws, trying to find a goddamn *point* to all of this.

But I couldn't. I hadn't the capacity, the experience, the skill, intelligence, or wherewithal to string all of this together into a neat little final theme that would not fall shrill and tuneless on my ears.

But I wanted to have that ability, that intelligence and skill.

Life is material. . .

That's when I decided I wanted to be a writer of horror fiction. I promised myself that I would always try to convey in my stories at least some small sense of what I felt at that moment during the summer of 1977 when I watched the police haul my father down the street. Horror is not merely creating unease or suspense, nor is it simply letting emotions both light and dark bleed all over the page or the screen. It should convey the genuine sense of tragedy that hangs over all our lives; it should *scare* us, yes, of course, no arguments, but there has to be an element of *genuine loss* connected to that fear — be it loss of life, limb, sanity, or loved one. Of all forms of fiction, horror shouldn't be satisfied with simply *engaging* the emotions — it should strive to make people every joy, every shudder, every tear and triumph; it must force them to assume the role of the story's characters, whether they want to or not, and live their tragedy as if it were their own. I will not apologize for this, and if it makes me pretentious in your eyes, so be it. But I know now that what I experienced that moment, looking through that window at my father as he was made a mockery of, is what all truly *pure* horror fiction should make its readers experience: the terror, tragedy, sadness, anger, and soul-sick absurdity of violence and grief and how we struggle from womb to tomb to reconcile them with the concept of a Just universe where, we're led to believe, the good are always rewarded and the wicked punished (insert rim-shot here). Sometimes a hand reaches out from the shadows to protect us, to lead us toward safety and acceptance; sometimes this same hand grabs your throat and begins to squeeze; and sometimes no hand reaches out at all, we're just left cowering in the basement, alone with the coldness and the darkness and the guns, bleeding and scared and helpless. True horror should leave you wrung out, physically and emotionally. The best of it can even change you.

Life is material. . .

I was changed that day, in that moment from the summer of 1977. It defined me as a human being, and that bleeding, frightened, pissed-off teenager defined me — and defines me still — as a writer of horror.

. . . you just have to live long enough to see how to use it.

My dad died of cancer on June 15, 2001, just a few days after his 75th birthday. Until he was moved to the nursing home where he died, he slept by himself in an old twin bed in my old room because my mom's snoring was too loud. There were no pictures hanging on the wall, no cases displaying his medals. There was a rocking chair in there, as well, one he never used. It was weighed down by photo albums of the past that he never looked at. He had to wear Depends all the time because the radiation treatments he received for his first batch of cancer pretty much ruined his bowels and bladder. His clothes — all of them — were folded neatly into a pile that set on a small table at the foot of the bed. He owned one pair of pajamas, one pair of slippers. Almost no one came to visit him, at home during the last few years of his life, and he stopped keeping a phone in his room because whenever there was a call, it was never for him. When he died, it took my sister and me all of an hour to pack his possessions into boxes. He never wanted much for himself, except to know that his hard work counted for something. Anything he had, he gladly gave to his children. Up until the end, even in the nursing home, when Gayle or I visited, he asked if we need any money or anything. This from a man who couldn't find enough to pay for all of his prescriptions. His mother never came around to see him after his illness entered its final months. She said it was because of her health, yet she somehow managed to continue seeing her other living children several times a week.

When Dad died he was sitting in a wheelchair waiting for the nurses to change his bed. He was parked at an angle by the door to his room — which meant that he was looking into the bathroom. He was alone, and sometime between the nurses' changing the pillow cases and unfolding a fresh fitted sheet, my father quietly, not wanting to bother anyone, died. Staring into a toilet. His mother did not come to his funeral, claiming health reasons (yet somehow managed to find the energy to visit with her daughters later that same day). Nine months after Dad's death, my mother passed away. Going through some of her things, I came across a letter that Dad had written to her when they were first married and both of them worked double shifts:

Dear Mary:
    I am so sorry that I did not have the money to buy you an anniversary present. I will make it up to you. I know I say that a lot. It always seems like I am making things up to people. But I wanted you to know how much I love you and am glad you are my wife. I'm sorry I don't have a present for you. Happy anniversary.

It always seems like I am making things up to people.
Someone should have made something up to him. Just once. My mother, as well (who, I should add, grew up in the county childrens' home and she, like my father, worked her fingers and spirit to the bone to give their children a decent life).

So this is what happens to the dreams of youth.

There once was a young soldier who dreamed of becoming a chicken farmer, but he worked the line instead. I am that young soldier's only surviving son, and am proud to have had him as my dad. He thought it was great that I write, and that I'd published books. He'd read a lot of my published work — at least, that work whose type-face wasn't to small for his eyes, which were never what they used to be for as long as I knew him.

I take horror — not, for the record, myself — damned seriously, and I have my dad and *Quadrophenia* and a certain film by John Frankenheimer to thank for it.

As a result of my attitudes toward the horror field, I tend not to find myself drawn to many of the more traditional books and movies that are so easily — even *too-easily* —

Recognized as being part of the genre. *Of course* the movies in, say, Romero's "Dead Trilogy" are horror films — and we'll talk about those shortly — but for my money, you have to expand not only your personal definition of horror but your willingness to look for books and films that are not marketed as being the same; by looking outside of the narrowly-defined and popular misconceptions of horror, by moving past the obvious, you can often enrich your appreciation of those things that are good about the field, and understand more clearly why the bad is so inarguably awful.

To that end, I want to look at three other "second chance" films that also qualify — strongly, in my opinion — as horror movies.

Just as complex as *Seconds,* though less overpowering in its execution, 1968's *The Swimmer* (directed by Frank Perry and written by Eleanor Perry, based on the short story by John Cheever) was a labor of love for its producer/star Burt Lancaster. In it he plays a businessman who, at film's start, has decided to spend a bright summer Sunday afternoon making his way from pool to pool, swimming his way across suburbia to his own home. He lives in an upscale and trendy community where everyone knows everyone else in their chosen clique, so it comes as no surprise to anyone when Burt wanders into their back yard and tells them he is swimming home. They laugh. They make martinis. They talk about what a card Lancaster is and what a simply mah-velous party story his little escapade will make. It seems like another *Peyton Place* soap opera at first.

But then people start asking about his wife and daughters:
"I heard what happened . . ."
"I was so sorry to hear . . ."
"How are you feeling now. . . ?"
"I didn't think you'd want to be around anyone for a while, not after . . ."

What exactly did happen in Lancaster's life that has everyone treating him either with extreme caution or overzealous joviality? Where exactly is he coming from at the beginning of the film? (Our first sight of him comes as he's running in his swimming trunks through the woods, already sopping wet, yet he tells the first back yard gathering he appears in that theirs will be his "first" swim on his way home.) And why can't he tell anyone what he's been doing lately?

These key questions are skirted for the first half of the film, but it's the very lack of ready answers that provides a good deal of tension. Hints are dropped, concerned looks are exchanged, surreptitious gestures made behind Lancaster's back, and soon the viewer wonders about Lancaster's mental stability as, piece by piece, the horror of his life comes together like a jigsaw puzzle that's missing the last piece — which may be the reason *The Swimmer* is such a turn-off for many viewers: there is no direct and final answer to any of the questions, no last-minute revelation, but if you pay close attention, everything you need to know is there.

Lancaster gives a typically terrific performance, one full of both internal and physical catharses; every pool is a new baptismal fount where he washes away past sins, yet by the time he reaches the next pool, a different load of sins have made themselves known. You may not have a lot of sympathy for this character — he's shown to be a shameless opportunist, an adulterer, two-faced, and self-aggrandizing — but you will nonetheless be fascinated enough to follow him through to the genuinely shocking conclusion of his journey.

The Swimmer may be the closest American films will ever

come to capturing the type of "quiet dread" so richly explored in the "Oxrun Station" stories of Charles L. Grant. Yes, it's difficult as hell in places, but it's also suspenseful, disturbing, and ultimately rewarding.

The next two movies have something in common the previous films don't share: both crippled their director's career for various reasons.

Sorcerer, made by William Friedkin after his triumphs and numerous awards for both *The French Connection* and *The Exorcist,* was his own *Apocalypse Now*; a film that went over budget and took three times as long to film as originally planned, but one denied *Apocalypse's* subsequent fame, notoriety, and audience interest.

A remake of Henri-Georges Clouzot's *The Wages of Fear,* *Sorcerer* tells the story of four men, all wanted criminals, who flee to a nameless Third World country to escape punishment, imprisonment, torture, or death. When a devastating oil rig explosion offers the chance to make some big money very quickly (they have to transport old crates of leaking nitroglycerine over 200 miles of treacherous mountain road), each sees a chance to get out of this hell-hole country and forge a new life elsewhere, far from their regrets and old enemies.

Screenwriter Walon Green (who co-wrote *The Wild Bunch* with Sam Peckinpah) foregoes a script filled with meaningful dialogue and concentrates instead on expressionistic imagery to tell large chunks of the story. This, coupled with Friedkin's flair for jittery realism, gives *Sorcerer* an effective and gritty documentary feel. There are three sequences in this film which remain to this day some of the most astounding ever executed in a fictional movie; a terrorist attack that makes you feel as if you're trapped in the middle of a Lebanon street war; a riot scene of raw and terrifying violence; and a bridge crossing sequence that should be help up to future directors as a quintessential example of how an expert filmmaker builds nerve-wracking suspense.

But, as in all these films, the final price of the second chance is extracted, and proves to be more than the characters bargained for. And if nothing else remains in your mind after viewing this movie, the one indelible image that will haunt you is the gaunt, drawn face of Roy Scheider as small-time hood Jackie Scanlon; Scheider is the embodiment of weariness and regret that struggles against all logic and hope to find something worth going on for. Schieder gives a marvelous performance in a role that relies more on physicalization than dialogue to define and express the character and his struggle.

I greatly admire both *Sorcerer* and *The Wages of Fear,* but find my preference leaning toward Friedkin's film, if for no other reason because *Sorcerer* takes the time to establish these men in their previous lives so the viewer can have some sense of what they've been forced to abandon. *Sorcerer* possesses emotional layers where *Wages* opts for the coldly intellectual, and though both films are potentially devastating to the viewer, *Sorcerer* remains the more humane and accessible of the two — that second word not being easily applied to the final "second chance" movie: Sam Peckinpah's *Bring Me the Head of Alfredo Garcia.*

Early on in *Garcia,* one secondary character remarks: "Be content with your lot in life, no matter how poor it may be. Only then can you expect mercy."

That line could have come from any of these films, and in each case would have been appropriate, but in *Garcia* it's doubly so, for no other American director has understood or been able to capture the Mexican "culture of poverty" as unflinchingly as Peckinpah. Though *Garcia* may not be Peckinpah's best film (it continues to appear on several "All Time Worst" lists), it is without a doubt his most personal. From its lovely opening image (a young pregnant Mexican woman resting by a river, sunning herself) to its harrowing closing shot (a smoking Gattling gun), *Garcia* is unique, for no other film of Peckinpah's has so seamlessly managed to contain every element this often-brilliant director was obsessed with exploring: love, betrayal, desperation, tenderness in the face of brutality, loneliness, helplessness, anger, the struggle of integrity vs. conformity, friendship, and, of course, the futility of violence.

Peckinpah was accused throughout his career of glorifying violence, but he insisted he was doing the direct opposite:

showing how repulsive it was by dwelling on it so much — and on no film was he more accused of glorifying the violence he claimed to disdain than in *Garcia*.

The basic story goes like this: The beautiful daughter of a wealthy and powerful Mexican land baron is seduced, impregnated, and abandoned by one Alfredo Garcia, a shameless gambler/drunkard/womanizer. The land baron, El Jefe, assembles his soldiers and declares his outrage at the loss of his daughter's (and subsequently the lessening of his own) honor, and shouts: "Bring me the head of Alfredo Garcia!" And like the Knights of the Round Table questing for the Holy Grail, El Jefe's army is off and running.

Into this scenario enters an American expatriate named Bennie (Warren Oates) who is biding his time playing piano in a sleazy Mexico City bar. He is approached by two gangsters he often works for as a bagman (Robert Webber and Gig Young) who have been authorized to offer him a substantial piece of change if he'll hunt down and decapitate Alfredo Garcia. Bennie, despite many indecent instincts he's been trying to kill, accepts the offer, telling them he can use the money to take himself and his girlfriend, Elita (Isela Vega, who remains the strongest female character to appear in a Peckinpah movie) somewhere far away and begin a new life.

Along the twisted way, Bennie proposes to Elita in what is arguably the most heartfelt and sadly moving scene Peckinpah ever filmed. The two run into and overcome several obstacles in their way (yes, I'm being deliberately vague here) before they find themselves at a rotting, neglected graveyard where the careless Garcia, shot by a gambling partner, is now buried.

The first half of this film has the loose narrative structure of an obscure European import; in fact, in places, it gets downright eccentric — but I still say this film was condemned only because it came from Peckinpah; had it come from a director from New Zealand or France, critics would have drowned it in praise. (Had to get that in.)

"Why does he think of this as a horror movie?" I hear you cry.

Because from the moment Bennie and Elita enter that

wretched graveyard in the middle of the night, *Garcia* employs not only the classic visual elements of old horror movies (circling bats, wolves howling in the distance, misshapen shadows skulking in the background) but its heart and soul surrender to the horrific as well. The shadow-drenched grave robbing sequence is truly nightmarish, and from that scene on, the film begins a fast descent through all nine circles of Dante's Hell as Bennie makes his way across country with Garcia's decomposing head inside a wet burlap bag that is perpetually swarming with flies.

"Just you and me, Al, baby!" says Bennie, who spends the second half of the film slowly going insane. Warren Oates (who was infuriatingly underrated for most of his career) gives a fabulous performance as Bennie, making the man at once repulsive, sympathetic, heroic, romantic, and tragic. His fascinating and complex characterization was easily the best American film performance of 1974, yet was ignored by virtually everyone when it came time to hand out those overrated golden statuettes.

Bennie's "relationship" with Garcia's head gets so creepy by the film's end that I refuse to spoil it for you by going into any more details; suffice it to say that Bennie not only talks to Al, but often stops in the middle of a sentence to listen as Al gives him advice. (And that's not even the weird part.)

That Bennie is doomed from the moment he comes into possession of Garcia's head is a given, yet the viewer is perversely compelled to watch his slow and painful deterioration. Of all the "second chance" movies mentioned here, *Bring Me the Head of Alfredo Garcia* is the one whose heart, blood, and soul lie strongly within the field of genuine horror. (I am convinced that John McNaughton drew some of his visual and thematic inspiration for *Henry: Portrait of a Serial Killer* from the second half of *Garcia*. Watch both films back-to-back and you might think you've just watched then first two movies in an uncompleted trilogy.)

In the end all four movies seem to have the same philosophy about the Second Chance: You're better off where you are, for there is no mercy regardless (a philosophy my dad would have agreed with — he wouldn't have *liked* agreeing with it, but he would have) — and if that doesn't qualify them as horror films, then maybe we'd all be better of reading Sidney Sheldon or sighting re-runs of *Will & Grace* and *Dallas* as examples of the well-told story.

2

For An Eye And a Tooth; Chowing Down; and The Emperor's New Clothes

"Violence, violence
It's the only thing that'll make you see sense."
— Mott the Hoople

*E*very year the tired old debate over that Ol' Debbil Violence on TV, in films, and in horror fiction erupts again, with proponents on both sides shrieking their intolerance of the others' views on the subject. The catalysts have ranged from the absurd bloodletting found in Brian DePalma's laughable remake of *Scarface* (with Al Pacino's brilliant 3-hour impression of Charro), to the intentional over-the-top absurdity of Edward Lee's *The Big Head* and Robert Devereaux's *Santa Steps Out*, to how many times Wile E. Coyote has plunged into that canyon in the Road Runner cartoons.

I think both sides of this argument would do well to consider something so obvious it almost depresses me to think it needs to be said outright: it's not the quantity of violence contained in television shows or movies or books — or, for that matter, even how graphically it is portrayed — it is the attitude *behind* the violence which should be called into question when someone is trying to determine whether or not something might be "harmful" to a viewer or reader. "An eye for an eye and a tooth for a tooth" might have worked well in the days of Saul and Moses, but the world has become less morally black and white since the stone tablets allegedly came down from the mountain. There has always been violence in the world, and there will always be violence in the world . . . and psychos with knives and rapists and sadists and pedophiles and bad folks with big guns *ad infinitum* and, eventually, like it or not, it will touch everyone in one form or another. I'm forty-three years old and have been (among other things) beaten up several times, stabbed twice, shot (see previous chapter) . . . and not once did I blame the actions of my attackers on their having viewed *Dirty Harry* or *Taxi Driver* or *Friday the Thirteenth* or *A Nightmare on Elm Street* one time too many — or having spent too much time re-reading *The Books of Blood* or *The Regulators* — a novel which reportedly began life as am original film script by Stephen King that was to be helmed by director Sam Peckinpah; ain't it annoying, the trivial shit I know?

I have been on the receiving end of violence more than a few times; I have also been on the delivery end of it; and I have been — like the character of Bonnie Winter in Graham Masterton's brilliant novella of the same name — among those whose duty it was to go in and mop up the aftermath.

Some of you may be familiar with my novella "Safe" which originally appeared in *HWA Presents: Robert Bloch's PSYCHOS,* and was also reprinted in *The Year's Best Fantasy and Horror,* as well as my collection *Things Left Behind* (under the title "Searching For Survivors"). The story concerns the after effects of a violent mass-murder on a mid-sized Midwestern town; the core of the story details the night a skeleton janitorial crew goes into the house where the first of the murders took place and proceeds to systematically scrape, mop, wipe, and carry away every trace of the tragedy.

"Safe" took the better part of twenty years to get onto paper because it hit too close to home. I worked with a janitorial company for several years in the late 70s and early 80s, and one night I was awakened at two in the morning by a call from my boss asking me if I would volunteer to join a skeleton crew for an emergency job. The night would pay $300.00 for each crew member. At first, still groggy, I couldn't understand why anyone would turn down 300 bucks for four or five hours of work; then he told me why he had to call and ask for volunteers.

Three days before, a local man had snapped, killing his family and then himself. The family was a somewhat prominent one in town, and the surviving relatives wanted the house cleaned as thoroughly and as quickly as possible. Two of the family members this man had killed (with a shotgun) had been children.

I wound up cleaning the childrens' room. You cannot help but feel the sick-making silence and overwhelming loss of life when you perform a duty like this. Three times I had to stop work to go outside to either cry or vomit. But I got that room cleaned; I wiped away every trace of those childrens' existence. There was a lot of blood, as well as other liquids, all of them dried. There was also, in places, bits of tissue mixed in with that blood.

When it was all over, we collected our pay and went back to our homes. I fell asleep somewhere around nine a.m. and didn't wake up until well after four. I had thrown my clothes from that night into the corner, along with the work boots I'd been wearing. As I was gathering everything up for washing, I for some reason checked the bottoms of my boots, and found a very small but — thanks to the mopping I'd done — still very wet piece of human tissue wedged into the heavy treads. I got sick all over again. This was all that remained of one of those children. But which one? And from what part of them had this been blasted? Had they died immediately or had they suffered? All this came to me in a rush and I just imploded.

I tell you this because it's important that you know I am not one of those writers who employs violence in their stories simply because "it's cool" to wipe out as many people in as many grotesque and creative ways as possible. I have seen too much violence, as well as the consequences of that violence, to be so blasé and thoughtlessly off-handed about its uses and depictions in fiction.

If you haven't already guessed, this is a subject about which I feel passionately, because violence, regardless of your attitude toward it, is an indispensable storytelling tool to those of us who toil in horror/dark fantasy — a field in which the tales rely heavily on the exploration of, and connections between, violence and grief and how we as human beings try reconciling their presence and consequences with the idea of a Just Universe.

For the record, I am not one of the Happy People (an admission which will come as a great shock to readers of my fiction); I tend to define myself only by what I do: I am a writer, a storyteller, a professional teller of lies. For most of my life — as absurd as tit may sound — I've never felt all that comfortable around people (which is why you don't see me at many conventions) and, as a result, I'm not all that close to anyone. What few folks can endure my company only feel comfortable approaching me as a writer —

everything that is asked about or expressed, all opinions and philosophies and feelings that are shared, are almost always done in the sole context of what I do. Who I am doesn't enter into it, because I usually won't allow it to. I keep people at arm's length both emotionally and physically, and often wish that I possessed whatever mechanism it is that allows one to drop one's guard and welcome human intimacy without fear and suspicion, but the truth is: I don't trust happiness. I never have and probably never will, and that is very often reflected in my fiction.

It is also reflected in my tastes in fiction and movies; I find myself drawn most strongly to those stories in which the central character, while respected and even loved by those around him or her, remains at a distance from everyone and everything, an observer on the sidelines of their own existence; more often than not, these characters are also a bit monomaniacal, even obsessive, over one thing in particular, an object or concept or single-minded notion they believe is the only thing that gives their existence any meaning whatsoever. Add to this mix the threat of, or consequences from, violence, and as both a reader and movie watcher, I'm there.

So it should come as no surprise that I responded fervently to director Jim (*MyLeft Foot, In the Name of the Father*) Sheridan's 1990 film *The Field*, starring the late Richard Harris in what is surely his finest performance on the screen. He plays

Bull McCabe, an Irish farmer who, for all of his life, has been tending a field that was passed on to him from his father, who was given it by his father, who was given it by his father . . . you get the idea. McCabe's dream — scratch that — his *sole purpose* in life, is to pass this field on to his surviving son. (We learn early on that his other son committed suicide years previous to the start of the story.)

There's just one problem: McCabe's family doesn't actually own the field, but merely rents it. It's a matter of deep personal pride to McCabe that he took this field, once no more than a barren, dirty, rock-covered plain, and, with a tenderness and care most men relinquish on the raising of their children, turned it into a piece of rich and fertile land that is not only stunning to behold but produces enough sustenance to keep his cattle fat and healthy.

The man who owns the field dies, leaving it to his widow. Upon learning that widow plans to move away, McCabe assumes that she will sell the field to him. Enter American businessman Tom Berenger, descendant of an Irish clan who fled the country during the Potato Famine. Berenger's company wishes to purchase the field for development, thus bringing industry and commerce to the area. McCabe swears upon the souls of his ancestors that "the Yank" (as he's called throughout the film, never being given a name) will not take what is "rightfully" his.

This doesn't even begin to set up the moral quagmire that the film grapples with. The widow does not feel a moral obligation to sell the field to McCabe — she'll sell it to the highest bidder. McCabe's son doesn't want to inherit the field, he wants to go to the city and make his own life, and so sets out on a campaign of terrorism against the widow so she'll sell to the American just to spite McCabe. McCabe, who sees the possibility of losing everything his life has been centered around, bullies the townspeople into siding with him. Add to this volatile brew the unspoken truth that McCabe's first son chose to kill himself rather than inherit the field and his father's way of life, and you've got a story where, from the outset, the question is not "Will it end well?" (you know it can't) but, rather, "Who will suffer the least?"

Though it lacks some of the subtle moral shades that characterized the John B. Keane play on which it is based, it's impossible to watch *The Field* and not be caught up in McCabe's passion, even when you begin to realize that his obsession with the field borders on the psychotic. There is ultimately no Wrong or Right in the film, only a thick, murky gray area where the best you can hope for is to make a choice and stick with it and hope it's a good one.

About two-thirds of the way through, McCabe visits with the local priest who has called a meeting between him and the American. The scene is terrifying on countless levels (physically, morally,- psychologically), and culminates in what has to be one of the greatest single speeches in film history, where McCabe, in order to make the American understand his love and loyalty to the field, recounts an incident from his childhood where he and his father had to choose between saving the life of McCabe's mother or tending to the field. They chose the field.

I don't "chill" easily, but this speech, brilliantly rendered by Harris, left me trembling. Violence, grief, obsession, confusion and self-loathing, passion and purpose, as well as fear of the unknown are all contained in this speech, and it is a testament to Harris's ability as an actor that he manages to convey all this not in stops and starts but an a hard, prismlike beam, delivered in a whisper that resounds stronger than countless roars. I defy you to watch this scene and not react.

In the end, though, Understanding crumbles between the warring factions and leaves only violence. And when it comes, it comes down hard, culminating in a final sequence of inescapable tragedy that manages to be not only affecting but highly
symbolic without resorting to heavy-handedness.

Though not billed as a horror film, *The Field* wrestles with issues and actions that are not uncommon to horror, and is, in that respect, a horror movie of the highest (though not most obvious) order, and should not be missed, if only for Harris's astounding acting. It reminds us that nothing in horror is so jarring as the genuinely tragic.

The genuinely tragic is the jumping-off point for director

Alan Arkin's 1971 film *Little Murders* — a movie that serves to underscore the notion that it is not the violence but the attitude behind it which must be examined, and here the attitude hits decisively at the core of the American family.

Based on Jules (*Carnal Knowledge*) Feiffer's stage play, it chronicles the story of milquetoast NYC photographer Alfred Chamberlain, superbly played by Elliot Gould. Gould's character is passive to the point of catatonia, not defending himself from a beating by street thugs early on because, as he says, "There's no way to talk someone out of beating you up if that's what they want to do." Enter Patsy Newquist (Marcia Rodd), a hard-as-nails urbanite who tries to awaken in Alfred some sense of moral outrage at the wretched state of the world. The two fall in love — insomuch as they are able. (Alfred's declaration of "I really truly nearly trust you!" is the closest he comes to voicing his affection, and is the ultimate turn-on for Patsy.)

The New York of *Little Murders* is just as ugly as that presented in films such as *Death Wish* and *Combat Shock* (a.k.a. *American Nightmare),* but unlike those movies, this ugliness is tinged with a sense of absurdity, a n onyx-dark humor that (intentionally) leaves the viewer unsure whether to laugh or cringe . . . so you do both. (And, as if to underline the film's intent, director Arkin chooses to give it a music score — written by Fred Kaz — that sounds as if it was lifted from something that starred Charlie Brown and Snoopy.)

After Alfred marries Patsy, the two move in with her family. Her father (Vincent Gardenia) is a button-down, extreme Right-Winger who makes George W. Bush look like a free-thinker, while her mother (the marvelous Elizabeth Wilson) is a "take everything one day at a time" type who, when asked why she didn't flinch after nearly having her head blown off by a sniper, smiles and says, "I get shot at every day. Why whine about it?" These characters are the conclusive evolution of the jaded city-dweller; violence and death are interchangeable with meat and potatoes in their lives, and are viewed in the same off-hand manner.

Little Murders defies easy analysis and must be seen to have its more trenchant moments fully savored. Every reel of the

movie is saturated in violence, even when it occurs off-screen
(which is often the case). With the exception of Patsy and her
father, the rest of the characters are one step above zombies
and remain so until the last fifteen minutes, when the depressing darkness of truth begins to overshadow the often
sidesplitting comedy.

After a family member is murdered by a sniper's bullet —
which comes through the window of the Newquist's apartment during dinner, and is reacted to by the mother in the
same way most people would react to a fly — the Newquists
turn their dwelling into a steel-doored fortress right out of a
Batman comic book — but even this doesn't protect them
from the encroaching insanity they try so hard to stay above.

A mind-blown detective (hysterically played by Alan Arkin)
shows up to
reassure the family that the NYC Police Department will
protect them; but the detective himself is so burned-out, and
rabidly paranoid, that he only serves to amplify their fear
rather than alleviate it. (Don't misunderstand, the scene is so
howlingly funny you might have to watch it twice in order
to hear the parts you were laughing over.)

Finally, Alfred surrenders to the violence, bringing home
a rifle which he proceeds to load in front of the family, then
smashes out a window and begins shooting at
passersby in the street. This act is not presented as evil and
deranged, but rather cathartic and healthy, for it snaps the
family out of its complacency and bonds them together more
firmly than any amount of love ever could. After each has
had their turn at blowing away innocent bystanders, the
family sets down to a nice American dinner while screams
from the street filter in from the window and the wail of
police sirens grow louder. Mrs. Newquist looks around the
table at her smiling, happy clan, offers a benevolent matriar-
chal grin, and says, "You don't know how good it is to hear
my family laugh again . . . for a while there I was really
worried." The camera lingers on her sublime expression as
the sirens scream and the madness outside covers everything
like a shroud. If it weren't so terrifying it would be funny —
or is, if it weren't so funny it would be terrifying? See it, and

judge for yourself.

The point *Little Murders* seems to be making, in direct opposition to that made by *The Field*, is that when we resort to violence, we become not worse than those who direct violence against us, but sickeningly the same; there's no way to tell the difference. And where can we go from there?

If we are to believe the answer offered to that question in Sam Peckinpah's 1970 *Straw Dogs*, then where we go is deeper into the enjoyment of that violence, for it is only in the amount and scope of individual brutality that there can there be found any hope of rising above the masses and establishing integrity of character. In short: if you're meaner than the meanest, that alone will redeem you in your own eyes — a theme that was both explored and eschewed by Peckinpah throughout his career.

Born in Fresno, California on February 21, 1925, Peckinpah grew up on a ranch in the California mountains. His father was a judge, and Peckinpah was a rowdy teenager who eventually enlisted in the Marines, though he never saw combat.

After his discharge, he discovered theater and eventually got his lucky break in the early 50s when respected Hollywood director Don Siegel hired him as an assistant at Allied Artists. Peckinpah began writing scripts (he helped rewrite and had a small role in 1956's *Invasion of the Body Snatchers*) and got his first job directing in 1958 when he did an episode of the television series *Broken Arrow*. His feature-length directorial debut was 1961's *The Deadly Companions*.

Peckinpah, with films such as *Major Dundee* and *Ride the High Country*, easily established himself as a great American director. Critics were quick (before *The Wild Bunch*, anyway) to mention his name alongside those of John Ford and Howard Hawks.

Peckinpah hated it.

He hated it because in the "good old" Western the only characters an audience was asked to sympathize with were, naturally, the good guys like Randolph Scott and Chuck Heston. When the so-called "bad guys" got blown away, it was supposed to make an audience cheer wildly.

Which, as Peckinpah was quick to point out, completely robbed the "bad guys" of any humanity whatsoever — after all, the "bad guys" in *Shane* and *Will Penny* were given full identities, so why couldn't this be a trend that could set itself firmly in the American Western?

Because no one is *supposed to care* about the bad guys.

So Peckinpah set out to make an "anti-Western," a film that, while it might be set in the West, horses and posses intact, had nothing else in common with the type of films he'd been making — and despising.

That film was *The Wild Bunch.* In it audiences met the likes of Pike (William Holden in one of his finest hours) and his gang, a run-down, over-the-hill bunch of outlaws who time and progress has caught up with. They were old, tired, anachronistic, looking for a way out. Audiences learned to sympathize with these men as the film progressed, even side with them and, in the film's historic finale — almost folklore now — watch them die in blood-drenched slow motion, every agonized twitch dwelt upon until their mangled bodies lay dead before the camera.

Here was Peckinpah's genius with his bloody ballet of death: he'd made a Western, all right, but he'd shown it from the "bad guy's" point of view, and no one cheered when they died. The black and white way of presenting right and wrong was forever destroyed, and the myth of the American Western was forever debunked.

Peckinpah was then asked why he chose to make the violence so bloody, and why he chose to film it in slow motion. His reply (which I am paraphrasing) was something along these lines: "I thought audiences should be given a good, clear look at what they've been cheering all these years."

That was in 1969. Vietnam was at its height. The Civil Rights Movement was the victim of more and more violent attacks. Students were being killed protesting. And a bunch of hippies had just gotten together for three days of peace and music at a place called Woodstock.

Things were nuts; and into this insanity Peckinpah unleashed *The Wild Bunch,* which many claimed was not so much an anti-Western as it was a thinly-disguised metaphor for the dangerously unstable state of American society at the time; that Peckinpah had set his morality tale in the Old West and not on some college campus only served to give credence to this argument.

To which I say: Yeah, right; whatever. Go back to your film-school textbooks and leave me alone to enjoy the movie.

After enduring an endless series of attacks in the press and horse-shit intellectual "dissections" over the violence and themes in *The Wild Bunch*, Peckinpah followed it up in 1970 with the gentle, lyrical, funny, and uncharacteristically warm *The Ballad of Cable Hogue*, a bawdy, character-rich Western with Jason Robards, Stella Stevens, and a wonderfully daffy David Warner as a whacked-out backwoods preacher. The movie was a critical success, did lukewarm business at the box-office, and was just inoffensive and uncontroversial enough for people to stop worrying about Peckinpah — which I think is exactly what he intended, because he was about to turn loose *Straw Dogs* — a film that not only escalated the levels of violence found in *The Wild Bunch* but moved it into the modern-day world.

In the movie, Dustin Hoffman plays David Sumner, an American mathematician who, having received a research grant, moves to England with his ultra-sexy wife Amy (Susan George, in what has to be one of the great smoldering-tease performances of all time). They take up residence in her former home, a remote village near Wales.

From the start Sumner knows he's not welcome; early on he enters a pub to purchase a pack of "American cigarettes" and is met at first by condescending smirks, then, by the time he leaves, barely-disguised hostility — even after he buys a round of drinks for everyone.

In an effort to behave in a neighborly fashion, he hires a group of local men to re-shingle the roof of his house. One of these men turns out to be his wife's former boyfriend, Scutt, who, (and not to much surprise), still harbors a torch for her — and she for him.

Things get bad in a hurry. The men set out on what is at first a subtle campaign of terror (which is eerily echoed in *The Field)*, intimidating Sumner at every opportunity. Somewhere in here one of them mutilates the family cat. But even after this, Sumner refuses to strike back, insisting that he is an intelligent and civilized man, and civilized men find other ways to work out their problems.

Failing to break Sumner, Scutt and the others change their tactics and invite him to go hunting with them — then, once he is safely isolated, humiliate him while Scutt makes his way back to the house and proceeds to rape Amy.

Viewing the movie again, you cannot help but be struck by the moral ambiguity of the prolonged rape sequence. In a time of ultra-lame-brained PC, filmmakers today are too nervous to try anything like this for fear of offending anyone. (An aside here: were Peckinpah still alive — and what a loss that he is not — and tried to release this film today, I am convinced that this sequence would either be heavily trimmed to make it one-sided, or excised altogether.)

In the scene, after the initial act of violence (a hard slap across the face which sends Amy slamming down onto the couch), Amy and Scutt set about wrestling with one another in a manner that, by turns, resembles both a rape and a mutual seduction of the soft-core S&M variety. Amy calls Scutt names while saying "No, no!" over and over, all the time undressing him and wrapping her legs around his waist. Whenever he physically overpowers her, we see in her face that she loves it; and when she fights back against his brutality, this turns him on all the more. This is the kind of sex she prefers (that much is made obvious), the kind Scutt is best at, and the kind lacking in her marriage. In a way, it's the inverse of the ultimate rape nightmare, because the viewer is left uncertain of: A) who assaulted whom, or, B) if a rape occurred at all — and when later Amy goads Sumner into making their sex more violent, the discomfort level is shoved up another fifty notches or so.

Throughout the film we get glimpses of a character named Henry Niles (the superb David Warner, brilliantly effective here in an uncredited role, which he played for nothing as a favor to Peckinpah) who is basically the village simpleton, a gentle giant right out of Steinbeck's *Of Mice and Men*. Peckinpah deftly establishes in a few brief scenes the sympathetic connection felt between David Sumner and Henry Niles.

Later, when Niles accidentally kills a local girl, he seeks refuge at Sumner's home while a drunken band of heavily-armed men (Scutt among them) surround the house and demand that Sumner hand over ". . . that idiot savage." Amy insists that they throw Niles out the door, but when a brick comes crashing through the window, Sumner turns to her and says, in a voice devoid of human emotion, "I will not allow violence against this house," and proceeds to defend his home against the invaders, accompanied by bagpipe music which blares from the stereo.

This last half-hour still remains in my opinion unparalleled in its heart-stopping and perversely beautiful depiction of savagery as Hoffman's character gradually begins to enjoy the violence. Peckinpah's maverick and trend-setting use of the now-legendary (and often-satirized) "slow-mo" technique was never more effective or affecting than it is here; this astounding sequence has lost none of its power or vicious grace during the 32 years that have elapsed since its initial release; employing everything from boiling liquids to splintered chair legs to a bear trap, Sumner — with an intensely calculated, automatonlike purpose — kills every single last one of the attackers: in the end, standing amidst the carnage, blood splashed across his face in ribbons, Sumner smiles. Even through the cracked lenses of his glasses we see the sparkle in his eyes as he says, "I did it. I killed 'em all." (A moment is in almost direct contrast to the closing moments of the novel upon which its based, Gordon M. Williams' *The Siege at Trencher's Farm*. Though an excellent novel, it, like James Dickey's *Deliverance*, approaches the violence from an almost mythic viewpoint, and offers a sense of justice that *Straw Dogs* goes out of its way to avoid. Back to the bloodied Dustin now.)

Leaving Amy wife to weep and shudder over the body of her former lover, Sumner puts Niles into the car and the two of them drive out into the darkness. After they've been on the road for a few minutes, Niles turns to Sumner and says, "I don't know my home." Sumner, his face illuminated by the dashboard lights, smiles, looks out the windshield with an expression like a serial killer on the prowl, and replies, "That's all right. Neither do I."

And they vanish over the hill into the seemingly permanent night.

What one comes away with after viewing these films is a somewhat nihilistic view of human nature; the sense that we, as a race, are hell-bent on complete self-destruction and only bother creating music and art and temples so as to have an interesting backdrop for the bloodletting. It's a disturbing notion, but one that seems more a warning than a prophecy. It helps to think of these movies as being cautionary tales, which (in my opinion) is what enables the best horror stories to transcend the ghettoization imposed on the field by those who would have you believe that only works which concern themselves with what is true and fine and noble in the human condition are worth one's intellectual and emotional investment.

Then how do you explain the controversy and animated discussions that *still* ignite when the subject of George A. Romero's *Dead* Trilogy arises?

I want to refer you back to that quote from Eliot's *The Waste Lands* that I used at the front of this book; now, while I doubt that Romero used this poem as a source of aesthetic inspiration for the first *Dead* movie, I find that Eliot's simple, eloquent imagery echoes the sad and cynical poignancy that can be found in Romero's justifiably ground-breaking horror film trilogy.

It can be argued that the *Dead* series challenges not only the notion of what constitutes cinematic Art (witness the still-raging debates over the original *Texas Chainsaw Massacre),* but rends that notion to shreds, reconstructing it for a generation of horror fans who, like myself, were too young to be tolerated by the folks who survived World War II and weren't old enough to be embraced by the Woodstock Nation: we took refuge in the products of our and others' imaginations, be it a late night rerun of *Frankenstein* or *The Masque of the Red Death* (or, nowadays, first-run showings of *May, The Ring,* or *28 Days Later),* telling ghost stories at sixth-grade camp (now: listening to Stephen King reading *Hearts In Atlantis* on compact disc or watching *Near Dark* on DVD), or huddling under the blankets at night with a flashlight and a pile of those nasty horror comic books our parents didn't want us to read (which have now become the Clive Barker/Peter Straub/Douglas Clegg/Anne Rice novels we proudly read in public). In short, the *Dead* films document (albeit covertly) the evolution of horror's moral and (you should pardon the word) aesthetic sensibilities.

Just so you know that I'm aware of something, allow me to quote the eminently-quotable Joe R. Lansdale; this is taken from his essay "A Hard-On For Horror" as it was reprinted in *Writer of the Purple Rage*: "I'm not saying that *Night of the Living Dead* and *The Texas Chainsaw Massacre* kept me awake at night pondering the meaning of it all. I have seen far too much attention given to the existentialist nature of these movies, and all I have to say to that is this: Bullshit, pilgrim!"

So understand that what follows — while heartfelt — might very well be just another steamy load of pilgrim bullshit.

Ahem . . .

Although the trilogy has been accused of dealing with everything from tribal mentality in the face of political paranoia to humankind's inability to seriously face its own encroaching mortality, the richness of the *Dead* films, for me, is in their exploration of the relationships that quickly develop among the human protagonists. In all three movies you have people who, under normal circumstances, would more than likely have nothing to do with one another, yet are forced to band together against a common enemy in order to survive. New enemies are made, to be certain, but so are new friends — and these latter relationships are always blood-brother/sister strong, and undeniably compelling.

But these movies are first and foremost scary as hell, fiercely executed to generate often dizzying levels of terror and revulsion — but Romero has never been satisfied with just giving his audience "a good scare"; he also wants to leave them with something to think about once the shock has worn off, and achieves this by offering "zombie" films that are also intelligent, literate, and populated (for the most part) by full developed characters with whom the viewer feels a immediate empathy. Add to this already sublime mixture heavy doses of dry humor, and you've got a unique horror film experience.

One element in all three movies that has been almost consistently overlooked is their commendably unsentimental poignancy; the unflinching manner in which they present emotional pain that always reaches, and sometimes even surpasses, the level of physical pain so graphically portrayed on the screen.

Early on in *Dawn of the Dead* then is a scene where a woman who's holed-up in her apartment opens the door to see her long-dead husband waiting outside. She embraces him and he immediately chomps a large chunk out of her neck and shoulder. The scene is powerful and affecting not so much because of the gore (Tom Savini's makeup effects remain among the finest in the field) but because of the expression on the woman's face when she sees her husband: in a few golden seconds her expression goes from shocked to confused to relieved and, finally, joyful; the viewer gets a real sense of her loneliness and longing before her screams pierce the air. Violence and grief become two sides of the same coin; rarely is one present without the other, and in the world of the *Dead* trilogy where your ". . . shadow at evening" (the dead, who are, ah all, ourselves) ". . . rises to meet you," that's precisely how should be: the traditional funeral intonation may be "ashes to ashes and dust to dust," but here where the zombies rule, our deepest fear (that all of us shall return to a state of dust one day) is held in their hands . . . and they shove the reality of Death down our throats over and over again. (It occurs to me that an attempt to distill the true subtext of these film so that all of us will come away in agreement is a little like throwing a hundred strangers into a room and trying to get them all to agree on seeing the same image in a Rorschach blot; so keep in mind that I'm speaking for myself and myself alone. One pilgrim's bullshit.)

In 1968, when *Night of the Living Dead* was released, such metaphorical notions were about as "different" as horror movies could get, and helped to establish Romero as a force to be reckoned with. He once told *Filmmakers Newsletter* that the movie was intended to be ". . . an allegory, meant draw a parallel between what people are becoming and the idea that people are operating on many levels of insanity that are clear only to themselves. The zombies are us. We create them so we can kill them off, justifying our own existence — it's a kind of penance, self-exorcism."

To understand just how effectively Romero practiced what he preached,

you would do well to remember that the Vietnam War was reaching its bloody height at this time; Had *NOTLD* been released earlier or later than that painful, historic year of 1968, I think it possible that its sometimes diatribe-level symbolism would have been lost on its audience.

Another element which set *NOTLD* apart from other horror movies of its decade was its then-radical use of a black hero *not* played by Sidney Poitier. In addition to Vietnam, the country was dealing with the violent opposition to the Civil Rights Movement; giving an unknown black actor the lead in *NOTLD* should have, given that volatile climate, signaled commercial and critical suicide for the movie. It's a testament to both Romero's integrity and the late Duane Jones' excellent performance as that this did not turn out to be the case.

Romero stuck his neck further out by having the script contain *not one* reference to Ben's being the only non-white among the main characters — and you can't help but wonder if this was Romero's way of paralleling the story with the Civil Rights Movement: a notion that, considering the violence which had befallen Malcolm X and was to soon befall Martin Luther King (not to mention the Watts Riots), makes Ben's death at the end of the film more sad and tragic than ironic.

If you think social irony isn't present in these movies, take a look at the way people's attitudes toward firearms are explored over the course of the trilogy. In *NOTLD*, guns are the source of salvation and power within the group — whoever holds the guns holds everyone's safety, and is subsequently the Leader (a role that changes several times during the film).

In *Dawn of the Dead*, guns — like the zombies — are rampant, and make their presence known almost immediately. Everyone has a weapon and an itchy trigger finger and is more than willing to shoot anything that moves — count how many times someone almost blows away a still-living character. Guns are almost glamorized here — a sentiment very much in vogue in a lot of the films of the 1970s. We're not supposed to blanch when a gun is pulled out, we're supposed to cheer. Pay attention to the sequence where the heroes, trapped in a large suburban mall, raid a gun shop and soon emerge looking like Pancho Villa's troops. This sequence contains some impressively intense editing, and is expertly calculated to make the viewer lust after the weapons just as much as do the characters. When the four of them run into hoards of the undead armed to the teeth, even the most passionate pacifist may find themselves shouting encouragement.

(An aside here: It was almost as if Romero saw the coming of the 80's arrogant, flamboyantly materialistic way of life — "He Who- Dies With The Most Toys Wins" — and found it as ridiculous then as we do now. So in one masterful sweep

he offers the ultimate Yuppie fantasy (a mall for the taking); then, after allowing us to experience the nirvana of "having the most toys," he gleefully slaughters us and our greed before our own eyes, chuckling the whole bloody way.)

Then comes *Day of the Dead,* wherein this underlying theme of guns = power reaches its zenith; trapped in an abandoned underground military complex, the protagonists find themselves at the mercy of two disparate but equally destructive forces — the zombies above and the macho bravado of the soldiers who have appointed themselves the rulers below. Many have said (and I agree) that the dichotomy presented in *Day* quickly crosses the line into heavy-handedness: on one side you have the scientists, most of whom are presented as wise, resigned, level-headed thinkers; on the other side you have the MAs (Military Assholes), a bunch of swaggering, barking, arrogant, groin-kicking borderline psychotics who are an almost laughable embodiment of the Freudians' theory of guns-as-penis-extension. There is no problem they won't solve by blasting it into oblivion: early in the film the leader of the MAs pulls an automatic pistol on the sole female scientist and threatens to blow her brains out because she won't sit down and listen to him rave on about why his way is best — thus almost totally reversing the attitude toward firearms; they are no longer instruments of salvation, but the implements of self-destruction and therefore evil. But a necessary evil, as the film's heart-stopping finale proves.

Day was released hot on the heels of Ronald Reagan's Star Wars ("Peace Through Strength") program, where the world's nuclear arsenal was at its peak and tensions between the U.S. and the (then) Soviet Union were approaching a boiling point (or so we were told) not seen since the Cuban Missile Crises — which may help explain the film's disgust with and anger toward the military, as well as its barely-restrained bitterness toward humankind's hope for the future. This last element, perhaps the darkest and most genuinely affecting of the film, is all but negated by a trite, seemingly tacked-on, and not at all believable "happy" ending that is made even sillier by its "Eve-In-The-New-Eden" symbolism — which is intended to echo the subtle power of the Pieta tableau early in the movie but instead trivializes it.

But let's get down to it: it's been 18 years since the third *Dead* movie was released, and *35 years* since the original. Do the movies still hold up?

You bet your ass they do. Admittedly, the effects in *NOTLD* pale in comparison to those found in the sequels (as well as director Tom Savini's exceptionally well-done but ultimately pointless remake), but the film still manages to retain a great deal of its power — this is one of the few movies where the limited budget is actually an asset. The grainy, often jerky black-and-white photography gives an disquieting documentary feel to everything, especially in the middle of the film after the survivors have barricaded themselves in the farm house.

If asked to name their favorite sequence in the original, a majority of people would probably pick the eerie graveyard opening. A good sequence, no argument there, but that scene has always struck me as somewhat self-conscious. Even when I saw it for the first time, lo these thirty years ago, I was painfully aware that I was watching a director trying to scare me — the kiss of death in any film that relies heavily on suspense.

My choice for the best sequence will always be the nerve-shattering race to the gas pump. When that truck blows up and leaves Ben stranded in the middle of the road with the zombies lurching toward him, it still ties my gut up in knots when I watch it today. The editing is inspired and muscular – Romero's trademark, as far as I'm concerned.

But let's face it; aside from that sequence and the little girl murdering her mother in the basement, the film isn't all that scary. Tense – yes; claustrophobic – yes; but for white-knuckle, sweat-inducing, Jesus-Am-I-Breathing? terror, it leaves something to be desired. (And the peripheral ersatz-explanation of the "strange" radiation that may be responsible for re-animating the corpses just gets in the way.)

A lot of the film's original infamy came, of course, from the shock of seeing the zombies chowing down on the limbs and innards of their victims, but that doesn't happen until over two-thirds of the way through. Until then we get a lot of panic, running around, and loud arguments – not to mention one close-up too many of the zombies, who look more like a bunch of folks after a three-day drunk than rotting corpses newly arisen from the grave.

I know this is probably blasphemous to those of you who would defend this movie with your last ounce of lifeblood, but it's the truth. There is more genuine terror in the last fifteen minutes of *Day of the Dead* than there is in the whole of *Night*. Which doesn't mean it isn't a good movie – it is easily that, and much more – it just isn't "The Scariest Movie of All Time," as some would have you believe

Dawn of the Dead, by far the slickest of the three movies, manages to strike a fever pitch of terror early on and sustains it for well over half the film, faltering only when the protagonists finally set up their little Utopia in a hidden section of the mall's upper floors. Romero spends quite a bit of time exploring the characters and their relationships (*Dawn* contains the richest characterization and best acting of the trilogy), but in the process the viewer almost forgets that the zombies even exist. I know this was the intent – we're supposed to be lulled into the same false sense of security and

superiority that the characters are experiencing — but somewhere in here (I think it starts to happen right around the
time the heroine, who is pregnant, and her hubby skirt
around the issue of abortion) the pacing comes to a screeching halt and you begin to feel that you're watching a daytime
drama. How much this "calm before the storm" section grates
on your nerves may depend on which cut of the film you see
— myriad prints run anywhere from 120 to 142 minutes. My
vote goes to the 142-minute cut now available on DVD,
wherein the length of the Utopian sequence seems to be just
right.

But when things pick up again, they do so with a venge-
ance; not only is the mall besieged by a group of the sleaziest
bikers you're likely to encounter, but one of the three remaining characters is killed by the zombies, then resurrects and
proceeds to lead the dead to the secret hiding place. (The other
now-dead character, a SWAT team member who is bitten when
his Gung-Ho mentality compels him to take an absolutely
idiotic chance, is neatly dispatched by a bullet to the head
from his friend's gun. We know from the start that this
particular character is Dead Meat, because he cannot live in
peace — he's used to violence and excitement and it's in the
pursuit of these that his tragic fate is sealed — perhaps an
augury of the antimilitaristic mentality to come in the third
film.)

Finally only two characters remain: Peter Washington and
Francine Parker — the black cop and the pregnant woman,
played to perfection by Ken Foree and Gaylen Ross. Ross, by
far the most effortlessly sexy of Romero's heroines, manages
to exude both Earth Mother pragmatism and innocent
naïveté, turning her character into a fully-realized human
being and not the whiny, self-righteous Grande Dame who
pops up in the third movie.

Foree, an immensely likable actor (who was one of the
many graces in the unjustifiably-maligned *Leatherface: The
Texas Chainsaw Massacre Part III)*, remains the most compelling hero of the series. There are endless levels of intelligence,
compassion, and barely-restrained violence behind his eyes.
Even in the scenes where he has little more to do than stand

around while the other characters argue, you can't help but watch Foree, whose natural charisma dominates the proceedings, easily securing the viewer's sympathy – and it is because of that sympathy that *Dawn* contains what may be the single most terrifying sequence in any of the films.

Foree's character, realizing that Ross's character has to get away, sends her to the roof to escape in a waiting helicopter while he distracts the zombies. Knowing this will cost him his life, Ross's character, Francine, begs him not to do it in a short but genuinely heart-wrenching scene. But Washington is burned-out; he can't stand the thought of living in this world anymore and would rather just go out fighting than fade away. (And there's none of that "noble warrior" crap made trendy in later movies such as *Rambo: First Blood Part 2.*)

Francine gets safely to the roof as Washington leads the zombies deeper and deeper into the guts of the mall's work tunnels. Armed only with an automatic pistol, he manages to corner himself, waiting until the zombies are mere yards away, then presses the gun to his own head (and the look on Foree's face at this moment will freeze the blood in your veins).

The zombies lurch and stagger toward him, he begins to squeeze the trigger –

– and then it happens. Like the Grinch finally realizing the true meaning of Christmas, we see the light of Life not only ignite but explode behind his eyes – this is a man who's decided he wants to live.

But he's got a long way to go in order to get to the roof, most of the zombies are closing in on him, and he doesn't have that much ammunition left in the gun.

Foree's mad dash to get to the roof alive is, hands down, one of the five or six most frightening and exhilarating sequences to ever appear in a horror film, and manages to end *Dawn* on a slightly hopeful, if darkly cautious note: if human beings can still find reason to not only go on living, but to choose to bring new life into such a world as this, can we really be doomed?

The ending is perfection, punctuated by a killer closing

dialogue exchange. *Dawn* is the most successful film of the trilogy, the only one that — despite its scant flaws — gets better every time I see it.

Now for the fun part.

As much as I respect *Night*, and as much as I admire *Dawn*, *Day of the Dead* may be my favorite of the bunch. I know, believe me, that in terms of overall execution — the script, the acting, the action, even a lot of the characters' motivations — it is by far the weakest of the series. It is in turn terrifying, thought-provoking, shrill, muddled, philosophically top-heavy, laughable, tender, sadistic — and endlessly watchable. *Day of the Dead* takes it rightful place alongside *Martin* and *Knightriders* as one of Romero's most thematically complex films — and I forgive it most (but not all) of its trespasses for that.

Day manages to encompass every theme previously explored in the first two movies, as well as introduce a few of its own: What is the true meaning of power? What constitutes genuine survival? How far will an individual's conscience allow them to go in order to protect themselves? Is there any value to human compassion in a world spiraling downward toward self-destruction?

It reminded me of David Cronenberg's *Scanners*, insomuch as just when you think the movie is going to run out of ideas, it machineguns nine more into your face. Unfortunately, these ideas are more talked about than illustrated — especially in the long, long, *loooong* initial confrontation scene between the sole female scientist and Captain Rhodes, leader of the MAs. This scene is overflowing with some of Romero's most brittle dialogue, but the actors give the words no texture whatsoever — Joseph Pilato, as Rhodes, screams continuously (I think he actually begins to foam at the mouth at one point) while the female scientist, Sarah (played by Lori Cardille) pouts and whines, only getting up some genuine backbone toward the end of the scene. One has to wonder why Romero — who usually solicits sparkling performances from his actors — allowed the thespians in this film to either badly overact or frustratingly under-act their choice roles. I am convinced that if the overall acting had been of the same high caliber as the dialogue and themes, *Day* would have fared better both at the box office and with fans of the series.

Oddly enough, the only character who emerges with a natural humanity (despite the philosophies espoused by the radio officer and black chopper pilot, who are so wise, warm, and fuzzy you just want to step on them) is "Bub" – a zombie who is in the process of being "domesticated" by a memorably daffy scientist named Logan (the late Richard Liberty, recipient of that year's Charles Laughton Award for Most Eccentric Performance). Bub is played by Howard Sherman, who is nothing short of astonishing in the role; even through the layers of Savini's makeup we can see every nuance of the dormant humanity that lies within. I don't know if it was Romero's intent to have Bub emerge as the most sympathetic character, but that's what happens. Add to this that, at movie's end, Bub is more than capable of organizing the zombies, and *Day* turns into not so much a movie as a long trailer for a possible fourth installment to the series (which reportedly, at this writing in August of 2003, will go into production as soon as Romero wraps his new movie, *The Ill*): if some spark of distinct personality remains in each zombie – a theory grappled with throughout the movie – and if they can be re-trained to think, to read, to behave with civility in a societal environment, then is it so Out There to foresee a time when some zombie *gestalt* might occur and the few bands of humans left alive will find themselves facing an organized army that simultaneously wants to chow-down on them but also learn how to live side-by-side?

In the end, I admire *Day of the Dead* more for what it attempts to achieve than what it actually succeeds with; it is not so much the ideas it explores, but those it leaves in the viewer's mind afterward.

But, damn, can a lot be forgiven in light of those last twenty minutes. The chase/escape through the zombie catacombs displays Romero at full-tilt-bozo, and the ferocious editing contained in this sequence is hands-down the most muscular and agitating to be found anywhere in the series.

I truly hope that Romero does make a fourth film to bring the series full-circle. Hopefully he will have the finances and capabilities to bring his vision to full life. The series should not end with a cluster of dangling, half-realized notions — fascinating though they might be. The series deserves one last grand hurrah, something that will leave its fans and admirers feeling the dead went out with a bang, not a sad, depressed, cynical whimper.

A final Big One before we get into the books and stories.

Thus far I have tried to avoid a simple, straightforward reprinting of any past film and review columns, simply because it is a format which, as I said earlier, grows wearisome and annoying in a hurry, but I'm going to make an exception with this next section. For one reason, there is no way to break this particular column up into bite-sized pieces that can be sprinkled about elsewhere; and for another, I want to offer up a coda with the luxury of 20/20 hindsight; I have, over the two decades since the following column saw print, changed my mind about certain things. The tone of this piece finds me in out-and-out Smartass Mode, and at the time of its appearance earned me so much hate mail I still sometimes start whenever someone at a convention mentions this column to me; some of that hate mail contained threats. I was "pissing on an icon"; I was "going after" Stephen King; I was "jealous and stupid"; "elitist"; "worthless"; and of such a low nature that it would be doing the world a favor if ". . . somebody blew your ignorant fucking head off your ignorant fucking shoulders."

We should all be exposed to such evangelical open-mindedness. Think of how it would broaden us.

I'm going to stop talking about the column and just let it speak for itself; I'll catch you on the flip side for the follow-up.

Bearing in mind that I was in my 20s, full of piss and vinegar and functioning under the delusion that the aroma of my bodily waste seduced the olfactory senses with the subtly sweet fragrance of exotic flora, I give you, from *Eldritch Tales #11*, the infamous column entitled "The Emperor's New Clothes":

*T*here is a moment in a certain motion picture where Richard Deacon (you'll remember him as Mel, the befuddled produced on *The Dick Van Dyke Show)* in the role of a shifty Hollywood producer, is negotiating with a certain female author for the rights to film her book; the author tells him that she wants to make sure the essence of her book is captured by the filmmakers, and to this Deacon replies:

> "Books, schmooks! Who do you know who reads books? Books are made for coffee tables or for something to look at while you're sitting on the toilet . . . but *movies!* Movies are for people with *vision!*"

Those of you who are late night flippers of the cable box will of course recognize this as a patch of dialogue from *The Happy Hooker Goes to Hollywood.* I found it funny the first time I heard it, and I find it sharply perceptive now, something you'd never expect from a nervous-Nelly soft-core porno movie.

What? I hear you gasp, how *dare* he begin a column that deals with the five recent films based on Stephen King's novels with something from a low-budget, sleazy (but high-spirited) dirty movie?

Ah, mmm, *well* . . .

Considering what had been done with Mr. King's work in its voyage from the printed page to the big screen, that may be more appropriate than you'd care to admit to yourself, but . . . all right. Perhaps I'm being a bit too harsh here. Let's turn to the words of Mr. King himself.

From page 195 of *Danse Macabre*:

> "I am no apologist for bad filmmaking, but once you've spent twenty years or so going to horror movies . . . you realize that if you don't keep your sense of humor, you're done for."

From page 207 (damn my eyes, the same *chapter,* even!):

"At this writing, three of my novels have been released as films . . ." (Referring, of course, to *Carrie, Salme's Lot,* and *The Shining*) ". . . I feel that I have been fairly treated . . . and yet the clearest emotion in my mind is not pleasure but a mental sigh of relief. When dealing with the American cinema, you feel like you won if you just broke even . . ."

Now, before going any further, let's play a game of Creative Cerebral Plagiarism: Let loose the writer of your psyche and have he/she combine the three quotes you've just seen; if you can do this and form one fluent paragraph, you just might be able to put your finger on the reason why all of the five films based on King's work are so damned *disappointing.* (Also ask of this writer if he/she thinks Mr. King gives a golden rat's ass . . . the reply will most certainly be, "He's crying all the way to the bank.")

Since the majority of you who read this publication have without a doubt read all of the works in question, I'm going to dispense with too much Belaboring of the Point and tell you a fancy tale from the Igneous Age of Celluloid. Our characters are Mr. Stephen King (henceforth to be known as The Emperor), and the Film Producers With a Glorious Vision (from this point to be known as The Munchkins of Authority). It's called, surprisingly enough, "The Emperor's New Clothes."

Part One: Barking Dogs Never Ride Your Leg

Once upon a time the Emperor wrote a good book about monsters, the type that exist in your mind, the type that exist in The Seasons, and the type that are, sometimes, in your own back yard.

The Munchkins of Authority wanted to make it into a movie, but they didn't like the way it looked, so they dressed it all up as a new version of Jaws on land, with a little General Hospital thrown in for good measure . . .

Louis Teague's film version of *Cujo* isn't a total disaster, but it's in walking distance of the neighborhood. Here is where the point I made in an earlier column shows its flips side. With one notable exception, all the characters who played a major role in King's novel are here, right down to The Sharp Cereal Prof. (Yep, lotsa problems here!)

What came across as claustrophobic ingredients in a microcosm of fate and circumstance in the book, here emerges as a muddled, pointless mess. There is some splendid camera work by director Teague (especially in the last third of the film), a solid performance by Dee Wallace, and some damned impressive stunt work by three sheepdogs and two German Shepherds dressed in Saint Bernard costumes. (My favorite is the shot of the Shepherd, wearing only a puppet head, clawing at the windshield of the yellow Pinto from on the roof. Skinniest damn Saint Bernard I ever saw!)

Despite the whoops and hollers of fear from the semi-illiterate teeny-boppers who populated the audience at the showing I attended, there was not, in *Cujo,* one genuine moment of suspense. At one point I thought I could almost forgive this film all its faults if it would just scare me *once!* But, even if I found that one scare, I couldn't forgive this film its final, cheap, uninspired out-of-your-seat scare tactic borrowed from *Friday the Thirteenth.* The Up-With-Families happy ending completely destroyed any lasting effect the movie might have had (and need I remind you that it was that unexpected twist at the end of the book — Tadder's death — that gave *Cujo* it's real lasting chill; guess what? There *are* monsters in the world, Tadder!)

I do have to admit a certain begrudging respect for the make-up men who drenched the dogs in mayonnaise and old mustard to give him a really decrepit, shambling-with-disease look. But, aside from the camera work and Ms. Wallace's performance, the thing that will stay with me from *Cujo* is the singular shot of the dog slamming itself head-first into the Pinto's driver door. I thought, "Gawd-damn! That musta hurt!" It's just a pity that the only beings who walked away numb from *Cujo* were the poor dogs who performed the stunts in it.

Part Two: Mr. Smith Goes to ComatoseVille

*T*hen the Emperor wrote a book about a poor man who, after a *terrible accident, wakes up with the gift of Foresight, sometimes Hindsight, but always something that only touches upon pain and human misery.*

The Munchkins of Authority said to themselves, "Well, this one's pretty good as it is. Let's just get a big name this time and let them do it like they want . . . up to a point."

Under his own definition, King may very well feel that he "broken even" with Teag's version of *Cujo*; if such is the case, he must feel a small profit from David Cronenberg's film of *The Dead Zone. DZ* is, quite simply, a good movie drawing from a good book as its source. There is, however, only one reason that *DZ* is a good movie, and — guess what? — it *ain't* Cronenberg.

When Cronenberg is let loose with an idea of his own, even if it an idea which fails (like *Videodrome*), one at least gets a sense of real passion in his work, even if it's a passion that gouts buckets of grue everywhere. Anyone possessing any doubts about this should pop into their local video store and rent copies of *Scanners* and *The Brood*; even if you don't care for these two films, you'll have to agree that there is passion there.

One of the things many critics liked about *DZ* was Cronenberg's restraint as a director this time around. Well, droogies, I don't think I have to hammer this point too much; Cronenberg's 'restraint' borders on the somnambulistic: at one point I was afraid the picture was going to put the audience into a deeper sleep than Christopher Walken had been in. It's been a long time since a director of Croneneberg's caliber made a film that is so devoid of passion.

Cronenberg does manage to inject *DZ* with his own darker form of excitement during the long sequence that involves the catching of the Castle Rock Killer; here the power is derived from the anticipation of the final confrontation, one that ends in a cookie-whoopsing image of the killer going through death-spasms in a bathtub, a long pair of sharp scissors jammed through the roof of his mouth and the center of his forehead: he jerks and convulses and spits out thick streams of dark blood. Just peachy. There isn't an audience anywhere (save NYC) that wouldn't feel their stomachs twist at this image, which Cronenberg lets his camera leer at for longer than is necessary.

Jeffery Boam is the credited screenwriter, though it was

rumored that up to four different writers had a crack at it. Of all the films based on King's work, *DZ* seemed the one most intent upon the most literate form of condensing his novel to the big screen, one-hundred-minute format. There's nothing particularly wrong with Boam's script, but there's nothing particularly outstanding, either. It just breaks even.

But, that aside, you undoubtedly noticed that of all the King-based films, *DZ* seemed to be around the longest. It was, as they say in Munchkin Land, a hit. There is a reason for this, and its name is Christopher Walken. Walken, who won the Academy Award for his wonderful performance in *The Deerhunter,* turns in a rich, flawless performance as John Smith, the protagonist of King's Rip Van Winkle terror tale. You like John, you care about him, and you feel his frustration and pain as he is forced to come to grips with a power he never asked for, but must live with, nonetheless. Every time John has a vision, it's an unnerving experience for both him and the audience, simply because Walken is so masterful at conveying compassion, pain, disgust, and fear; not individually, but in a swirling kaleidoscope of conflicting emotional reactions, all of them inexorably placing him in the middle of other people's lives with their pain, loneliness, fear, and sometimes, their pettiness and perversions. It is solely because of Walken that *DZ* holds up all the way and manages to keep your interest focused when Cronenberg falls asleep and lets the film become stoic and unconvincing.

Martin Sheen is used to good sleazy advantage as Greg Stillson, as is Herbert Lom as Dr. Sam Weizak; in Lom's case he achieves his convincingness not with sleaze, but with a tired, cynical type of compassion that is sparked by an occasional burst of good humor. However, were it not for Walken, their two good performances would have been lost amongst Cronenberg's celluloid sleeping tablet. One can only hope that, in the future, Mr. Cronenberg will keep himself to himself when making films; I'll take passion that fails of safe somnambulism any day of the week.

Part Three: Kiddies of the Porn

*A*nd so the Munchkins of Authority sat in their high offices and said to themselves, "We don't seem to be having a great deal of luck with these movies of his longer works, what say we try beefing up his short stories. He did write shot stories, didn't he?"

One of the secretaries runs out to check, comes back a few minutes later and confirms that in fact The Emperor did, indeed, write short stories. None of The Munchkins of Authority had read any, however, but that would not stop them from taking a fine piece of his short fiction and dressing it in a sacrificial gown.

Fritz Kierch's film version of *Children of the Corn* appears in this section of the column under protest and only for the sake of continuity; it took a great deal of self-control not to place this sickening glop of cinematic afterbirth in the Tarnished Bedpan Award Winner's Circle (note: The Tarnished Bedpan Awards was a section in each column devoted to the absolute *worst* horror movies imaginable). I had a good deal of hope for this movie when I first saw it advertised. The best laid pans, etcetera . . .

An annoying pontificating pause here:

Stephen King's novels do not condense well. King is the master of intricate plotting in the horror novel and, even more than that, he understands and utilizes the importance of the minor character and the small, seemingly insignificant detail. A minor character, for instance, may do something that seems inconsequential at first, but stems from deeply rooted motivations in their system that have taken years to manifest themselves. (The mailman's forgotten trip to the

Camber's farm in *Cujo* is a good example of this.) Because of this, King's novels are rich in character, plot, and terror. There are a lot of heavy-handed episodes in his books, but there are an infinite number of subtleties also. It's these missed subtleties that so righteously muck-up his books when brought to the screen. That's why *Children of the Corn* seemed such a good candidate for a film. Rather than screw up a full-blown novel, why not take a short story (though it borders on the novella) and beef it up a bit, say to ninety minutes, you'll get all the characters, detail, and terror, yet have some room to fill in some extra goodies. Sounds logical, right? Right. A good road to follow, right? Right. Easy to success with, right?

Ahem . . .

Outside of the fact that this film (and I use that term loosely) takes every chance it can to grout grue and guts all over the floor, it takes a nose-dive into the idiot-pits yet undreamt of when it turns He Who Walks Behind the Rows into some sort of mythic super-gopher that burrows under everything in an effect that was used to much better advantage in John Carpenter's *The Thing*.

Kerisch and screenwriter George Goldsmith have taken a story that had "success" written all over it and turned it into another one of those horrid, tasteless, bucket-full-of-steaming-innards movies that only hold appeal to the idiotic, pre-pubescent teens with zits on their faces who to go these things with their boyfriend or girlfriend so they can act scared and/or grossed out so they'll have yet another excuse to grope each other's budding anatomies in the dark.

Children of the Corn could have been a decent film; there are one or two good images that are cut away from before they can work up any power, and the acting is just above that found in *Plan 9* but not nearly at the level of something like *The Exorcist*, and Jonathan Elias has provided it with a much better musical score than it deserves. This movie only goes to prove that bigger isn't always better.

Part Four: Would You Buy a Used Car From This Man?

*T*hen there was The Emperor's tale of love between a boy and his *fiery red 1958 Plymouth; it was an intelligent, intense, and poignant tale of alienation, loneliness, and final revenge for all the wrongs done to an individual by the growing pains of youth.*

The Munchkins of Authority decided that no one could really take a story about a haunted car seriously – obviously they didn't and theirs is the opinion that counts – so they dressed it up in a stand-up comic's garb, complete with arrow through the head and whoopee cushion. Hardy-har. It is, as they say, to laugh.

Christine is the biggest disappointment of all the King films, and there are two very big reasons behind this; first, but not the biggest, is that King's own agent, World Fantasy Award-Winner Kirby McCauley, was heavily involved in the production end of this film. One would think that, with such a literary man as McCauley helping to oversee the film, it would hold true to the vision that was presented in the book; nothing could be more off-base.

The second reason is, unfortunately, director John Carpenter, who shows with *Christine* that he is not above compromising his craft for money. This film may be the sloppiest one he's ever made, and it pains me to say this because I've grown to respect Carpenter over the past few years, especially after *The Thing*. (For more on that, consult ET#9)

Christine is so self-enamored of its own smug-assed humor

that, after a while, you begin to feel as if you're not being let in on someone's personal joke. The movie treads dangerously close to mocking King's novel, which — even with its own good sense of humor — was a dark and saddening tale. Carpenter's film turns it all into one, long punchline that is badly in need of a joke with which to be prefaced.

Not to be totally disheartened, there are some gems in this film as far as moments go; the opening sequence, where Christine is rolled off the Detroit assembly line, has some of the best tracking-cam work you'll ever see, and with George Thorogood crooning "B-b-b-b-bad to the bone" under it all, it comes across extremely reminiscent of the opening sequence of Paul Shrader's *Blue Collar*.

*K*eith Gordon is wonderful as Arnie Cunningham, displaying (as much as the muddled script allows him) all the frustration and alienation that causes Arnie to be at first enamored of, and then possessed by Christine. It is only through Gordon's winning performance that Carpenter's film holds any lasting connection to the work upon which it was based.

Carpenter, who had been busy shooting *Firestarter*, scrapped that project in order to do *Christine*; the film came out astoundingly fast after the release of the book. Everyone swears that the film rights were purchased and the final script approved before the book was even released, but you should take those statements with a grain of salt; *Christine* was a rush job, and it looks it.

The car itself never really comes alive as far as character is concerned; in the book she was a fire-blazing bitch on wheels; possessive, jealous, and vengeful; Carpenter turns her into nothing more than an expensive central prop.

And in the cheapest bit in the movie, Carpenter utilizes the same uninspired gimmick that Teague did in *Cujo*; I don't have to tell you what I'm referring to, do I? Didn't think so.

Under King's own definition of "The Horror Movie as Junkfood," I think that *Christine* fits in quite well; all taste with no protein. Dare I say that *Christine* runs out of . . . nah!

Even *I* won't stoop that low.

All things considered, Mr. Thorogood's theme song was well-chosen.

Sorry, John.

*B*efore going on to the final film, let's check back with The Emperor once more. He offers an analogy of all this that is better than any I could ever come up with, and I never try to improve upon perfection.

From page 210 of *Danse Macabre*:

> "You don't appreciate cream unless you've drunk a lot of milk, and maybe you don't even appreciate milk unless you've drunk some that's gone sour. Bad films may sometimes be amusing, sometimes even successful, but their only real usefulness is to form that basis of comparison: to define positive values in terms of their own negative charm. They show us what to look for because it is missing in themselves."

Beautiful, just beautiful.

Part Five: Zen and the Art of Lighting a Gas Grill

*A*nd so The Munchkins of Authority chose The Emperor's tale of fire and love and pursuit. This time their boss, He Who Caters to *the Distributors, told them to follow the book to the letter. The Munchkins bowed in obeisance to their boss while giving The Emperor's readers The Finger. Then someone lit a match to see how high a flame would have to go in order to burn another person's ass . . .*

If you follow such fine magazines as *Twilight Zone* or *Cinefantastique* then you already know that, of all the King film, *Firestarter* was among the first to be started and the last to be finished. This undoubtedly gave you reason to be optimistic; with all the failures thus far, perhaps more care was being taken and the result would be a better finished product. ("Movies are for people with vision!")

Director Mark L. Lester's (*Stunts, Class of 1984*) version of *Firestarter* just misses being on target; there are many instances during the film when you want to jump up and shout, "GET YOUR ASS IN STEP!" in the hopes it will make everything synchronize; it doesn't, but you have to appreciate the effort, nonetheless.

The screeplay by Stanley Mann is pretty good as it goes, though I'd be willing to wager that a full 95% of the dialogue was lifted straight from the book. (King supposedly offered advice on the script, and I get the impression that if King had written the screenplay himself, it wouldn't have been much different than Mann's.)

Lester does a fairly competent job of stringing things along, but it seems more like a child following the instructions of a paint-by-number kit than a director trying to interpret something onto film. You also get the same feeling by watching this movie that you might get when listening to a live symphony where the orchestra, somehow, gets ahead of the conductor. Everything about *Firestarter* seems to be on the verge of connecting and turning itself into something pretty spectacular, but it never gets there.

What does recommend *Firestarter* is the acting. As I expected, George C. Scott's John Rainbird dominates the screen from the moment he first appears. It's nice to see that King's material is starting to attract such wonderful talents as Scott, Walken, Sheen, and Art Carney. Maybe someone will find a good role for Olivier in the film version of *Pet Sematary,* which will probably be out before this column sees print.

Scott, though badly miscast (Will Sampson should have played it) is chilling to watch as he struts around with his Neanderthallike gait, smashing in people's faces and spouting existentialistic philosophy. It's only a pity that his make-up for the bad eye keeps changing from scene to scene.

David Keith is solid as Andy McGee, conveying all the panic and anger that is required for the role, though I got a little tired of the heavy-handed way he and Lester presented "the push."

Art Carney is just perfect as Irv Manders, and you'll find yourself wishing that he was used more in the film. It amazes me how, even in the worst of films, Carney seems able to submerge himself completely in another character — the whole point of fine acting. It's a pity he wasted so much time playing second fiddle to Jackie Gleason for all those years. He and Scott provide *Firestarter* with many memorable moments.

Then we come to Drew Barrymore's performance in the extremely difficult role of Charlie. In a surprising contradiction of Hollywood logic, the producers have cast an eight year old to play an eight year old.

Barrymore, who so charmed audiences in *E.T.,* here shows that she is a damn good little actress. There are times in the film when the script crams too many words into her tiny mouth and you get the impression of a children *trying* to act, but there are more than enough moments of real performing to erase the lesser ones. In a moment that will make you want to cheer, she turns to one of The Shop's members and says, "Get out of here you bastard or I'll fry you!"

I believed her. (Gulp!) And that's all you need here, just enough convincing moments to make you swallow everything.

Martin Sheen is back again, rapidly becoming the quintessential King villain; well-dressed, greasy hair that looks almost plastic, and a smile that Hitchcock would've loved. It's also good to see this fine actor pop up again in a King film. (In case you weren't already aware of this fact, the role Sheen plays — Cap — was originally going to be done by the masterful Burt Lancaster, who had to bow out when heart surgery needed to be performed.)

But, in the end, *Firestarter* never manages to get all its good elements in synch, something that will leave you half-hearted and none the warmer. (Sorry, I couldn't resist just one comment along those lines.)

One last pontification and then we'll look in on *The Keep*.

King and his literary peers (Peter Straub, Charles L. Grant, Karl Edward Wagner, Ramsey Campbell, Dennis Etchison, just to name a few of the biggies) all agree that the best type of terror (?) is the type that lingers in the mind long after the last page has been turned or the last reel has rolled through the camera. I don't think there's anyone who reads this publication who would argue with that.

When that statement is applied to the five films reviewed previously, it can be stated (and without too much fear of protest) that there can be found more "lingering terror" in the grave-robbing sequence in *Bring Me the Head of Alfredo Garcia* than in all five of these movies combined. I don't possibly see how King could feel that he's "broken even" with this batch of movies. Perhaps he'll never see a really find film made from any of his fine (and, in some cases, brilliant) novels. But something tells me that, in the end and with all his seven-figure advances, Mister King probably doesn't much care how he is treated by Hollywood; and so the big question: If Stephen King doesn't care, why should we?

Epilogue: The Nick-Nack Paddywack Burial Ground

*A*nd so The Emperor left the golden land of Hollywood, none the worse for the wear, but richer. And, in the night, if you turn your ears towards the West and listen very carefully, you'll hear an ominous sound.

There! Here it? That sound like desiccated flesh being set aflame? Not to worry, though . . .

It's only The Munchkins of Authority counting their box office receipts.

MAN IN THE LOW CASTLE

*D*irector Michael Mann's version of F. Paul Wilson's *The Keep* shot in and out of theaters in less than twelve days, after an extensive publicity campaign. I'll not hold you in suspense about this: Gary A. (that crazy sonuvabitch likes *anything*) Braunbeck did not, overall, like *The Keep*, but that does not stop me from recommending that you see it in the event it pops up at the local drive-in, or a cheap-seat matinee showing, or on a pay cable film channel.

Michel Mann, who created one of the better (which I know isn't saying a whole hell of a lot) television detective shows, *Vegas*, had directed only two films previous to *The Keep*: *The Jericho Mile* and *Thief* (the latter being one of the best psychological studies of the criminal mind in a long, long time). He proved with his two films that he was a impressive technician and damned literate script writer. There was also a very muscular feel to both these films, an intense and often overwhelming power that left movie-goers breathless and stunned. Unfortunately *The Keep* doesn't exercise these traits nearly as well as the other two films. What starts off brilliantly for its first thirty-five minutes quickly degenerates into a muddle of mixed-metaphors, unconvincing characterizations, and buckets of quasi-mystical-super-psycho-gobbledy-gook. Mann stated that he was inspired by Jean Cocteau's *Beauty and the Beast*, and he wanted to turn Wilson's novel into a seductive fairy-tall of evil.

Mann has managed to give *The Keep* a wonderful look (it is undoubtedly one of the most beautiful *looking* films of recent years), and there are dozens of images that will stay with you long after the film has finished, but *The Keep* leaves you with a sense of being cheated; of being given a gorgeous package with nothing inside.

The film does have a few good moments during the first third; the Nazis' entrance into the town and then to the Keep itself moves along with the same feverish pace that marked the opening robbery in *Thief* (*The Keep* was shot in 70mm), and the Keep itself, though it differs radically in structure from the way it's described in Wilson's terrific novel, does have a murky, subterranean look that creeps up your spine.

But one of the best things about this mish-mash of a motion picture is the stunning musical score provided by Tangerine Dream (who also provided *Firestarter* with an equally excellent soundtrack). If the name of this three man group from Germany sounds familiar, it may be because they've done several soundtracks in the last few years, among them *Sorcerer, Strange Invaders, Strange Behavior,* and *Thief.* If you were a follower of the music column in Twilight Zone magazine, you probably didn't find Tangerine Dream listed anywhere, and more's the pity; their particular brand of synthesized electronic wizardry is well suited to genre films, and it's good to hear them being utilized to such an advantage. Give them a listen the next time you read something by Charles L. Grant, and you'll see what I mean.

Finally, it should be noted here for the record that Michael Mann, though he's scored his first miss with *The Keep,* is a director who, If he can put aside his more condescending notions concerning the genre, may very well make a substantial contribution to horror/fantasy films one day. He possesses just enough scope of vision, cynicism, and hard-edged compassion to recommend him. Perhaps, after all, director Michael (and I couldn't resist this one) is The Mann Who Should Do King.

God save us from the echoes of our younger selves.

Is it just me, or can you still smell that column's stench hanging in the air? The overuse of exclamation points! The sudden attacks of Capitalization Disease. The magnificently awkward, convoluted, self-conscious turns of phrase (". . . another one of those horrid, tasteless, bucket-full-of-steaming-innards movies that only hold appeal to the idiotic, pre-pubescent teens with zits on their faces who to go these things with their boyfriend or girlfriend so they can act scared and/or grossed out so they'll have yet another excuse to grope each other's budding anatomies in the dark"); what in the *hell* made me think I could ever make a living out of this?

Talk about your pilgrim bullshit . . .

This is not meant to serve as an apology; when I turned in that column, I thought it was a fairly good, clever piece of writing, and think it still has a few things to give it merit or — believe me — I would not have reprinted it here.

A little background on how that column came to be

written.

First of all, I was in my early 20s; secondly, I was drunk and upset most of the time, no more so than when I wrote it; third and lastly, my life and my budding career had come to a grinding, miserable halt and I was pissed off at everything; not yet 25, I had already buried my first marriage and my only child, and was making a vocation out of collecting rejection slips. In the meantime, I worked as everything from a janitor to a fry cook to a sometimes-actor and a the-less-said-about-it-the-better musician. I was as directionless as they come. Welcome to the beginning of your third decade, you pathetic loser.

Looking back on it, I think there was an element of jealousy that colored my opinions (and if you're a professional writer who finds that they practically have to threaten editors and publishers with bodily harm before they pony-up the long green you've been waiting months for, then you cannot possibly tell me that, on some level, you *maybe* begrudge King his phenomenal and well-deserved success; at least, not with a straight face, you can't).

I still maintain that this column was not an attack on King, despite some of the more sarcastic asides; it was and remains a badly-written assault on what I at the time perceived to be a batch of pretty mediocre-to-abysmal movies. (I can't help but add that, when the film version of *Pet Sematary* finally came out, it was even more horrendously awful than I'd feared it would be — though the production design and the late Fred Gwynne's pearly performance as Jud Crandall remain impressive, as does the heartfelt turn by Miko Hughes as the doomed Gage Creed.)

So, how do these opinions hold up at this end of the time-slip?

Not very well, overall.

I still stand by my comments about *Children of the Corn* and *Firestarter,* but find that I've softened my attitude toward *Cujo* quite a bit, *Christine* only slightly, and have done an almost complete reversal on my opinion of *The Dead Zone* — this last, when viewed today, can easily take its place alongside *The Shawshank Redemption, The Green Mile, Stand by Me, Misery* and the unjustifiably-maligned *Hearts in Atlantis* and *Dream-catcher* as one of the best adaptations of a King novel (and Cronenberg has gone on to prove himself one of the few genuinely maverick directors working today, as such films as *Crash, M. Butterfly,* and the phenomenal *Spider* readily prove; his work on *The Dead Zone* is as pure an example of intense restraint as I've seen, and I couldn't have been more wrong in my assessment.) Christopher Walken's performance remains one of the best he's ever given, and Tom Skerritt's understated turn as Sheriff Bannerman just gets better with repeated viewings.

The softening of my attitude toward *Cujo* is so intertwined with my reasons for disliking it the first time I still find it difficult to discern where one ends and the other begins.

Got another laugh-filled personal pause here, so whip out the whoopee cushions and that well-thumbed copy of *The Big Book of Fart and Booger Jokes.*

I once had a daughter. She died when she was very young. She had been sick from the moment she was born and never got better. She never learned to walk, never made a sound, never blew out the candles on a birthday cake. The only home she ever knew were the sterile walls of an ICU. She was very tiny and she fought very hard. The last seventy-two hours of her life were agonizing, and when she died it was without the benefit of a warm, loving human touch lingering on her skin: Her mother, exhausted and sedated, was asleep on a couch in the hospital's lounge; I'd not eaten for almost a day-and-a-half and so had gone to the vending machines one floor below to get some coffee and a sandwich. The entire trip took four minutes. The coffee was lukewarm and weak, the sandwich stale and tasteless, and by the time I came back to the ICU, my daughter was dead and gone.

Her death was not a surprise, her mother and I had known for a while that it was (as the tired cliché goes) "only a matter of time."

Not a surprise, but still the ice-pick in my throat.

I remember seeing the curtain pulled around her incubator.

I remember the sounds made by the various machines hooked up to the other patients in the unit.

I remember wanting to cry but being unable to.

Then it was shuffling, being taken aside, muffled words from weary nurses, uncomfortable-looking orderlies, a gurney with a squeaking front left wheel, and the last sight of my daughter: Bumps and curves and patches of pale flesh inside a translucent plastic bag, rolling away, away.

Her mother and I were both young and foolish and not nearly strong enough to handle this. Our relationship crawled along for a few more months, a joyless thing, back-broken and spirit-dead, before ending in infidelity, accusations and poison.

It's been almost twenty years since she died. I have since seen my writing career at last get on its feet, and finally gotten — albeit sporadically — the upper hand in the battle with my recurring bouts of severe depression.

Still, there are times — periodic though they may be, usually very late at night or first thing in the morning — when it all comes back, diminished not one whit by the passage of years, and I crumple. Simply crumple.

Don't believe what the pop-psychologists or self-help books or daytime talk-show hosts tell you about it: You *never* fully recover from the death of a child. The grief eventually works its way into the shadows, back there someplace, a whisper, an echo, a tendril of smoke perpetually curling in the air over a just-emptied ashtray . . . but it never completely goes away.

And the bitch of it is, you never know when it's going to come snarling to the surface, or what may cause it to rally and bear its teeth.

In my case, it was both the novel *Cujo* and its respectful — if not altogether successful — film adaptation.

In the novel, when "Tadder" dies despite all his mother has gone through to protect him, it drilled right into my core; whether he intended it to or not, King's simple, elegant description of the boy's death and the emotional aftermath echoed what I myself was going through at the time. For that reason alone — even if I hadn't found the rest of the novel intense and compelling — *Cujo* remains one of my six favorite King books. (The other five, if you're interested, are *The Dead*

Zone, Night Shift, Hearts in Atlantis, Roadwork, and *From a Buick 8* — this lat one read while in the bin after the meltdown following my second divorce and the deaths of my parents. I don't think any other book but King's wonderful round-robin narrative would have kept me in one piece during that time.)

When I saw the film version of *Cujo,* I was actually quite pleased with the way it was unfolding (anorexic St. Bernard notwithstanding) and — as sadomasochistic as this is going to sound — I was *looking forward* to seeing Tadder's death and its emotional aftermath portrayed onscreen. I wanted to see how if the moviemakers were going to get it right — and I wanted, if just for a moment, the audience to feel some small part of the crumpling grief I was still experiencing.

So imagine my reaction when "the Tadder" suddenly pulls in a wheezing, life-giving breath, opens his eyes, and begins coughing as Mommy and Daddy move together for a warm and fuzzy group hug as the picture freezes and slowly fades to black.

"Goddamn *cowards!*" I said loudly, much to the annoyance of the others in the packed theater and to the embarrassment of my mom, who'd come to see it with me. "Goddamn spineless, wimpy, gutless cowards!"

Mom smacked my arm. "It's only a movie, Gary. Calm down. And watch your language. We're in public."

Here's where the old debate between novel vs. film adaptation comes seriously into play.

My mom — who had not read the book — was pleased that Tadder did not die; in fact, she smiled and got a little teary-eyed, she was so happy. That stuck with me, and over the years when I talk to others who have seen the movie but *not* read the book, the majority of the reactions have been positive; they like it very much (anorexic St. Bernards . . . cha-cha-cha).

Re-watching the movie, I realized that Teague and screenwriter Don Carlos (*Impulse)* Dunaway were not attempting to *dramatize* King's novel (as I had unreasonably expected) but rather re-interpret it as a dark fairy tale with a happy ending. If you watch the movie — and you don't have to watch it all that closely — there are several hints throughout that Tadder is going to make it and that Mommy and Daddy will be reunited. With the sole exception of the makeup used on the dogs, *Cujo* succeeds in what it sets out to do, and to that end must be respected. What is there is simply a solid, if not particularly distinguished, movie.

I have warmed slightly to *Christine,* as well. It still isn't a very good movie, but the tongue-in-cheek supporting performances of Robert Prosky, Harry Dean Stanton, and the sly cameo work of Roberts Blossom as George LeBay give the film an effortless, understated black humor that the rest of the movie strains to achieve. And Alexandra Paul is just gorgeous. (Gimme a break; I've loused-up two marriages. Any fantasy helps.)

As for *The Keep* . . . well, F. Paul Wilson's understandably low opinion of this film is well known, and almost every fan of the book agrees. However, despite all the pissing and moaning and assorted brouhaha, it's not a lousy movie; it is *one half* a lousy movie, one half a stunning and sure-handed adaptation of the novel. Its gorgeous photography and production design still hold up, as do the fierce performances of Jurgen Prochnow and Gabriel Byrne; the confrontation scene between the two near the 3/4 mark in the movie is almost up there with the Burt Lancaster/Fredrick March scene from *Seven Days in May;* both actors are on fire and the dialogue crackles.

I suppose it's only fair I offer some comment about the performance of Ian McKellen in the pivotal role of Dr. Theodore Kuza. This was McKellen's American film debut; he was just coming off his award-winning triumph playing Antonio Salieri in the Broadway production of Peter Shaffer's *Amadeus;* in the play, McKellen had to portray an old and crippled man who, before the audience's eyes, is transformed into a healthy, vital, younger man, before returning at play's end to his former old and crippled state; to stretch his acting range for his film debut, McKellen took on the demanding role of an old and crippled man who, before the audience's eyes, is transformed into a healthy, vital, younger man before returning at film's end to his former old and crippled state.

McKellen — who, for the record, is one of the four or five finest actors alive — was a bit too histrionic here, playing Kuza as if he wanted to make sure ticket buyers in the loge seats would be able to read his every expression. The performance is far from an embarrassment — McKellen is incapable of giving a bad performance — but it lacks the subtlety and richness he has since brought to his subsequent roles, particularly his excellent portrayal of Gandalph in Peter Jackson's magnificent *Lord of the Rings* trilogy.

Michael Mann has since gone on to prove himself a great director, with films such as *Manhunter, The Last of the Mohicans, Heat, The Insider,* and *Ali.* He is arguably the successor to John Frankenheimer, and I maintain to this day that a Stephen King novel adapted and directed by Michael Mann would be a wonder to behold.

Before moving on to the next section, I want to offer a short list of other movies that, though not marketed as horror films, nonetheless fall easily into the category and should be required viewing for any serious student of the field. Don't be surprised if you haven't heard of most of them, just know that they are all available on either VHS or DVD, so you don't have much of an excuse not to seek out at least one of them:

The Offense: This 1973 film, directed by Sidney (*Network, The Hill, Dog Day Afternoon*) Lumet and written by John (*Murder by Decree*) Hopkins (based on his stage play *This Story of Yours*), is one of the most nerve-wracking and emotionally devastating studies of moral and psychological deterioration ever filmed. Sean Connery, in hands-down the most intense, multi-layered, and moving performance of his career, stars as Detective Sergeant Johnson, a bitter, angry, hard-drinking London Police Force detective whose tenuous grip on sanity is finally pushed past the breaking point during his interrogation of a suspected child-molester (the late Ian Bannen, who matches Connery every step of the way in an equally powerful performance). Decades of dealing with rapes, murders, beatings, and other serious crimes he's had to investigate have left a terrible mark on Johnson's psyche. His rage and disgust have been suppressed for far too long, and during the course of the interrogation he reveals that the state of his own mind is just as bad, if not worse, than that of the suspected child-molester's.

The Offense does not unfold in a traditional linear fashion; there are flashbacks, flash-forwards, and scenes that appear as brief fragments reflecting the crumbling state of Johnson's mind. (I firmly believe that writer/director Christopher Nolan had to have found at least part of the inspiration for *Memento*'s structure from watching this film.) The sequence where Johnson breaks down in front of his wife and delivers a shattering, stream-of-consciousness monologue (wherein he begins mixing up the specifics of various cases until they all become one massive, bloody pile of bodies) was and remains Connery's finest moment on the screen. The entire cast is first-rate, Lumet's direction is tense and claustrophobic, and Hopkins' brittle, literate dialogue is some of the best you'll ever encounter. When anyone asks me to name the five most terrifying movies I've ever seen, *The Offense* is always one of them.

The Tenant: Based on the superb novel by Roland Topor, this 1976 film remains one of Roman Polanski's most personal movies; aside from directing, Polanski (*Chinatown, Rosemary's Baby, The Pianist*) also co-wrote the script and stars as Trelkovsky, a bookish clerk who comes into possession of an apartment whose previous tenant, a woman, committed suicide. As an ever-increasing series of bizarre events sends Trelkovsky into a downward spiral of sleeplessness and paranoia, he begins suspecting that his landlord and neighbors are trying to turn him into the previous tenant so he too will commit suicide.

Polanski offers a subtle and sly performance as Trelkovsky, and is given solid support from Melvin Douglas, Shelley Winters, and the luminous Isabelle Adjani, whose sexy, shaded, off-putting portrayal of Stella (the parallels to *A Streetcar Named Desire* deliberate) make her one of the most fascinating female characters ever to appear in a Polanski film.

The rich, deep-focus, brooding photography by Sven Nykvist (*Fanny and Alexander, Crimes and Misdemeanors, Chaplin*) is a real asset, employing negative space to great advantage, especially during the second half of the film when Trelkovsky's already too-insular world begins shrinking even further.

The only shortcomings in this otherwise excellent film are some ill-advised dubbing by American actors of the French cast's voices (not all the French actors were dubbed, which creates at times an annoying inconsistency), and a tendency in Polanski's and Gérard (*Dario Argento's the Phantom of the Opera)* Brach's script to, in places, make literal those elements of Topor's novel that should have been left unexplained. But even these problems do not fatally detract from one's enjoyment and appreciation of this tense, haunting film, one whose closing sequence ranks just below that of *Seconds* in its power to shock and terrify.

*Child's Play: Not the 1988 Tom Holland movie that shoved Chucky, The Doll From Hell, up our noses and down our throats, but the 1972 Sidney Lumet film based on the stage play by Robert Marasco (*Burnt Offerings*). Child's Play – one of the best stage-to-screen translations made during the 70s – tells the story of an new gymnastics instructor (Beau Bridges) at an exclusive boy's prep school who's drawn into a feud between two of the older instructors, and soon discovers that things at the school are not as staid, tranquil, and harmless as they seem.*

The instructors are played by James Mason and Robert Preston, both cast effectively against type; Mason, usually the strong and confident intellectual, is an open nerve, a man whose grip on his self-respect and faith in his fellow human beings is being systematically chipped to pieces, causing him to question not only his worth as a teacher, but his sanity, as well; Preston (the one and only Prof. Harold Hill of The Music Man*), typically the boisterous, good-natured, fast-talking rascal you can't help but like, here is as eerie and intensely low-key a psychotic as filmgoers had met until the appearance of Hannibal Lecter early in the next decade.*

Drenched in quiet dread and oppressive atmosphere, *Child's Play* also boasts a memorably creepy ending that culminates in a final, understated, chilling image whose unapologetically dramatic presentation only serves to empower rather than detract from the film's lasting effect.

Okay, time for a quick recap:

If you're doing research and want to know what it feels like to be shot, stabbed, beaten up, not invited to many parties, and generally have most people cross to the other side of the street when they spot you coming their way, then I'm your guy.

If you're hoping for one last personal tidbit to close this section, here it is: I worked for a short time as a clown for childrens' birthday parties. Hand to God, I did. My professional name was "Rags." I wanted to call myself "Scuzzo the Marginally Humorous" or "The Banal Mr. Wiggles" but was worried folks might get the wrong idea about the nature of my show.

If you're looking for horror movies that fall well outside the often short-sighted boundaries of the popular definition of the field, then here's a roll-call of the movies I've been attempting to foist on you:

Bring Me the Head of Alfredo Garcia; 1974, directed by Sam Peckinpah

Child's Play; 1972, directed by Sidney Lumet

The Field; 1990, directed by Jim Sheridan

Little Murders; 1971, directed by Alan Arkin

The Offense (a.k.a. *The Truth or Something Like It)*; 1973, directed by Sidney Lumet

Seconds; 1966, directed by John Frankenheimer

Sorcerer; 1977, directed by William Friedkin

Straw Dogs; 1970, directed by Sam Peckinpah

The Swimmer; 1966, directed by Frank Perry

The Tenant; 1976, directed by Roman Polanski

Onward . . .

Part Two:

Proud Words on Dusty Shelves

"Persons attempting to find a plot will be banished.
Persons attempting to find a moral will be shot."
— Mark Twain

**Statistics; Subtext; Fans vs. Admirers; and Why Horror
Will Never Be Considered Serious Lit-rah-chure, No
Matter How Much We Stamp Our Feet and Threaten
To Hold Our Breath Until Our Faces Turn Blue and
Pass Out From Lack of Oxygen Which, If We'd Been
Using It Properly In The First Place, Would Have Gone
To Our Brains And Made Us Realize That We Need To
Make Our Writing More Than Merely Competent,
Only Now We're All Passed-Out On The Floor And
Have Wet Ourselves And Little Kids Are Sticking
Uncomfortable Things Up Our Nose And Who's
Going To Take Us Seriously After That.**

I realize that the unclear nature of the above title might be
a little bewildering, and for that I apologize, but if you'll just
stick with me I promise you I'll do everything I can to clear
up the confusion and make this section's schema a bit less
nebulous.

Here's a real interesting pair of statistics for you to mull
over before we get any further along:

In 1978, according to study done by the University of California at Berkley, only 9% of this country's then 200,000,000-plus population bought books; of that 9%, only 2% bought more than a single book a year, and the other 7% bought only the flavor-of-the-month popular bestseller.

In 2000, this same study was conducted again, and on the surface the results seemed more optimistic; that 9% from 1978 had risen to a whopping 11%, and the 2% who bought more than one book a year had risen to 5%. Looks good at first, until you consider one itsy-bitsy teeny-weeny little fact: the population of this country in 2000 was nearing 300,000,000.

Grab a calculator and do some quick math; g'head, I can wait.

Uh. Huh.

Factoring in the rise in population, you have just discovered that not only have the stats from 1978 *not* improved, they have actually worsened by a margin of something like 7/10 of 1%. Which means that the other 6% of that 11% are still buying as their sole literary indulgence each year the latest Grisham, Collins, or current self-help-trend manifesto typed out (notice I didn't say "written by") whichever self-proclaimed "expert" the vapid, glassy-eyed hosts of daytime television talk shows are told by their focus groups will nab the biggest audience.

Excuse me while I go whip up a Bailey's and Drano® cocktail . . .

Yeah, I'm overstating things just a smidgen (but only just) in order to make a point: horror fiction is still the deformed drooling bastard child that picks at its scabs and who Literature keeps locked up in the cellar when company drops by, but for all our complaining about its being the last "ghetto" of fiction, has anyone given serious thought to the single greatest reason why?

I refer you back to the subtle and evenhanded title of this section.

Horror will never be taken seriously by a majority of readers or the so-called "academicians" who would have you believe that unless you can savor the metaphoric layers and protests against the restraints of language throughout something like Joyce's *Ulysses* you're Missing The Whole Point of Reading — *none* of them — readers, teachers, scholars, your sweet Aunt Eunice, *nobody* — is going to let horror out of the basement until horror writers do one simple thing: stop being, at best, merely competent.

. . . he said with some truly convoluted syntax, thus nearly defeating his own point.

Ahem . . .

No, I am not claiming right to pontificate from some higher ground because my own writing is so without flaw that I can say, "Listen to me because I and I alone am correct." God knows my own work has more than its share of problems: my attempts to consciously create "atmosphere" are sometimes laughably bad, my aversion to having so-called "villains" in my fiction creates gray areas that work against my themes about a quarter of the time, and you can count on one hand the number of simple sentences found in any single story of mine — my tendency is to use the longer, sometimes circular, always complex breed of sentence because it enables me to establish both tone and rhythm . . . and sometimes indulge it a little too long; case in point, the sentence you're reading.

Understand that everything which follows is prefaced by these unwritten words: In my opinion.

All clear? Good.

Onward.

Many horror writers cry that it's the Curse of Categorization that keeps horror trapped in the literary cellar, and readily point to the publishers on whom they are all too willing to lay blame. Here's a Muppet News Flash: it isn't only publishers who categorize our fiction; it's also the readers, the editors, and even (sometimes especially) the writers, as well. No one here is blameless, regardless of how much chest-thumping and eloquent self-serving grandstanding is done to the contrary. There is a market for horror, so there exists a genre label for horror, because there are writers of horror who want to sell their work to a horror publisher in order to reach the horror-reading market. (Can you say

"Ouroboros Syndrome?" Good, I knew you could.)

All this brouhaha over labeling and categorization is just a rubber sword wielded by writers of limited talent and imagination to make themselves and their work seem more polished and important than either really is; with a handful of exceptions – Harlan Ellison, Dan Simmons, Dean Koontz, to name three – I find those who bitch the loudest about their fiction being categorized are usually those whose work is the most limited in its vision, scope, execution, and expertise; they aren't getting a wider audience because their work doesn't *deserve* a wider audience ... and in some cases doesn't even deserve the limited one it already has.

All of which is a smokescreen, because nowhere in this self-manufactured "controversy" is there directly addressed the question of quality in the field, of which there remains a noticeable want.

Face it; the majority of horror published during the standards-free *tsunami* of the 1980's was worthless; it lacked depth, it lacked thoughtful characterization, it lacked even a nodding acquaintance with the concept of "theme," let alone an ability to have its plot stick to the ground rules established in the story – if, indeed, the effort to establish same had even been made. It seemed that any idiot with access to a typewriter (who'd also read all of Stephen King's books and seen every *Friday the Thirteenth* and *Nightmare on Elm Street* movie) decided that, in order to become a published horror writer, all you needed to do was take a graphic description of a day's work at the local slaughterhouse, set it in a remote town, throw in a couple of sex scenes, add some dialogue here and there to give the impression something worthwhile is actually happening, then slap it all together as thinly-veiled *homage* to Freddy or Jason or that chick who vomits pea soup in *The Exorcist* and – *voila!* – you have a saleable horror novel.

And here's the thing: it worked. That *is* all you had to do in order to sell a horror novel in the 80s. (Slightly overstating again to make the point – but only slightly.)

Where'd I set that Bailey's and Drano® cocktail. . . ?

Many lament that we are still paying for the cornucopia of conscienceless crap that littered bookshelves back then, and they're right, we are; we're still paying for it because we *should* still be paying for it. The majority of horror in the 80s was a supreme embarrassment to the holy craft of storytelling; there was no excuse for it then, and there's even less of an excuse for it now, nearly two decades later, when the field is finally enjoying the start of a resurgence in popularity. Unfortunately, many of the new breed of horror writers cut their literary teeth *on* that cornucopia of conscienceless crap for which we're still doing penance, and despite their potential, enthusiasm, or varying levels of skill, you cannot build a literary foundation on the influence of that which the field is trying to overcome.

A well-respected and excellent writer I know who used to write horror under a pseudonym during the 80s once said the following to me: "I did it because it was decent money, it didn't take long, and I sure as hell didn't have to worry about whether or not the book had any kind of *value*; people just wanted a lot of violence as soon as possible, not too much thinking, and as much shock-value as I could deliver in 300 pages. It was nothing more than bloody junk-food. I never blew a brain cell on it."

To this writer's credit, the novels written under their pseudonym were much better than their above words would lead you to think; in fact, they were some of the better horror novels being produced at the time. That might seem to denote that horror wasn't as bad as I've made it out to be; the more likely subtext is that this writer had personal standards which so far surpassed those of the field that even their "bloody junk-food" writing outshone everything around it.

Nothing that I have said up to this point has been said while wearing my writer's cap; I am in full Reader mode for this central section, and if my tone comes off as arrogant or know-it-all, there is what I feel to be a pretty good reason: I am a *merciless* reader; I have zero tolerance for sloppy, uninspired, hollow-cored storytelling, pedestrian prose, or characters whose sole purpose is to wander onstage, do something stupid, and then be graphically Slurped by the Glop. I may occasionally slip on my writer's cap for an aside here and there, but the bitchy guy you're dealing with now is Gary, the

Reader.

Let me tell you *why* I rank among the most unforgiving of readers:

I read *very* slowly.

Where most people I know ripped through Stephen King's marvelous *The Girl Who Loved Tom Gordon* in three hours, it took me three days. The upside to this — and what makes me a sloppy writer's worst nightmare — is that, because I read so slowly, I notice more detail than most people and have a greater awareness of the micro-writing. Not a bad thing at all.

The downside is that I can't read as many books in the course of a week or month as I would like to. I envy people who read two, three, four books a week. I wish I could devour literature the same way, but I can't.

When I was in the second grade at St. Francis de Sales School in Newark, Ohio, our English teacher, Sister Mary Elizabeth, required that we read aloud on Mondays and Fridays. Coming from a hard-core blue-collar background, reading was not something that was encouraged in the Braunbeck household. Not that my parents *dis*couraged it, but because both of them worked long hours at hellish factory jobs, they were either too tired or too busy with things like bills and home repairs to find time to read much. Neither of them completed high school, and neither of them ran in social circles where "intellectual" pursuits such as reading were the norm.

No, I'm not blaming them, far from it; Mom would always buy me a book if I found one I wanted, and Dad was more than happy to read to or with me. (Aside: Mom was a big Mickey Spillane fan, and read his books whenever she could, but the only two books I ever saw her re-read were Blatty's *The Exorcist* and F. Paul Wilson's *The Keep*, which she thought was ". . . one of the best books I've ever read. I hope he writes another one.")

Okay, so I'm sitting there in English class one Friday, and we're taking turns reading paragraphs from some book — I wish to hell I could remember its name — about this kid named Johnny who works odd jobs so he can earn money to go to the movies because he likes to imagine that he's the cowboy hero or brave fighter pilot or smart detective.

Gets to be my turn, and I'm reading along — slower than the other kids, but smoothly, nonetheless — when I encounter a word I'd often heard but had never actually seen in print before: "aisle."

I stopped, stared at the word, and tried to figure out how to pronounce it.

Sister Mary Elizabeth made quite a show out of my inability to read this word aloud, so finally, embarrassed beyond belief, I gave it a try.

What I said was something akin to "i-sell."

Everyone laughed. Sister Mary Elizabeth told me to try it again.

I-sell. Again.

I couldn't figure out any other way to pronounce it.

Sister then pulled several other books from the shelf and opened them to selected pages, thrust them under my nose, and ordered me to read about twenty-five different words at her random choosing, all of which I'd *heard*, none of which I had ever seen in print before, among them "redundant," "envelope," "digestion," "automatic," and — my personal favorite to this day — "repetitive."

I missed every last one of them.

And everyone got a dandy guffaw out of that.

Most of the kids who attended St. Francis came from fairly well-to-do families, families who financially contributed heavily to both the church and school, who held positions on the school board or church board, and who got to wear dresses and ties to their jobs and sit behind desks.

I was one of a small handful of kids who came from, well . . . *not-so* well-to-do families, and there was a marked difference in the way we were treated — both by our fellow students and the teachers. If one of the rich students was having difficulties, well, then, hire a tutor, arrange for special sessions with teachers after school, cut them as much slack as possible.

But if one of the poorer students was having trouble . . . tough shit. Their families were barely making the quarterly tuition payments, so it wasn't worth anyone's time to give them any extra help.

Three days a week, I was provided with a free lunch because my parents couldn't afford to pay for an entire week's worth. Somehow, Sister Mary Elizabeth managed to work that into her scolding of me in front of the class that day, as well as several observations about the limited selection options available to me for my wardrobe.

"Go sit out in the hall, you're holding everyone else back, you dumb-bunny."

Dumb-bunny. Never forgot that one.

So I went out into the hall and sat there.

Which is how I came to find myself transferred to the "special" English class the following Monday.

Here is what the "special" English class consisted of:

Some assistant coach (or Darrell Sheets, the marvelous, kind man who was the school's janitor) sat at a table in the cafeteria while the rest — there were five of us — were seated at another table. On this table was a stack of childrens' books. Twenty of them, in fact. I remember this because these books never changed. Ever.

These were books written for children at the pre-school/kindergarten level.

This is Dick. This is his sister, Jane. Dick and Jane are playing with their Dog, Spot. "Run, Spot, run!" See Spot run. Run, Spot, run.

Goddamn page-turners were these books.

From Grade 2 until Grade 5 that is how I spent my English classes; down in the cafeteria, sitting at a table with four other "special" students, reading the same twenty books over and over. (We were not allowed to bring our own books, we had to read only those that were deemed to be "within" our "ranges of comprehension." At least at the beginning of every year they gave us twenty different books than the year before. Our big exam was to read two of them aloud at the end of the year.)

As a result of this, and the lack of reading time/assistance at home, I read at a first-grade level until the sixth grade. Even then, I was way behind the other kids. (The "special" program had been 86'd at the end of my fifth grade year because they could no longer find assistant coaches or assistant janitors who were willing to baby-sit us.)

I somehow managed to bluff my way through sixth grade English — I squeaked by with a "C" — but even that summer, I found that I was still having trouble reading books that, by all accounts, I should have been able to breeze through four years ago.

I was given a reading comprehension test at the start of my seventh grade year.

I was reading at a third-grade level . . . and just barely at that.

But I got lucky. My English teacher that year was a terrific guy named David Kessler who had been made aware of my "learning disability" and who, even though he wasn't allowed to give me any extra help either in or outside of class, did provide me with books designed to help me read better. I guarded these books as if they were my life savings. Whenever either of them could, Mom and Dad helped me, or one of the neighbors if I offered to cut their grass. But mostly I had to do it on my own.

By the time I left the Catholic School system at the end of my eighth grade year, I was reading at the fifth-grade level.

For me, it was a personal triumph.

I haven't bothered getting myself tested in decades, because whatever level I'm reading at right now is the level I will read at until I take the Dirt Nap.

But there remain times . . .

There were several sections in Dan Simmons's brilliant *The Hollow Man* that I had to re-read more than once before fully understanding what I was reading. As much as I admire and enjoy the work of Joe Haldeman, Harlan Ellison, and Gene Wolfe, there are times while reading them that I feel genuinely *stupid*, as if I'm standing there in front of Sister and the class trying to decipher "aisle" once again.

It took me three days to read a short novel that most people read in three hours.

To this day, I remain angry about that.

To this day, I still have trouble reading at times, and always will, and that has caused some measure of enjoyment to be subtracted from my life, and that saddens me whenever I think about it for too long.

Because the ability to read is one of the most precious gifts we possess, and few things piss me off more than to meet someone who has the ability to read — odds are, at a level higher and faster than myself — who chooses not to because reading is "boring" or "a waste of time."

One of those few things that *does* piss me off more is to have my time, trust, and skill as a reader taken for granted by sloppy writers who think that "bloody junk food" is the best they need strive toward, and as a result waste my time, insult my intelligence, and needlessly slaughter acres of trees whose continued existence the rest of us could use to help us breathe easier.

Okay, I can go on tossing out generalities until we're all lulled into a coma. It's time to get specific.

Instead of sighting dozens of examples of bad writing in horror — which I pray to God or Whatever's out there you can readily recognize on your own — I'm going to illustrate what I find to be both right and wrong with the current state of horror fiction by examining only two short stories that, respectively, encapsulate both the best and the worst elements to be found in the field. The stories, "Megan's Law" and "Gone," are by one the field's leading practitioners, Jack Ketchum. Both can be found in his recent Subterranean Press/Leisure release, *Peaceable Kingdom*.

While you seek out and read those stories, we need to establish a couple of things; first and foremost: the difference between a "fan" and an "admirer."

I don't haunt many on-line discussion boards because I've found that a majority of them are frequented by pointlessly mordant, juvenile-minded muckrakers whose only purpose in life seems to be insulting everyone and everything they can in an effort to draw attention to themselves; there is, however, one discussion board that has almost never fallen into this trap: the always-refreshing Book Forum at Gorezone: *http://pub70.ezboard.com/fgorezonefrm3*. It's been around for over five years and has proved its staying power, so I feel confident that you'll still find it up and running strong by the time this book sees publication. The Book Forum is moderated by a gent named Mark Sieber who is the type of reader any writer dreams of having; he's intelligent, articulate, open-minded, and, above all, courteous, and expects the same of anyone who participates in the discussions. If you've never been to the Gorezone Book Forum, visit it soon; you'll go back.

A while back there was a discussion thread about the work of the late Richard Laymon. One of the participants in the discussion, having never read Laymon's work but having encountered on the board countless kudos about it, sought out and read several of Laymon's novels and short stories, then chimed into the discussion with these word: "I just don't get why this guy is so revered."

They went on to say that, while they found Laymon's work to be beautifully paced, delivering of decent enough shocks at times, and offering the occasional memorable set-piece, they just didn't think the writing itself was good enough to warrant all the praise. On any other discussion board this person would have been impaled and roasted over hot coals for saying this; they would have been accused of attacking Laymon himself, not his work, and charged with pissing on his memory.

But not at Gorezone.

Instead, there was a lot of "I'm sorry you feel that way," "Maybe his stuff just isn't for your taste," et cetera, but one specific response stood out, at least to me: "I feel that I have to defend his work, because I love everything he writes."

And *there*, my friends, if you can read between the lines, you have a glowing example of the difference between a fan and an admirer; while the former participant in the discussion found elements in Laymon's work that they appreciated, overall his work did not appeal to them; the latter participant, however (while not refuting anything said by the former), bravely and admirably proclaimed their love for "everything" Laymon wrote.

God bless fans, and I mean that from the bottom of my heart and with not an ounce of patronizing; fans are worth their weight in gold and should be treasured and thanked whenever possible; a fan will read everything they can get their hands on by a favorite writer, and will forgive that writer damn near anything. Quick example: in Stephen King's *The Tommyknockers*, much is made of everyone in town losing all of their teeth, yet roughly seventy pages later, everyone has their teeth back and no explanation is ever offered. Point this out to a King fan and they will defend it unto death: "His workload was very heavy at the time," et cetera. King fans forgave him that mistake (one that should have been caught by whichever copyeditor fell asleep at the wheel) because they *love everything he writes.* King's admirers — among which I proudly count myself — did not, because there is *no* excuse for such an amateurish gaffe; that doesn't mean we were attacking him personally, or saying that all his work was rubbish, drivel, and gobbledygook; it's simply that we respect King's work and know him to be a far better writer than a blooper like this would lead one to think. (And I have to agree with something Ed Bryant once said in *Locus*: that because King is a giant, the flaws which occasionally crop up in his work are often unjustifiably magnified well beyond their actual harm.)

Back to Jack Ketchum.

"Gone" was the recipient of the 2000 Bram Stoker Award for short story, and rarely have I outright cheered such news as I did that announcement. Make certain you've read both before continuing, because what follows is going to include so-called spoilers. Don't say I didn't warn you.

I'll state for the record that I am a great *admirer* of Jack Ketchum's work (one of the stories in my upcoming collection *Destinations Unknown* is even dedicated to him); I am *not*, however, a fan. If you don't understand the difference, then you've just been skimming, and shame on you. Me works hard to be entertaining and illuminating.

I've never met Jack Ketchum. I've been at conventions which he has also attended, but have never been introduced. I only know him as, 1) a writer, and, 2) a mid-sized, lean fellow who looks like the less-stable twin Willem Dafoe keeps chained up in the family cellar. Everyone I know who's met him says that he's a terrific guy, and I do not doubt this; I am not here to discuss him as a person but as a storyteller.

Ketchum's average as a storyteller with me has been a consistent 50/50; the stuff of his that I like, I like tremendously; the stuff of his that I dislike, I dislike *intensely*; but I admire *all* of it because his work never fails to solicit a strong reaction from me. (The worst thing anyone can say about a writer's work is that it left them feeling indifferent. You can't say that about Ketchum's work, and bravo to him for that.) The best of his work is literate, stylish, oft-times feverish in its emotional intensity, and unflinchingly brutal in its depiction of the violence we either inflict on one another or, through inaction, allow to be inflicted upon others — and nowhere is this sentiment more beautifully expressed than in the closing passages on his introduction to *Peaceable Kingdom*: "And that, finally, is my wish for us all, concealed or obvious somewhere in each of these stories — *they shall not hurt or destroy.*"

How the hell could I *not* admire the work of a fellow writer whose core agenda is so close to my own heart? Ketchum's overall body of work functions at extremes: from the visceral, no-holds-barred horror of novels such as *The Girl Next Door* and stories such as "The Passenger," to more gentle but no less affecting works such as *Red* and "Mother and Daughter," Ketchum has proven himself time and again to be a writer of undeniable power, even when that power is misdirected and undisciplined, which brings me to the other 50% of his work that I in no way think of as his best.

The work of Ketchum's I dislike, I dislike because I find it structurally unsound, thematically unfocused, sloppily executed, or, at its very worst, self-consciously shocking — that is, being shocking for its own sake and not because the story justifies it; for me, this last is perhaps the most unpardonable misstep committed not only by Ketchum, but by many writers in the horror field, be they the young Turks or the more seasoned pros who should damned well know better; that a horror story *has* to have some kind of heavy-handedly shocking, grisly, or hideous element that readers can look at and say, "See here? *This* makes it a horror story because there's an axe murder/torture scene/rape/cannibalism/S&M/lots of blood/violence/telemarketers/Oprah's Book Club selections (et cetera) in it!"

(Which prompts me to ask: Do horror writers put these often-superfluous elements into stories because readers *expect* to find them, or do readers expect to find them because the writers always put them there? See "Ouroboros" note from earlier.)

Now, if you've managed to track down and read both stories, we can get started on "Megan's Law" — which remains one of the most frustrating and brilliant failures in the horror field I've read in ten years.

The bare bones of the story are this: a man discovers that a recently-paroled sex offender has moved into his neighborhood; fearing for his daughter's safety, he decides to kill the other guy, and then does just that.

As tidy and concise a plot as there is to be found.

The title of the story refers to an expansion (Chapter 908) made in 1996 to California's Child Molester Identification Line, which made registered sex offenders' whereabouts available to the public; Megan's Law made it mandatory that all members of any given community be informed in a timely fashion of any registered sex offender who was living in, or about to move into, their community. It is named after 7-year-old Megan Kanka, who was raped and killed by a known child molester who had moved across the street from her family without their knowledge. In the wake of the tragedy, her parents sought to have local communities warned about sex offenders in the area, and the result, thankfully, was Megan's Law . But like any law implemented in these ridiculously politically correct times, there is a proviso (this quoted directly from the web site of the Office of the Attorney General, State of California, Department of Justice; italics are mine): *"The law is not intended to punish the offender and specifically prohibits using the information to harass or commit any crime against the offender."*

So, starting with its very title and all it references, you know that "Megan's Law" isn't going to be a romping Waldropian chuckle-fest. We're not even into the first line of the story yet, and already Ketchum has masterfully agitated the reader. This is not happenstance, folks; Ketchum knows, as does any writer worth their carbon, that it really isn't the first line of your story that serves as the so-called "hook" for the reader, it's *the title*, and with this one Ketchum, quite covertly but nonetheless deliberately, has already jarred loose specific associations in the reader's mind.

Everything's good so far.

And it gets even better with the opening passage, with its musical, brittle cadence worthy of Paddy Chayefsky or Rod Serling:

> Well, what the hell would *you* do?
>
> A cop walks up to your door, knocks. You look out the window and see his squad car parked in front of your house. You open the door and this kid half your age with a gun and cuffs and bullet pouches on his belt and pad, pencil, and some flyers in his hand says *'scuse me, sir, good morning, Mr. Albert Walker?* and you say *yes, what can I do for you, Officer?* and he introduces himself and proceeds to inform you on this fine sunny summer nine-thirty Saturday morning smelling of fresh cut grass and dew that there's a goddamn *rapist* moved in two doors up, a fucking *child molester* by the name of Philip Knott, a tier-three high-risk sex criminal and he's informing you by order of the county prosecutor's office.

Looking at this opening passage from a straightforward technical standpoint, Ketchum could not have possibly gotten this *more* right; in four sentences, he establishes time, place, situation, character, and introduces the central conflict — Who, What, When, Where, and Why; the *how* which completes this formulae is the basis of the rest of the story.

But it's the rhythm of these opening sentences, as much as their content, that draws you in. With the first sentence — "Well, what the hell would *you* do?" — he immediately sets up an easy three-quarters-time tempo that clicks in the reader's mind, and even goes so far as to emphasize the word "you" at precisely the place where a natural down-beat would occur if this were a line being sung in a song. With the opening sentence of the next paragraph, it would be justified, in order to keep the flow uninterrupted, to repeat this cadence — and, in fact, he nearly does: had the next line gone "A cop walks up to your door and knocks," the "and" would have been at the same down-beat point as the previous sentence's "you" and the repetition of the rhythm would have further eased the reader into the understated musicality that begins building toward its climax with the very next line — however, he doesn't do that. Instead of maintaining the tempo established in the opening sentence, he eschews the use of a down-beat "and," replacing it with a comma that creates a skip in the measure and catches the reader off-guard; the flow is disrupted just enough to inform the reader, albeit on an unconscious level, that the rest of the story — evidenced by this deliberate stop-and-start-again blip — is going to take every opportunity it can to agitate you.

The following line — "You look out the window and see his squad car parked in front of your house" — returns to the cadence of the first line, the down-beat coming here on "window," "squad," and "front." While this echoes the meter of the first sentence, it also expands on it, preparing you — whether you know it or not — for the crescendo that follows.

The fourth and final sentence is a solid illustration of the old "know the rules before you break them" creed; it would have worked just fine if Ketchum had decided to follow the standard rules and broken this up into two or three shorter lines; you would still have gotten all the necessary information for the setup, but there's much more he's indirectly conveying here, information the reader would not so readily perceive if this fourth sentence was not the glorious, near-operatic run-on that it is: namely, Albert Walker's immediate and mounting panic, a panic echoed at first in the agitating repetition of the word "and" (". . . and gun and cuffs and bullet pouches . . ."), then with an unbroken string of seemingly banal details (". . . this fine sunny summer nine-thirty Saturday morning smelling of fresh cut grass and dew . . .") that seem at first almost ridiculously out of place — a technique often employed by the Two Johns, Cheever and Updike — until you reach ". . . there's a goddamn *rapist* moved in two doors up, a fucking *child molester* by the name of Philip

Knott . . ." at which point the sentence switches to a rapid listing of details concerning Knott — details that serve to lend sudden, intense importance of the more banal fine points of before (". . . fresh cut grass and dew . . ."), because it's now those taken-for-granted everyday details that are threatened by Knott's presence.

Another subtle trick that Ketchum uses to great advantage is opening the story with six paragraphs written in second person ("A cop walks up to your door, knock. You look out the window . . .") before making the jarring transition to first person at the beginning of the seventh paragraph (italics are mine): "He goes on to say that should *my daughter* be approached by Mr. Knott for any reason . . ."

Two things are accomplished by this: 1) The second person passages at once draw the reader into the narrative by making them a part of the situation, so that by the time the seventh paragraph switch to first person occurs, they are, 2) Firmly in Walker's corner and very much sympathetic to his mindset.

It also sets up and justifies the POV change that occurs after the scene break, where the reader is introduced to Philip Knott through Knott's first-person internal monologue:

> *It isn't fair. I'm worried damn near all the time now.*
> *In some ways, it's worse than fucking Rahway. In Rahway I had Jumma to protect me and even if the price for that was so fucking high I'm lucky I can walk straight, here I got nobody. Nobody I can trust to watch my back. The guys at the garage, I trust the owner but not the rest of those dumb white-trash assholes. They know I'm a damn good mechanic but they'd just as soon kick my ass as look at me.*

Notice how the cadences which comprise Knott's interior monologue echo those which close the opening passages where Walker starts giving in to his panic; here, Knott is fully in the grip of the anxiety that Walker is only beginning to experience, and throughout the rest of the story, as the POV switches between Walker's actions and Knott's interior monologue, the rhythm of both men's thoughts become more and more attuned to one another until, in the closing sections, the meter of the language is exactly the same for both characters; Walker has reached an almost euphoric calm in his decision to kill Knott, and Knott has found a consoling internal balance, realizing that he not only *can* overcome his demons, he *wants* to, and that makes the *first* ending of "Megan's Law" chilling and genuinely tragic: Knott vows to overcome the darkness that compelled him to commit his atrocious crimes in the first place, and in that respect becomes the embodiment of a potential "rehabilitated" criminal; Walker, on the other hand, is shown in deft strokes to become every inch the monster he thinks Knott still is and always will be, and his matter-of-fact manner in justifying his actions are as cold and calculating as those of any serial killer. ("I was suddenly all will. All purpose and design.")

Throughout all of this, Walker's daughter, Michelle, is kept almost completely in the background; we know that Walker feels very protective of her from the days when Walker's late wife, an abusive alcoholic, would terrify Michelle when Walker wasn't around. It is not until the closing passages of the story — after Walker has killed Knott and effectively disposed of what scant evidence there is to link him to the murder, then gone on to work as if it's just another dull old day — that Michelle comes onstage, and even then her presence is represented rather than illustrated:

> "That night when I came home Michelle told me that the police had been here and talked to her. That they were questioning everyone on the street. I figured that was only natural. As his neighbors we were the likely suspects after all. They told her to have me call when I got home from work so I did. We set up an interview for tomorrow morning. Nine o'clock sharp.
> "I have no problem with that at all. I probably won't even be late for work, they said."

Had the story ended there (as it should have), Ketchum would have produced another unflinching, trenchant, drenched-in-gray-area tale that could stand alongside the best of his short stories, such as "The Rifle," "Gone," and "Father and Son," to name but three excellent pieces.

But it doesn't end there; what follows the above passage are nine more sentences that, not content with merely shooting the story in the foot, shove the business end of a double-barrel shotgun into its mouth and trip both hammers:

> Michelle, though, Michelle was pretty shook up over the whole thing. You couldn't blame her. The murder. The police and all.
> So I did what I usually do.
> I took her to bed.
> I comforted her.
> What would you do?

In exactly forty words, and for no good reason other than to deliver a cheap shock, Ketchum completely destroys what was until then an first-rate, cold-blooded study of a normal Joe committing a psychopathically misguided act of vigilantism because of his mistaken perception that another man was a threat to his daughter, his community, and his way of life.

Fans of Ketchum's work have defended this ending by saying that he was trying to illustrate Nietzsche's warning that "Whoever fights monsters, should see to it that in the process he does not become a monster."

To which I, as an admirer of his work, repeat Joe Lansdale's succinct quip: "Bullshit, pilgrim."

Nowhere — *nowhere* — previous in the story is this supposed "twist" hinted at, foreshadowed, or even alluded to; the best "twist" or "shock" endings emerge naturally from the flow and content of the narrative that comes before — witness Charles Beaumont's "The Crooked Man," Philip K. Dick's "Frozen Journey," Rod Serling's "The Escape Route," or William F. Nolan's "Dark Winner"; while each of these stories contains an effective twist at its conclusion, these jarring turn of events have been set up well beforehand, with hints and clues dropped subtly but judiciously so the ending doesn't feel like something that was tacked on as an afterthought in order to placate the lazy habits and short attention spans of horror readers who, since the 80s, have come to expect everything to be spoon-fed to them — because God knows you don't want to have to *think about* the ending of a story. (For the best recent example of how well so-called "twists" can work when they work well, watch M. Night. Shyamalan's *The Sixth Sense.)*

There is no such set up in "Megan's Law."

By ending the story as he does, Ketchum was clearly trying to hammer home the the that Walker has not *become* a monster, but that he's been one all along.

The thing is, we *already knew* this. As his actions and the reasons behind them have shown the reader, Walker is, in his way, just as much a threat to the world — and *potential* threat to Michelle — as he perceives Knott to be. With those last unneeded and unnecessary sentences, Ketchum not only trivializes the themes of responsibility and accountability that he has so adeptly grappled with, but effectively reduces an incisive, literate, and affecting sociological horror story to little more than a pointlessly heavy-handed diatribe, one seemingly directed toward an audience who either can't recognize subtle implications or who are too lethargic to fire off a few synapses in order to complete an obviously unspoken final thought.

Remember earlier, when I said that no one is blameless? That includes lazy readers, too.

Go back and re-read "Megan's Law," only this time use a bookmark or piece of paper to cover up the last nine sentences — the final five, short paragraphs — and read it as if the story ends with "I probably won't even be late for work, they said."

For me, as a reader, "Megan's Law" would have been a brilliant story had it ended there, leaving me with a lingering sense of dread and paranoia that would have lasted well beyond my turning the final page; instead I was cheated because Ketchum felt compelled to add this last, useless, gratuitous shock; as if the reader wouldn't know this was a horror story unless some "yeech!" element was involved.

No such element rears its unwanted head in Ketchum's other story, "Gone," which remains for me one of the most elegant, chilling, and genuinely disturbing he's written.

In it we meet Helen Teal, *nee* Mazik, a divorced woman whose house has for the past five years been shunned by the neighborhood children on Halloween. The other neighbors think of Helen as being a bit unstable, but if this is the case; she's got good reason: her three-year-old daughter was snatched from a parking lot five years ago, sending Helen into a downward spiral of depression and drinking that drove away her husband and left her branded as that "... lady down the block" by everyone.

This year, however, Helen has at last begun to get a handle on her depression, and has turned on the porch lights, stocked up on candy, and — as the story begins — is waiting for the first of trick-or-treaters to come to the door:

> Seven-thirty and nobody at the door. No knock, no doorbell.
>
> *What am I? The wicked old witch from Hansel and Gretel?*
>
> The jack-o-lantern flickered out into the world from the window ledge, the jointed cardboard skeleton swayed dangling from the transom. Both there by way of invitation, which so far had been ignored. In a wooden salad bowel on the coffee table in front of her bite-sized Milky Ways and Mars Bars and Nestle's Crunch winked at her reassuringly — crinkly gleaming foil-wrap and smooth shiny paper.
>
> *Buy candy, and they will come.*
>
> Don't worry, she thought. Someone'll show ...

Already you can recognize the familiar, sure-handed use of cadence — one of Ketchum's stylistic signatures — easing you into the one-set, four-character narrative (and take note of the splendid imagery, particularly the way the candy bars "... winked at her reassuringly. ..." This is good stuff.)

As Helen waits (and waits ... and waits ...) for the first of the trick-or-treaters to come knocking, she broods about the loss of her daughter and how she herself has "... gone from pre-school teacher, homemaker, wife, and mother to the three *p's* — psychoanalysis, Prozac, and paralysis."

Almost ready to give up, Helen is preparing to make herself another strong drink when three children — dressed as, respectively, a witch, a werewolf, and an alien, all of whom identify themselves as brothers and sister and are *not* from the neighborhood — come to the door. Seeing them gives Helen hope:

"She felt a kind of weight lifted off her, sailing away through the clear night sky. If nobody else came by for the rest of the night that was fine too. Next year would be even better."

Having been frightened of so much as looking at another child in the years since her daughter's disappearance, Helen revels in the presence of these children, happy that she feels no sadness or regret from enjoying their brief company; a quietly moving sequence where the compassion of and for this character shines through.

Then, just as the children are readying to leave, one of them asks Helen is she's the lady:

"Excuse me?"
"You're her?"
"Who?"
"The lady her lost her baby? The little girl?"

Helen answers that she is, the children apologize for having asked, wish her a happy Halloween, then turn and walk off the porch.

What follows the childrens' exit is one of the most well-crafted and -executed sentences Ketchum ever wrote, one whose unspoken subtext starts as a paper cut and ends as a dagger in the gut:

"They turned away and headed slowly down the stairs and she almost asked them to wait, to stay a moment, for what reason and to what end she didn't know but that would be silly and awful too, no reason to put them through her pain, they were just kids, children, they were just asking a question the way children did sometimes, oblivious to its consequences and it would be wrong to say anything further, so she began to close the door and almost didn't hear him turn to his sister and say, *too bad they wouldn't let her out tonight, huh? too bad they never do* in a low voice but loud enough to register but at first it *didn't* register, not quite, as though the words held no meaning, as though the words were some strange rebus she could not immediately master, not until after she'd closed the door and then when finally they impacted her like grapeshot, she flung open the door and ran screaming down the stairs into the empty street."

Note how Ketchum once again uses the repetition of "and" to great advantage in the early portion of the sentence to build the tension, then switches to "but" to achieve the same effect, result in a passage where the two words are repeated with the panicked near-stutter of a crime victim trying to describe what just happened to them to a confused police officer.

Had Ketchum chosen to end the story with this powerful passage, the story would still rank as one of his best, but an argument could be made that the knife needed to be twisted, quickly, just once, to make sure Helen's pain is driven into the reader's core; the forty-four words that comprise the coda of "Gone" — unlike those which end "Megan's Law" — are not only well-chosen, but build upon the and add to the previous revelation, rather than throw in a pointless shock of their own:

> She thought when she was able to think at all of what she might say to the police.
> *Witch, werewolf, alien. Of this age and that height and weight.*
> Out of nowhere, vanished back into nowhere.
> Carrying along what was left of her.
> Gone.

I rarely gets any better than that, folks. "Carrying along what was left of her. Gone."

Some writers would kill for an ending that concise and affecting.

Oddly enough, "Gone" is a story that many of the Ketchum fans I've spoken with like well enough in a luke- warm kind of way, but don't think of as being among his best. After much prodding, pushing, and pouting on my part, I managed to got them to admit to me what it is about the story that leaves them shrugging.

At least one-third of the Ketchum fans I have spoken with are wary of "Gone" for one simple reason: They don't under- stand the ending. And I purport that if readers of this story are left scratching their heads after the last six paragraphs are read, it is not through any fault of Ketchum's — everything you need to know is there, very clearly, done with amazing subtlety and grace, but *there*, nonetheless; you may have to read the closing passages slowly, with a greater attention to detail than you've become accustomed to, but everything you need to know about Helen, those three kids, and the fate of her lost daughter is right in front of you, and if after re-read- ing "Gone" you still don't get it, it's not necessarily all your fault; it's not that you're some stuttering kid standing in front of his second grade class trying to fathom how to pronounce "aisle" or "repetitive," it's not that you're stupid or a slovenly reader, it's because, since the 1980s, both horror writers and horror readers have become deadened to, respectively, the use and presence of subtext in the field. Writers avoid it because they have come to think that every last detail must be de- scribed and every last question answered or else it's a cheat to the reader; readers tend to be mystified by it because they've grown habituated to not having to *think* about anything while reading.

Which has the makings of genuine disaster all the way around, because subtext, like hesitation, is one of the greatest tools available to writers of dark fiction.

Raymond Chandler (creator of Philip Marlowe, hero of such classic novels as *The Big Sleep* and *The Little Sister)* once gave the single most illustrative example of what constitutes subtext that I've ever encountered (and I am paraphrasing here):

A man and women, both middle-aged, are waiting on

an elevator. It arrives, and the man helps the woman get on. For the first several floors they are alone, watching the blinking lights. They do not speak and stand well apart from each other. The woman wears a very nice dress. The man wears a suit, tie, and hat. The elevator stops — not their floor — and a young woman gets on; she smiles at both the man and the woman, who smile at her in return. The man removes his hat. The ride continues in silence. The elevator stops, the girls gets off, the man puts his hat back on. A few floors later, the man and woman get off and walk toward a door at the end of the corridor.

It was usually at this point that Chandler would stop and ask the listener: "What's written on that door?"

So I'll put the question to you: what words are written on that door which our middle-aged couple are heading toward?

How the hell am I supposed to know? some of you may cry. *No one in that goddamned elevator said shit to anyone else, and on the basis of all the* nothing *that happened during that boring, boring, boring ride, I'm supposed to guess what it says on that stupid door?*

Yes, you are.

Because an awful lot happened during that elevator ride: 1) The man and woman never spoke to each other, even while they were alone; 2) They also made it a point to stand well apart from each other even though the man *helped* her get on; 3) When they young woman got on, the man, out of respect and courtesy, removed his hat; 4) Once the young woman disembarked, he put the hat *back on;* and, 5) The man women got off on the same floor, and are heading toward that door together.

Still say nothing happened and that you have no clues to go on in order to take a guess?

Subtext: the *unspoken* information that is conveyed to a reader through a character's behavior, actions, or lack thereof. In acting, it's referred to as "nuance." It's subtle, but its implications are quite direct *if* you care enough to pay attention.

That is, in my opinion, what the field has lost over the last few decades: a willingness to employ and appreciate the quieter, more delicate, and less obvious details of character and scene that can make horror fiction so much richer and rewarding.

Last chance; take a guess what it says on that door.

Try: **Marriage Counselor.**

Now, apply Chandler's terrific example to the closing passages of "Gone."

What do we know about what's happened? 1) That this is the first time in five years (since her daughter's disappearance) that Helen has turned on her porch light to draw trick-or-treaters for Halloween; 2) She's been waiting for hours because the neighborhood children have been avoiding her house at the urging of their parents; 3) When finally some trick-or-treaters do arrive, they are not from the neighborhood; 4) Even though they are not from the neighborhood, one of them knows to ask if Helen is the ". . . lady who lost her baby" — not only that, but knows that the "little baby" was a girl; and, 5) As they are leaving, one of them comments, in a low voice, how it's "too bad" "they" didn't "let her out tonight . . . too bad they never do. . . ."

Subtext. What is conveyed through action and situation but not outright stated.

Now do you know what happened?

The three little trick-or-treaters *not* from the neighborhood came to Helen's house *specifically*; they came there specifically because they *know* Helen's missing daughter, who either lives *with* them, or with someone who lives near them; whatever the case, these three kids are terrified to tell Helen anything because of what might happen to them or Helen's daughter if they do.

Which is what turns "Gone" into the stuff of classic tragedy; Helen's closing the door before the kid's words finally register is akin to Romeo walking past the nurse who carries Juliet's note, and, like with Romeo, by the time she realizes what it means, it's too late, the kids are nowhere to be seen, "Carrying along what was left of her." It's not hard to imagine Helen, after this night, doing a Miss Amelia from *The Ballad of the Sad Café* or a Miss Havisham from *Great Expectations* and forever sealing herself up in that house, boarding up the windows, remaining alone with her grief and regret, never venturing out into the world again — an added dash of profound sadness that only serves to amplify the initial horror of her loss.

One last time: subtext. Just because Ketchum doesn't spell it out in exact terms doesn't mean it isn't there.

Subtext.

We need to get it back into horror; the sooner, the better.

Because until we do, until we avail ourselves of those storytelling tools that have so well served the work of such writers as John O'Hara, Raymond Carver, Carson McCullers, Eudora Welty, Charles L. Grant, M.R. James, Kate Wilhelm, James Agee, Jack Cady, James P. Blaylock, Tim Powers, and others, until we are no longer satisfied with the "bloody junk food" we developed a taste for in the 80s, until we as readers and writers say that we are no longer content with stuff that simply gives us a good scare, then horror is going to stay locked up in the literary basement, picking at its scabs and drooling on itself and wondering why in hell no one seems to care about it.

Thus raveth Zarathustra.

Onward . . .

Part Three:

Horror as a Way of Life

"I have the horror of death with the still greater horror of living."

— Oscar Wilde,
Letter to Robert Ross from Reading Goal Prison,
March 10, 1896

I

Fear; "But That's the Way It Really Happened!"; and Staying the Hell Out of Your Own Way, for Chrissakes

*I*f horror is indeed the literature of fear, then everything is a horror story. From the intense terror of films such as *Alien* and *The Ring*, to lighter fare such as *E.T.* and *Stir Crazy*, novels from *The Shining*, *Ghost Story*, *Interview with the Vampire* to books like *What Color Is Your Parachute*, *Who Moved My Cheese?*, and *Nickel and Dimed* — hell, even the most lame of thin romance novels — fear lies at the core of everything we do. We work in order to make money and pay bills because we're afraid if we don't, our families will wind up on the streets; we do what we can for those who love us because, on some

level, we're afraid that if we don't, we will lose them; we keep
up on work-place practices because we're afraid of losing our
jobs or being passed over for promotion; we take vitamins
and go to the doctor and workout three times a week because
we want to stay healthy and look good because we're afraid
of growing (and looking) old, which leads us back to Ye Olde
fear of death — the ending to every story, fictional or otherwise — that we want to stave off for as long as possible.

But let's keep this in the context of fiction; choose any
novel or short story from any genre, remove from it the
element of fear, and see how much of a story you have left.
Odds are, not much of one.

It is my fervent belief that, like it or not, it is ultimately
fear that lies at the core of all our actions, and since horror
writers deal primarily in the exploration of this fear, that
exploration has to include the re-shaping of things from the
writer's own life experience.

For the record, any writer who claims that their fiction is
not based on or drawn from some aspect of their own lives —
be it past, present, or worries about the future — is one of two
things: a liar or unpublished.

I know fear, and I know regret; I know sadness, and I know
anger; I know the fragile nature of joy, and the ethereal state
of hope; I know integrity, and I know duplicity; I know the
wonder of finding a true friend, and I know the pain of how
it feels to lose one; I also know that the more I learn, the less
I know; and that no discussion of the craft of writing can be
restricted to just the nuts-and-bolts aspects lest it read like
some dry, outdated textbook on the subject.

For this final section I'm going to discuss writing. Since
the only thing more tedious than listening a writer go on
(and on. . .and on. . .) about writing is having to *read* one
going on about writing, I am going to try and make this as
direct and clear as possible, with a minimum of technical
jargon, and will dissect for your glee some of my own stories.

Over the years, I have been fairly up-front about the influence my life has had not only on what I choose to write but
how I choose to write it, so be warned that no discussion of
my work can come without equal discussion of those events

and people and sensibilities that led to the writing of a particular story or novel.

Have you ever been present at a writer's workshop where, after hearing their story critiqued by the other members, a writer will point to a certain event depicted in the story — an event the others have dubbed "hard to swallow" or "unbelievable" — and say, *But that's the way it really happened!?"* Well, I've been at these meetings, and I've said there what I'm about to say here: Fiction doesn't give a Sumatran-rat's ass about how something *really* happened; it has no use for your real-life experiences if you are hell-bent to depict them as they actually occurred; the story doesn't care about your trivial little self-exorcisms, it cares only that you tell it as well as possible, and that you care enough to be quiet and stay the hell out of its way.

One of my most popular stories, "Union Dues" (which originally appeared in *Borderlands 4,* edited by Tom and Elizabeth Monteleone) was almost crippled beyond repair early on because of my bull-headed insistence on portraying an event as it ". . . really happened." As a result, "Union Dues" remains only one of three stories that I had to re-write four times before I got it right (I can usually get it in two passes, three if there's a serious glitch; I almost *never* have to go that desperate, ulcer-inducing, sleep-depriving fourth pass; I tend to have everything thought out well before I apply ass to chair and hands to keyboard).

Here's a section from the scene in question:

"Sheriff Ted Jackson held a handkerchief over his nose and mouth as he surveyed the wreckage of the riot.

A cloud of tear gas was dissipating at neck level in the parking lot of the factory, reflecting lights from the two dozen police cars encircling the area. Newspaper reporters and television news crews were assembling outside the barricades along with people from the neighborhood and relatives of the workers involved. Silhouetted against the rapidly-setting cold November sun, the crowd looked like one massive duster of cells; a shadow on a lung x-ray — sorry, bud, this looks bad.

Men lay scattered, some on their sides, others on their backs, still more squatting and coughing and vomiting, all wiping blood from their faces and hands.

A half-foot of old crusty snow had covered the ground since the first week of the month, followed by days and nights of dry cold, so that the snow had merely aged and turned the color of damp ash, mottled by candy wrappers, empty cigarette packs, losing lottery tickets, beer cans, and now bodies. The layer of snow whispering from the sky was a fresh coat of paint; a whitewash that hid the ugliness and despair of the tainted world underneath.

A pain-filled voice called out from somewhere.

Fire blew out the windshield of an overturned semi; it jerked sideways, slammed into a guardrail, and puked glass.

The crowd pushed forward, knocking over several of the barriers. Officers in ftdl riot gear held everyone back.

The snow grew dense as more sirens approached.

The searchlight from a police helicopter swept the area.

A woman in the crowd began weeping loudly.

You couldn't have asked for an uglier mess.

Jackson pulled the handkerchief away and took an icy breath; the wind was trying to move the gas away but the snow held it against the ground. He turned up the collar of his jacket and pulled a twenty-gauge pump-action shotgun from the cruiser's rack.

"Sheriff?"

Dan Robinson, one of his deputies, offered him a gas mask.

"Little late for that."

"I know, but the fire department brought along extras and I thought — "

"Piss on that." Jackson stared through the snow at the crowd of shadows. The strobing visibar lights perpetually changed the shape of the pack; red-*blink*-a smoke crowd; blue-*blink*-a snow-ash crowd; white-*blink* —   a shadow crowd.

"You okay, Sheriff?"

"Let's go see if they cleared everyone away from the east side."

The two men trudged through the heaps of snow, working their way around the broken glass, twisted metal, blood, grease, and bodies. Paramedics scurried in all directions; gurneys were collapsed, loaded, then lifted into place and rolled toward waiting ambulances. Volunteers from the local Red Cross were administering aid to those with less serious wounds.

"Any idea how this started, sir?"

"The scabs came out for food. Strikers cut off all deliveries three days ago."

"Terrible thing."

"You got that right."

They rounded the comer and took several deep breaths to clear their lungs.

Jackson remembered the afternoon he'd had to come down and assist with bringing in the scabs — the strikers behind barricades on one side of the parking lot while the scabs rode in on flatbed trucks like livestock to an auction. Until that afternoon he'd never believed that rage was something that could live outside the physical confines of a man's own heart, but as those scabs climbed down and began walking toward the main production floor entrance he'd felt the presence of cumulative anger becoming something more fierce, something hulking and twisted and hideous. To this day he couldn't say how or why, but he could swear that the atmosphere between the strikers and scabs had rippled and even torn in places. It still gave him the willies.

He blinked against the falling snow and felt his heart skip a beat.

Twenty yards away, near a smoldering overturned flatbed at the edge of the east parking lot, a man lay on the ground, his limbs twisted at impossible angles. A long, thick smear of hot machine oil pooled behind him, hissing in the snow.

Maneuvering through the snowdrifts Jackson raced

over, slid to a halt, chambered a shell, and dropped to one knee, gesturing for Robinson to do the same.

Jackson looked down at the body and felt something lodge in his throat. "Damn. Herb Kaylor."

"You know him?"

Jackson tried to swallow but couldn't. The image of the man's face blurred; he wiped his eyes and realized that he was crying. "Yeah. Him and me served together in Vietnam. I just played cards with him and his wife a couple nights ago. *Goddammit!*" He clenched his teeth. "He wasn't supposed to be workin' the picket line today. Christ! Poor Herb. . . ."

The stumbling block came with that ". . . smoldering over-turned flatbed at the edge of the east parking lot"; there was, in the first three drafts, a little boy hiding inside that truck.

Here's what *really* happened (which I should have remembered fiction doesn't give a shit about):

When I was seven years old, the workers at the Roper Manufacturing plant where my dad was employed went on strike. This strike, occurring as the war in Vietnam was gearing up for its final, protracted, bloody hurrah, went on for nearly six weeks. The men who walked the picket line did so 24/7. A group of wives, my mother included, arranged to take turns providing the picketers with food; each of them would, on their assigned day, make sandwiches, potato salad, cold chicken, whatever they could afford (the strike fund ran out very quickly, so most of this food was paid for with money no one could afford to be spending) and deliver it to the workers.

My parents did not own a car; we couldn't afford one. Since the plant was only a fifteen- to twenty-minute walk from our front door, it was decided that seven-year-old Gary would do his part for the American Worker and be the one to deliver the food on Wednesdays, Mom's assigned day. I had no problems with this; I'd load up the sacks of sandwiches and chips into my trusty old Radio Flyer wagon and trundle on down to the picket line. (Mom would always sneak in a couple of twelve-packs of Blatz beer donated by other wives or neighbors and tell me, "Make sure you keep this covered so that no one can see it. We don't want anybody getting into trouble." Yeah, I could have been technically charged with bootlegging at age seven, ain't life cool?)

On this particular Wednesday I was running a little late. I was supposed to be there no later than two p.m. because Dad, for some reason, wanted to make sure I was out of there by two-thirty; neither he nor Mom would tell me why. That bugged me, because usually on Wednesdays I got to hang around, carry a picket sign, and talk with the guys. It made me feel all accepted and liked and grown-up. But today wasn't going to go like that, and I resented it, as well as not being told why I couldn't hang around. So I piddle-farted around (Mom's term) longer than necessary and didn't get out the door until five minutes until two. I arrived at the picket line somewhere between two-ten and two-fifteen.

I knew as soon as I got there that something wasn't right.

Aside from the dozens of workers manning the picket line, there were three large flatbed trucks with a bunch of other guys riding in them. The workers were standing in front of the trucks, and the guys riding in the backs looked really scared — I figured that must be the case, since not one of them was making a move to get out.

I didn't know or understand about scab labor in 1968, so I had no way of knowing that the guys standing in the backs of these flatbeds were considered to be the lowest of the low on the totem pole of blue-collar workers. And I sure as hell didn't know that the strikers had gotten wind of the company's bringing in scab labor and so had gathered *en masse* and armed themselves to prevent the scabs from getting inside the plant.

A little pause here to make something clear about so-called "scab" laborers: until I hit my late twenties I was a feverish — almost rabid — pro-union guy; in truth, I still think labor unions are, *in theory*, a great thing, because God knows the blue-collar worker in this country doesn't have anything else in his or her corner, but I saw "the union" eventually turn its back on both my parents when they desperately needed the support; I saw the look on Mom's face when she and I had to go downtown to the welfare offices twice a month to stand in these ungodly long lines waiting for our free allotment of bread, cheese, food stamps, and milk coupons (when these last were available, which wasn't often); I saw the shame on Dad's face when he had to accept charity from neighbors who were employed and wanted to help us out; I saw the way people in the grocery store lines would wrinkle their noses and shake their heads in disgust when Mom pulled out food stamps instead of cash; and I saw the way the cashiers would roll their eyes, *tsk* none-too-quietly, and make a show-stopping production number out of having to reenter numbers when Mom discovered that we didn't have enough to cover everything and so had to choose what items to put back — to this day I want to roundhouse-punch both cashiers and other people in line who act like someone's having to put an item back because they don't have enough money is somehow an insult, embarrassment, and inconvenience to *them*; after all, who *cares* about how the person putting the items back must feel, they're the ones holding up the line, they're the ones who should have done their math, who should have kept their jobs or had fewer children or borrowed from family members so they'd *have* enough money to pay for their groceries and not fuck-up everyone else's day. I lost count of how many times Mom walked out of a grocery store in tears because she'd been humiliated by cashiers, managers, and other customers in line behind her.

What does this have to do with "scab" laborers?

Simple: When you consider what my parents — who were supposedly under the protection of their unions — went through while towing the line and sticking to the rules, can you imagine how desperate, how at the end of their ropes, a worker would have to be in order to work scab? These are the people who, for whatever reasons, cannot get hired on at plants or anywhere else, and so are reduced to hanging out in front of the unemployment office every morning like beggars at the entrance to a bus station in the hopes that someone is going to drive up in a flatbed truck and say they need able bodies to work, payment in cash at the end of the job. These workers go into a situation like this knowing that they're going to be threatened, spit on, and probably physically assaulted, all so they can hole-up inside a factory where they'll have to remain, day and night, until the outside situation has been resolved; only then can they collect their pay which, odds favor, will be about one-third to half of what a regular union worker gets for the same job. So the next time you read about a factory that is brining in "scabs" to work the line while the other workers are on strike, bear in mind that neither the workers nor the "scabs" are to blame; both are desperate and doing what they think is best for themselves and their families.

Gray areas.

I deal with those a lot in my fiction.

Even when it's a gray area from real life that I try to graft onto a story because I make the mistake of putting my ego and not the story's own good first.

Let's get back to seven-year-old Gary with his Radio Flyer full of sandwiches and beer.

The first thing I think when I see these guys in the trucks and the workers on the picket line is: *I don't think there's enough sandwiches for everybody.* Still, I figured, if some of the guys were willing to split their sandwiches (bologna and cheese, pimento loaf and cheese, ham and cheese) with the other guys, we might be able to make it stretch (which is actually what Jesus said right before the whole loaves-and-fishes thing; "Thou needeth nay to get thy shorts in a knot; yea, for I can maketh this stretch").

So I trundle on down right toward the middle of it and I'm about ten, twenty yards away when a gun goes off and the guys in the trucks jump down and the picketers surge forward and then there's nothing but clubs and fists and things smashing and people falling all around me and police cars and sirens and visibar lights and fire trucks and then tear gas and I wet myself I was so frightened because I couldn't find Dad and then a couple of guys fell over my wagon and knocked the sandwiches and bottles all over the parking lot, and I screamed and started running away but I tripped and fell face-first onto the asphalt and skidded a few feet, tearing up the side of my face and my arms and knees and it hurt like nobody's business, and I couldn't get up to run so I sort of crawled over to where this truck had been knocked over on its side and I hid underneath its bed and just lay there, shaking and holding my ears because of all the noise. In the midst of all this I see two guys fighting their way over toward the truck; one of them kicks the other's feet out from under him, and when the second guy is on his back the first guy drops down on him like a curse from heaven and starts hammering at his skull with an unopened beer bottle — one of the Blatz bottles from my wagon — and there's blood and screaming and then the bottle shatters and the guy who's been getting pummeled by it wrenches the remainder of it from the first guy's hand and slashes it right across his face, and the second guy falls backward, clutching at the blood on his face and scrambles around until he finds something on the ground, then he comes back up with this mother of a crowbar that must have fallen from the truck I'm hiding underneath, and he strikes the second guy in the head once, twice, three times, and once the second guy's down the first guy still doesn't stop, he hits him a couple of more times, hard, then takes off, and me, I'm lying there underneath the truck and the second guy, he's lying a few feet away with blood all over his face and body and he's shuddering and jerking and the whole time he's looking right at me.

And I watched him die.

Beaten to death in part by a bottle of beer that had fallen from my wagon which, if I'd been on time, if I hadn't piddle-farted around, would have been drunk and disposed of well before the trouble started and maybe wouldn't have been used to make this guy horizontal in the middle of a riot.

So I watched him die.

I found out what his name was later, which helped a little because it gave me something to put with that face, and I did eventually realize that it was the beating with the crowbar and not the beer bottle that killed him, but, still . . . no snowflake in an avalanche ever feels responsible.

When it came time to write "Union Dues" I was determined to have a little boy (standing in for me) hiding either inside or underneath that ". . . smoldering overturned flatbed at the edge of the east parking lot" because, goddammit, *that's the way it really happened.*

Little son-of-a-bitch kept getting in the way. The whole time I'm writing and re-writing this story, this whiny little useless literary construct (a person or thing in a story that serves no other purpose than to be a convenient symbol or plot device) kept calling out from that truck and causing Sheriff Jackson and Deputy Robinson to drop everything (forward momentum and internal logic of the story included) and run over there to drag his pointless ass out of the wreckage. I kept struggling with his presence, and finally managed to work out a logical way for the kid to be there and contribute something to the scene (he was initially the one who recognized the dead man) but then another problem arose: once I had dragged his butt from the wreckage and used him to identify the dead man, I had no effing idea what to do with him; he was in the sheriff's way, he was in the deputy's way, he was in the story's way — a story in which he now served no further purpose — and he was in my way, but I was going to keep him there because, goddammit, *that's the way it really happened,* sniff-sniff, wah-wah-wah, boo-hoo, stamping foot on the floor.

I was — to paraphrase "Megan's Law" — suddenly all will, all purpose and design — note that last word, because once "design" enters into the storytelling equation, you're dead in the water, you're not "following an outline" or "sticking to the plot" or "expanding on the theme," you're *grafting* onto the narrative something that probably has no business being anywhere near the story, let alone in it.

So, reluctantly (and after a major chewing out from Tom Monteleone, who informed me in no uncertain terms that I should with all haste slip my sphenoid bone and everything attached to it from the protective covering of my sigmoid flexure and remove it hence through the sacro-iliac symphysis — "Get your fuckin' head out of your ass, Braunbeck!" is I think the way he actually phrased it) I cut The Little Boy Who Couldn't out of the story —

— and every last problem that I'd been having with "Union Dues" vanished completely, resulting in what is, if I do say so myself, one of the best short stories I've yet written, and one that serves as a loving and respectful testament to my dad's memory.

All because I finally realized that in order to give a story its due, you have to care enough to be quiet and keep yourself out of it.

Because fiction doesn't care about how something "really happened."

It's a rare occurrence when a writer is able to lift something whole-cloth from his or her own life, portray it as it "actually happened," and have it positively serve the story; it's even more rare for that positive service to include enriching the story in simple terms of storytelling and structure.

Of the two-hundred-or-so short stories I've published, only four times have I lifted an event whole-cloth from my past and been able to use it with no embellishment to the advantage of the narrative. I don't know that I'll ever do it again, especially after the fourth and most recent occurrence — which I will discuss at the close of this book — but before getting in to those examples, we need to look at some of basics of the craft so you will understand what, in my opinion, constitutes good storytelling. Non-writers always hear writers going on (and on . . . and on. . .) about "knowing the rules," about "following structure," about "maintaining a consistent tone," and dozens of other seemingly secret-code catch-phrases that soon puts a tired gleam in the eyes of everyone within hearing distance as they surreptitiously start looking for the nearest exit.

The next section is not at all meant to be patronizing, condescending, or ,God forbid, Instructional; it is simply meant, for the non-writers among you, to shed a little light on this not-at-all-mysterious process we call writing.

2

Brought to You by the Law Firm of Beguile, Intrigue, and Assault

Opening lines.

I have grown to hate them.

One of the unpleasant realities we have to face as writers today is that we have, on average, about 500 words in which to grab and hold a reader's interest when writing a short story, 25–50 pages if it's a novel. I for one think this unfair, but I also voted for Dukakis, so what the hell do I know? Yes, it would be nice, be wonderful, be just oh-so-*peachy* if we lived in a world where readers have the patience and the time to be eased into a narrative, to be seduced by the ebb and flow of the language, the musical composition of sentences, the overall rhythm and atmosphere filtered by the writer through their own sensibilities and re-interpreted for you here on the printed page as a magnificent feast of words.

I also voted for Al Gore.

Back from Oz now, the harsh reality is and will remain that you absolutely *have* to hook and hold a reader's attention with your opening lines; if they get to the second or third page of your story and are still not interested in what's going on, they'll turn to the next story in the anthology. So your opening lines have to be intensely immediate, somehow grabbing the reader's attention while simultaneously establishing time, place, situation, character, and conflict.

Here is what remains for me the greatest opening line I've

ever read; from Dan Simmons's short story "Metastasis":

> "On the day Louis Steig received a call from his sister
> saying that their mother had collapsed and been admit-
> ted to a Denver hospital with a diagnosis of cancer, he
> promptly jumped into his Camaro, headed for Denver
> at high speed, hit a patch of black ice on the Boulder
> Turnpike, flipped his car seven times, and ended up in
> a coma with a fractured skull and a severe concussion."

It's really too bad that Simmons meanders around the
action like he does, being all wishy-washy and passive and —
— oh, wait, hang on a second; I was reading an opening
line from one of my old stories; never mind.

In one powerful sweep, Simmons not only grabs your
attention and holds it, but establishes everything that a good
short story needs to establish as soon as possible. Whenever
someone asks me for a good example of the opening line,
"Metastasis" is always the story to which I refer them.

Take note of Simmons's expert control of cadence while
you're at it, as well as the sly manner in which he keeps
punching that cadence with carefully-chosen verbs: Steig
jumps into his Camaro; he *hits* a patch of black ice; he *flips* his
car — words that have definite associations for the reader,
summoning up specific impressions in their mind which they
then use as points of personal reference to draw them deeper
into the narrative and make themselves a part of the story.

I have, through the experiences of my own reading and
writing, come to the conclusion that there are three and *only*
three types of opening lines, which can best be summed up
by the following words: Beguile, Intrigue, Assault.

The opening line of "Metastasis" is one of the more obvious examples of the "Assault" brand of opening line; it
machineguns so much information at you so rapidly and so
skillfully that it might as well grow a leg and kick you in the
teeth; no, it's not heavy-handed or consciously forceful, its
power emerges naturally from the rhythm of the words and
the situations those words are being used to convey. I say it's
"one of the more obvious examples" because you'd have to

be asleep or clinically brain-dead not discern Simmons's intent ; you know this is going to be a story that deals with high stakes in a head-on manner.

Don't let me mislead you; an "Assault" brand of opening line doesn't *have* to be jam-packed with details and action; it can achieve its desired effect with only a few words, such as this expert stab from Dennis Etchison's "The Dead Call," one of the most famous opening lines in modern horror:

"Today I rubbed ground glass in my wife's eyes."

Or this, from Harlan Ellison's "In The Fourth Year of the War":

"In the fourth year of the war with the despicable personage that had come to live in my brain, the utterly vile tenant who called himself Jerry Olander, I was ordered to kill for the first time."

Or this modest example, from my own short story "Saviour":

"I laid out the rifles, loaded the shotguns, and stacked up the cartridges along the wall."

Or this, from, William F. Nolan's "Fyodor's Law":

"They were at nearly every street corner in Greater Los Angeles, standing or sitting cross-legged in their ragged, dirt-stiffened clothing, their faces stubble-bearded, eyes slack and defeated, clutching crude, hand-lettered cardboard signs:

HOMELESS!
HUNGRY!
WILL WORK FOR FOOD
PLEASE HELP???
GOD BLESS YOU!!!"

And as a final example of the more obvious "Assault" opening, try this, from another story of mine, "The Projectionist":

> "It was an old movie theater full of winos and thugs and snoring bums and it stank horribly and was overcrowded and overheated and usually showed lousy movies but the projectionist didn't mind; it was better than the two-room shit-hole he called his "place" and gave him something to look forward to, especially on those days when the movies changed because then he got to splice the reels together and that made him feel like he was creating something, like he was part of the movie: It gave him the only taste of real power he'd ever known."

Working backwards on the list, next we have the Intrigue brand of opening line. While not as immediately overpowering to the reader, the Intrigue opening is nonetheless just as effective — and in some cases, more so — than the Assault approach; the idea here is to tap the reader on the shoulder and whisper something interesting in their ear, not too much, just enough to make them turn your story's way and see what they can make of this. The Intrigue opening can be a bit mysterious, off-putting, even whimsical, and while it doesn't offer as easy an opportunity to establish all the setup information right away, if you do it correctly, the reader will go along with you for a little while before they start asking Who-What-When-Where-Why-How. The Intrigue opening can be just as subtle as you'd like, or as hard as a slap across the face.

From the first chapter of Joe R. Lansdale's *Cold In July*:

> "That night, Ann heard the noise first."

From Tom Piccirilli's "Inside The Works":

> "Art, sex, and madness crawled and spun side by side down deep inside the Works; the walls dripped with

drama, floors covered in genius, soul, and a phalanx of talent."

Peter Crowther checks in next, with this beauty from his short story "Cleaning Up":

"Mostly it was only in his room when Chris woke up or as he waited for sleep, but just now and again, particularly on dry nights when he wasn't dodging puddles, he would think of Susie when he went out to the park for his evening toiletries."

Not to keep my own work from your discerning eyes, here's the first line of my story "All Over, All Gone, Bye-Bye":

"There should have been more left once the children were gone, more than just empty bedrooms, broken toys discovered in the backs of closets, the occasional pair of gym socks or pantyhose found hiding under the furniture, collecting dust like the little ones used to collect dolls or model cars."

From Gene Wolfe's "Black Shoes" (a personal favorite of mine):

"I heard this story from an old college acquaintance, a man I had spoken to for twenty years; I do not vouch for its veracity, but I do – I will – vouch for this: he believed every word of it."

And, from Rod Serling's novella, "The Escape Route":

"He lay on sweat-logged, soggy sheets — his ice-cube-blue eyes, set deep in a bald, bullet head, staring up at the cracked ceiling; his aching, middle-aged body pleading for sleep, but his mind a runaway dynamo, racing back and forth across the bombed-out landscape of his life."

In each case, if the writer has done their job correctly and the Intrigue opening has been accomplished, the reader's first reaction should always be this: *Well? What happens next? Go on.*

Which brings us to the last and infinitely most difficult type of first line, the Beguile Opening (almost sounds like the name of Robert Ludlam novel, doesn't it?). This type of opening combines the elements of Assault and Intrigue while adding a heavy dollop of the enigmatic to the recipe.

Take, for instance, this opening volley from Shirley Jackson's "I Know Who I Love":

> "Catherine Vincent began her life in a two-room apartment in New York; she was born in a minister's home in Buffalo; the shift from one to the other might be called her tragedy."

From John O'Hara's magnificent story "Afternoon Waltz":

> "In many American towns it often happened that on the main residential street there would be one or two blocks that for one reason or another gave the impression of retiring."

The Beguile opening of Jack Cady's "The Burning" goes like this:

> "Sunlight gleamed as Singleton and I walked down the hill to the charred wreckage of what had been a truck."

Compare that to the opening line of Karl Edward Wagner's "More Sinned Against":

> "Theirs was a story so commonplace that it balanced uneasily between the maudlin and the sordid – a cliché dipped in filth."

I'll throw my two cents' worth into the mix and offer the first line of my story "She So Loved Her Garden":

"After the death of her husband the old woman spent countless hours alone in the house for the purpose of making it emptier; it was a game to her, like the one she'd played as a child, walking on the stone wall of the garden, pretending it was a mountain ledge, not daring to look down for sight of the rocks below, knowing certain death awaited her should she slip, a terrible fall that would crush her to bits, walking along until her steps faltered and she toppled backward, always thinking in that moment before her tiny body hit the ground: *So that's when I died.*"

Rising star Kealan-Patrick Burke chimes in with this, from his story "Not Quite Ghosts":

"God was scraping His heels against the carpet of the sky as Angela turned up the lapels of her raincoat and bowed her head against the promise of rain."

And the finest example of the Beguile Opening comes to us courtesy of *Last Call* and *Earthquake Weather* author Tim Powers, from one of his rare short stories, "Night Moves":

"When a warm midnight wind sails in over the mountains from the desert and puffs window shades inward, and then hesitates for a second so that the shades flap back and knock against the window frames, Southern Californians wake up and know that the Santa Ana wind has come, and that tomorrow their potted plants will be strewn up and down the alleys and sidewalks: but it promises blue skies and clean air, and they prop themselves up in bed for a few moments and listen to the palm fronds rattling and creaking out in the darkness."

I readily admit that I may be stuffed full of wild blueberry muffins when I say there are only three types of opening lines, but remember: nothing I've said thus far is meant to be taken as an absolute; some opening lines can arguably fit in categories other than those I've assigned them here, but for my experience, I find that most memorable opening lines are usually brought to you by the law firm of Beguile, Intrigue, and Assault.

Now a little exercise, just for fun.

Below you will find an assortment of opening lines, all culled from my own stories; see if you can figure out which of the three types of openings each line is; there are no right or wrong answers, nor will any answers be offered in footnotes or appendices — mostly because this book ain't got none.

Here are the lines. Have fun:

"Lucinda turned her wheelchair away from the painting, adjusted her belly-bag, and decided that sadness was the color of rain."
　　　　　　　　　　　　— "At Eternity's Gate"

"A weary remnant of the young woman she once was, Fran McLachlan stood in the center of the midway holding her five-year-old son's hand and trying not to think about the way her life had gone wrong."
　　　　　　　　　　　　— "In a Hand Or Face"

"The ghosts of New Orleans are restless tonight"
　　　　　　　　　　　　— "Down in Darkest Dixie
　　　　　　　　　Where the Dead Don't Dance"

"Sarah Hempel glimpsed her reflection in the protective glass of a vending machine in the nursing home's tiny lounge, looked into her bloodshot eyes, and thought: *The question is, can she do it?*"
　　　　　　　　　　　　— "Rights of Memory"

"Blood from the wound on my neck matted the fur on the left side of my chest and piercing agony throbbed somewhere in my center as I reeled shrieking to the side, my heart triphammering."
　　　　　　　　　　　　— "Some Touch of Pity"

"The customers in the truck stop restaurant paid no

attention to the man in the parka until he started shooting."

— "Haceldama"

"Jeremiah Culpepper screamed over the boom of cannon and crack of gunfire as he saw his son Joshua take the full force of a Yankee musket ball directly in the center of his chest, stagger backward, crumple against the trunk of a pine tree, then slump to the gore-muddied ground where he curled into a ball like a little child, his face turning white as blood seeped through his heavy wool uniform."

— "News From the Long Mountains"
(co-written with Lucy A. Snyder)

"The baby rolled over inside the trash dumpster and coughed as blood trickled from its mouth."

— "Drowning With Others"

"He lowered the towel, unveiling the rest of his face, and looked into the reflection, past his eyes, past the skull underneath his skin, past the veins and blood and gray matter until it seemed he was staring into the ancient heart of some holy mystery whose answer had been, until this moment, out of his reach."

— "Geoff #1: Dreams and Permanence"

"The thing which most bothered Levon about the other members of the grief support group — besides their voices seeming too loud because he was starting to get one of his corkscrew headaches — was not so much that they looked like prisoners awaiting the hour of their execution, but that every last one of them had the air of a *falsely-accused* prisoner, one who'd resigned him- or herself to dying for a crime they knew they did not commit — *'Tis a far, far better thing I do now than I have ever done before* and other such urp-inducing romantic fal-de-ral."

— "One Brown Mouse"

"When Quasimodo awoke he found that sometime during the night he'd turned back into Simon Kaiser and the woman who was his Esmeralda had broken into particles of dust that drifted before his eyes like so many unobtained goals."

— "For Want of a Smile"

By now you've undoubtedly notice the preference I show toward writing which has a solid grasp of cadence. Not to hammer this into the ground, but as a writer I strive toward giving my prose a certain musical quality; if it reads smoothly aloud (and I at some point read everything of mine aloud), then it's going to read twice as smoothly when it's just the story and the reader and, maybe, if I did my job correctly, something akin to the A-word (Art) might happen.

I want to talk about Art for a second.

I do not in any way, shape, or form consider myself to be an artist or think that what I write qualifies as art. Art is a word that gets bandied about with effortless carelessness by everyone, but especially by filmmakers and writers.

Here's the thing: it was either Moliere or Ben Johnson who said, "The purpose of all true art is to disturb." Taken at face value, that statement could help to explain why so many people have an almost evangelical fervor for, say, *The Texas Chainsaw Massacre*. That film *does*, indeed, disturb the viewer, but in the end its rabid need to disturb is the only thing that justifies its existence — which in and of itself is okay; we need books and movies that serve only to keep our juices moving and our nerves tingling. We could debate the issue of moral content until it clears the room of humans but that's for another time and venue; we need concern ourselves with those aficionados who — though they might love being scared or grossed out — have come to want something more, something richer and deeper, from horror fiction.

If Moliere or Johnson were still with us, I would urge whichever one of them quipped the above to consider this slight revision: "The purpose of all true art is to *pointedly* disturb."

And I would remind you that "disturb" means not only

"to make afraid" but "to destroy the tranquility of." If you have ever cried at the end of a movie (say something like the magnificent *Iceman* or *Field of Dreams*, a movie that rakes me over the coals every time), if something in it has moved you to tears, then you have been disturbed by it; if a book or short story you've read has angered you, or surprised you, or forced you to think about something in a different way, then you have been disturbed.

There is, in my opinion, not one writer/actor/painter/sculptor/dancer/director/musician/etc. living today who has the right to call him/herself an artist: To sit down at your keyboard (I'm restricting this to the act of writing at this point) and say, "I'm creating a piece of art!" is to invite pretension and arrogant high-mindedness; it is to loudly declare to anyone who cares to listen that you're so cocksure your work will have a profound impact on everyone who encounters it that they should feel privileged to read it.

Art is not something that can be consciously created; it has to *occur.* Usually it's a happy accident. Timing, luck, happenstance, a person's mood at the time, all of these come into play — and the creator's underlying intent is always secondary. Always. It's more than just "liking" a piece of work, it's experiencing a complete, pure, and total communion with the work; for one second — maybe longer if you're blessed — you are submerged in the emotions summoned up by the piece and the world is reduced to only your burning core and what this work *does* to it, *gives* to it, asking for nothing in return, and what, finally, this communion *means* to the rest of your life: You come away from the work *more* than you were before.

Art lingers as a ghost called emotional resonance, and from that moment on *you*, not the creator, have the right to call this something a "work of art."

What's this got to do with my comments about cadence?

Simple: the first time I was aware of art "happening" to me, was when I was a little boy and was watching a first-run *Night Gallery* episode with my mom. The episode was "The Messiah on Mott Street," starring Edward G. Robinson, Tony Roberts, and Yaphet Kotto, about a dying Jewish man on

Christmas Eve whose grandson – oh, for chrissakes, I don't have to actually *tell* you about this episode, do I? Didn't think so.

(Yes, I remember when each episode of *Night Gallery* was brand-new and never-before-seen. Thus endeth the Old Fart moment.)

I realized about two-thirds of the way through that there was this little *lump* in my throat, and by the time the episode reached its unapologetically sentimental conclusion, I was bawling like a baby. So was my mom. Until the day se died, "The Messiah On Mott Street" remained her favorite Christmas episode of any television show. We had both been moved by Serling's simple tale of redemption and miracles among the tenements, and as Mom was pouring herself and me some hot chocolate afterward, she wiped her eyes and said, "Oh, I swear, that Rod Serling can sure write good stories."

That's when art happened for me. It wasn't until Mom said those words that I came back to reality long enough to realize that Rod Serling (who I knew from *The Twilight Zone)* had *written* the words that those people had said, and that his story had made both me and Mom cry (in that good but embarrassing way you never want to tell anyone about later), and that meant that words and stories could *affect* people.

Not a major unveiling as far as art exhibits goes, but it did the trick for me. Watching that episode, knowing my reaction to it, Mom's reaction to it, and then her reaction *about* her reaction, brought it full-circle and I started crying again (silly, sentimental boy), and when Mom put her arm around my shoulder and told me it was all right, it was okay, it was just a television show, just a story, all I could manage to say was, "No, it wasn't," before I started in with the spluttering again.

I hadn't the experience or the brains to fully realize what was happening to me, so how in hell was I supposed to articulate it? It seemed to me then that, if this were a fair world and just universe, everyone would be able to articulate their thoughts and feelings as well as the people on *Night Gallery* had, and then maybe people wouldn't find themselves standing around with snot running down their face and tears in their eyes, frustrated because they couldn't find the words to express all they needed to convey.

So I began seeking out Rod Serling everywhere I could. I found collections of his short stories at the local library (Serling was a much-underrated prose writer) and read them all cover to cover, then started in again. Anytime a movie written by Serling came on television, Mom or Dad would call me down to watch it. I became a *TZ* re-run junkie (still am), and you can bet *your* ass that *mine* was there in front of that television set every Wednesday night at 9 p.m. tuned to NBC for the next new episode of *Night Gallery* (I have every episode, uncut, on videotape), and as I grew older and sought out more information and programs and books and stories about Serling, I also studied the work of other writers from the days of live television drama — Paddy Chayefsky, Reginald Rose, Robert Alan Arthur, Ernest Kinoy, Ronald Ribman, Horton Foote, J.P. Miller, many others, and I began to detect a certain recurring element in all of their scripts: the cadence of their dialogue.

And their dialogue *had* to have that musical quality to it; after all, movies were still their biggest competition, and their dramas were being watched mostly by a generation home from World War II or on its way to Korea, a generation whose only two outlets for entertainment had been either the movies or the radio, so there was both the visual and audio aspects to compete with; given the financial and physical constraints of live television, the only hope these dramas had was for the scripts to be overflowing with magnificent, musical dialogue that the actors could sink their teeth into and make the audience forget about the radio or the latest big Hollywood movie.

And their cadences were — and remain — a wonder to behold.

Not that all of them wrote in the same meter or consciously attempted to emulate each other's style, far from it; each writer's meter was very much their own, but thing is, these crackling, brittle cadences were *always* present in every line of their dialogue. It sounded like music when spoken by the actors, but somehow reading it silently to myself was even better; what was restricted to one reader's or actor's interpretation when acted or read aloud, inside my head produced concertos, symphonies, *operas* with only the *spoken word.* It stunned, amazed, and mystified me that anyone could sit down at a typewriter and create something as glorious as this using *mere language.* The work of Serling and the other television dramatists led me to the work of Charles Beaumont, Jerry Sohl, William F. Nolan, George Clayton Johnson, Theodore Sturgeon, James Blish, and Harlan Ellison; Ellison led me to the work of Dan Simmons, Kobo Abe, Borges, Pushkin, Schiller, José Ortega y Gasset, and numerous other, who led me to the work of other writers I had never read before, on and on and on, this incredible circle of storytellers and thinkers creating concertos upon symphonies upon operas in my head as their words poured off the page and ricocheted inside my brain, forcing me to think outside the boundaries of my everyday world and consider things such as Imagination and Meanings and Possibilities that never, ever end — and, above all, most importantly, first and foremost, what a puny little kid from Newark, Ohio might one day know a taste of if he dedicated himself to the sole purpose of making sure that each time he sat down to write something he strove to make his words one-tenth as skilled, polished, and honest as those which lay between the covers of the books lining his shelves.

Craft.

But it all comes back to that moment I stood there in the kitchen with Mom after watching *Night Gallery* and realized the power words could have; which means it always comes back to the one man whose work had the first and most profound effect on me; Rod Serling, to whom I'd like to stop and pay tribute before we move to the next section.

I never knew Rod Serling; I never had a chance to meet the man; never had the opportunity to shake his hand and thank him for all that his work has given to me as both a writer and as a human being, never had the chance to express my appreciation for all he taught me.

And Rod Serling *did* teach me.

He taught me that it's okay for characters to express their humanity with words — and not the introverted running monologue that underscores the action in a novel or short-story narrative; I mean *solely through what they say*:

> "I've been living at a dead run, Dad. I was so tired. And then . . . one day . . . I knew I had to come back. I had to come back to get on a merry-go-round and listen to a band concert and east cotton candy. I had to stop and breathe and close my eyes and smell and listen." ("Walking Distance")

> ". . . something's happening to me. I keep getting beckoned to by ghosts. Every now and then it's 1945. And if you think that sounds nuts, then try this one — I wish to God those ghosts would stick around. They're the best friends I've got. I feel a whole helluva more comfortable with them than I do with all those warm, living, flesh-and-blood bodies I ride up and down the elevators with! I rate something better than what I've got. Honest to God, I do. Where does it say that every morning of a man's life he's got to Indian-wrestle with every young contender off the sidewalk who's got an itch to climb up a rung? I've put in my time. Understand? I've paid my dues. I shouldn't have to get hustled to death in the daytime and then die of loneliness every night. That's not the dream. That's not what it's all about." ("They're Tearing Down Tim Riley's Bar")

He taught me that the natural human predilection for repetition in everyday speech was not a liability to the writer, not something that has to fall shrill and tuneless on the ear; it was, rather, a grace-note:

> "Odd? It's not odd. Odd is when you go thirty days on the line and not lose a man. That's odd. Odd is when you walk twenty-five miles and don't get a blister. Now you're talking odd. This isn't odd, Captain. This is . . . this is nightmare. This is a lousy dog-face line officer who can see death on peoples' faces. A lousy dog-face officer who'd like to give back the power to whoever

gave it to him." ("The Purple Testament")

He taught me that a character's helplessness and rage can be expressed not through the lazy tool of violence, but through a simple, eloquent sadness whose clarity hits as hard as any fist:

"I would prefer, though never asked before, a job — any job at all where I could be myself! Where I wouldn't have to climb on a stage and go through a masquerade very morning at nine and mouth all the dialogue and play the executive and make belive I'm the bright young man on his way up. Because I'm not that person, Janie. You've tried to *make me* that person, but that isn't me. That isn't me at all. I'm . . . I'm a not very young, soon to be old, very uncompetitive, rather dull, quite uninspired, average type of guy . . ." ("A Stop At Willoughby")

He taught me that even the shabbiest, most downtrodden, cheerless, and inelegant of characters, when filled with enough need, can express themselves with a simple, dark poetry:

"Listen, boy, I been wishin' all my life. You understand, Henry? I got a gut ache from wishin' and all I got to show for it is a face full of scars and a head full of memories of all the hurt and all the misery I've had to eat with and sleep with all my miserable life." ("The Big, Tall Wish")

He taught me that anguish has a language all its own and, when it is given the proper voice, can move even the most hardened of hearts:

"I don't know how to tell at all. All I know is that I'm an aging, purposeless relic of another time and I live in a dirty rooming house on a street that's filled with hungry kids and shabby people, where the only thing that comes down the chimney on Christmas Eve is more poverty . . . I wish, Mr. Dundee . . . one just one Christmas . . . only one . . . that I could see some of . . . the hopeless ones and dreamless ones . . . Just one Christmas I'd like to see the meek inherit the earth!" ("The Night of the Meek")

He taught me that when a character offers a moment of self-revelation, a whisper always rings louder than any scream:

"Because I'm sad. Because I'm nothin'. Because I'll live and die in a crummy one-roomer with dirty walls and cracked pipes. I'll never have a girl because I'm an ugly little gnome. I'll never be anybody because half of me is in that horn. I can't even talk to people . . . not without the horn. That's half of my language." ("A Passage For Trumpet")

Rod Serling was the best teacher I never knew I had.

I would have no career if it hadn't been for the effect his words had — and still have — on me; he taught me the importance of cadence, the necessity of compassion, and the impact of narrative control; he taught me the difference between style and substance; and, above all, he taught me that the direct and simple expression of human emotion is perhaps the single most powerful tool at the writer's disposal.

And so to the teacher who never knew he had me for a student, to the man whose stories sparked the desire in a young boy from Newark, Ohio to try his hand at writing, to the man from *Night Gallery* who my mom thought wrote such good stories, to the tour guide with the clipped speech who every week took us into a dimension beyond that known to man, I offer, at last, four simple words of gratitude, expressed about thirty years too late, but whose sentiment is, I hope, timeless and sincere:

Thank you, Mr. Serling; whenever someone tells me that my dialogue reminds them of yours, I feel like I might be on the path to finally getting it right.

3

Three-Part Invention

*T*his essay has never seen print. It was originally written as the Afterward to a deluxe limited edition for my novel *The Indifference of Heaven.* Due to the collapse of the novel's publisher, the deluxe limited edition never happened.

In the years since the novel appeared and disappeared seemingly overnight, a lot of readers and fellow writers have asked me how I came to write it. Since this last part of the book is detailing specific areas of writing, I felt that this essay should be included.

If you have not read *The Indifference of Heaven* then much of what follows will make no sense; however, Leisure books will be releasing the mass-market paperback edition of the novel (under the new title *In Silent Graves*) in April of 2004, so odds are by the time you're reading this, it will be readily available in bookstores and on the shelves of your friendly neighborhood Walpurgis-Mart. So if you want to skip over this part and come back to it sometime after you've read the novel, go ahead. My feeling won't be hurt.

If, however, you're one of the good folks who *have* read the novel, then you're going to find what follows garsh-darned fascinating; so, here, in its entirety, is the Afterward to the deluxe edition that never happened:

Okay, so you've now finished *The Indifference of Heaven* and have discovered this chapbook with the deluxe edition wherein (as you've been promised and have shelled out the

Serious Bucks for) I am going to reveal to you How I Did It.

Ah, hmmm, *well.* . . .

A couple of things about this have given me pause ever since Matt Johnson first proposed the inclusion of "bonus material," not the least of which is I am not sure how interesting most readers find the writing process; you pays your money for a book, you want a good story, a compelling read, and hope that you can turn the final page feeling that you've gotten your money's worth. If you really liked the book, maybe you'll read it again someday, or perhaps pass it on to a friend with your heartfelt recommendation that they read it.

Cool so far.

But here you are now, the story over, and find yourself confronted with fifteen or sixteen thousand additional words — including a short story sandwiched between two sections of an essay — and you're thinking to yourself: *Do I really need to know this much about how this story was created?*

Which leads me to repeat myself: Ah, hmmm, *well.* . . .

As a reader (and a rabid collector of special editions), I find when it comes to "bonus material," I tend to do one of two things when it comes to material like this: I either read the extra material before I read the book itself, or I wait until a week or so after finishing the book before tackling the extras. The first option, more often than not, gives me some hints about what was going through the writer's mind as she/he was grappling with the creative process; the second gives me the necessary distance to let my reaction to the book settle comfortably into place, and more or less guarantees that I will not feel that I've gotten too much of a good thing.

To me, there is no greater disservice to one's readers than to wear out one's welcome, so if you're among those who have decided to exercise option #1 and are reading this bonus material *before* reading the actual body of the story, I beg of you to stop at the end of this paragraph and read the book before returning here. Yes, I'm going to talk about the process of writing *Indifference,* but in the course of explaining some choices I made, I'm going to discuss certain revelations in the story that, for lack of a better term, were/are intended to be surprises; which is a roundabout way of saying that the remainder of this essay is going to contain a lot of spoilers (and they're called that for a reason). I don't want to ruin any of *Indifference* for you so, please, stop reading in about thirty-eight words, go back to the book, and read the story. What's here (barring some massive quantum accident) will still be here when you're done. I promise.

Now go on, go back, read the book.

*O*ne of the perks about writing this essay now — the trade and limited editions of *Indifference* were released about two months ago — is that I have some idea of what the critical reaction to the novel has been.

I am pleased to say that, with one exception, all of the reviews for the novel have been excellent, and I like that right down to the ground (and in all honesty, even the bad review had several good things to say, much to my surprise). Readers seem to think I have a certain flair with the English language, that I've created believable, compelling characters, and written a story which frightens, entertains, and moves them.

Hoo. Ray.

Sincerely.

When people ask me how I can tell whether or not something I have written is any good; my answer is always the same: If I absolutely, positively, no-holds-barred *hate it,* if I utterly loathe and despise it, if all I want to do is erase it from my hard drive and burn all manuscript pages and deny that the damn thing ever existed . . . then I know it's probably okay.

It's when I finish a story or book and *like* it that I know I'm screwed.

Indulge me a little on this.

It has been my experience that when I like a piece of my work upon its completion, odds are I've let my ego get in the way of the story; I have reveled in the land of "Look-Ma-Ain't-I-Writing-Good?" that will sink you every time; I have taken the lazy way out, either by saddling the work with pat characters, by-the-book dialogue, an obvious *denouement,* or — the worst sin of all — liberally doused it with unabashed heavy-handed emotional manipulation in order to guarantee that reader's gut reaction to the piece will be *exactly* what I want it to be (which, to my mind, inexcusably insults the reader's intelligence).

That is why I have a filing cabinet that is filled to bursting with stories of mine that I liked.

That is why no one will ever see these stories of mine that I liked so well.

Because they *don't* suck eggs.

If, on the other hand, the work fulfills its obligation to make me hate it, it's because the story — and *only* the story — has been the primary force; I had what I felt was a good idea, and when I sat down to write it, I took myself and my desire to be acknowledged as a *good writer* out of the equation. As a result, the story (and not my ego) took the spotlight, which is the *only way* it should ever be.

The moment I finished it I not only hated, loathed, and despised *The Indifference of Heaven* so much that I would have sold my soul to expunge it from the Universe, I actually considered selling my computer and typewriter, breaking all the fingers of my right hand so I would never be able to take up pen or pencil again, and having my tongue surgically removed so I wouldn't be tempted in a moment of weakness to use one of those voice-recognition programs should the desire to write ever bulldoze its way back into my psyche. I considered, yet again, a career in cesspool cleaning. Or law school. If all of that failed, well, there was that well-thumbed copy of *Final Exit* that I keep within easy reach.

I tend to put myself through this with damn near every-thing I write. Judging from peoples' reaction to my work, I gather that most of the time I succeed in hitting deep emo-tional chords, and for that I am grateful. For me, as both a writer and reader, the best stories are those that — even if their craftsmanship is a little clunky in places — leave you with a deep, *deep* emotional resonance that never quite goes away. Give me that, and I will forgive a lot.

To get back on track here: I try to instill my work with an extra layer or two of emotional depth because I like it as a reader. This is not to say that it's something I am consciously aware of while I write; that invites self-indulgence and the horrible possibility that I'm actually going to *like* it when it's finished; no, what I try to do (and this drives everyone around me crazy) is to decide before I even write the first word what the theme of the piece will be, then the subject in which I will explore the theme (and don't let anyone try to convince you that subject and theme are interchangeable items, folks), and then lastly − but far from least − the single emotion which will dominate the tone of the piece, and from which all others will spring. Once I know that, I go sort-of Zen or Method acting and dredge up everything I know of, have observed, or experienced wherein said emotion is the over-whelming factor and, whenever possible, try to find within the story a central image with which that primary emotion will be associated. (This central image isn't always evident at the start; sometimes it emerges while the story is unfolding − which is pretty cool, as well; it's nice to surprise yourself as things progress − and sometimes the story rears back its head and announces that no, there isn't going to be an associational central image, so get over yourself and let me finish, will you?)

In the case of *The Indifference of Heaven,* the theme was loss, the subject was child abuse, and the single emotion from which everything else was to spring was, simply, grief. Grief, in my world, begets fear, which begets loneliness, which begets anger, which begets fury, which begets . . . on and on.

And grief would be associated with *matryoshka* dolls.

Hopefully you're getting the idea by now.

Like all of you, I have experienced grief. In my lifetime I have held the hands of four people − one of them a child − at the moment of their death.

That is not something you are ever likely to forget.

I have also witnessed and experienced the act and aftermath of child abuse.

Another thing that sticks with you.

So, having decided that grief would be the core emotion of *Indifference,* I did that Zen/Method Thang and dredged up every memory and emotional residue of the grief I have known, be it directly or indirectly. I looked at it, it looked at me, announced it wasn't going anywhere for a while, and off we danced down the Yellow Brick Road.

I was an absolute emotional wreck during most of the time it took to write *Indifference,* and if any of that managed to work its way onto the page, if somewhere in the course of the book you found yourself being taken a level or two deeper into the emotional core of the characters' hearts, and if you came away from the story with at least a lingering sense of have experienced and not merely *read* a story, then it was worth it.

I'm not trying to make this process seem romantic, believe me; there were easily ten thousand other things I'd rather have done than spend nineteen hours a day feeling sad and depressed and helpless and alone, losing sleep, being cranky, alienating every human being I came into contact with, breaking into tears for no discernable reason while watching re-runs of *Green Acres,* and re-awakening an ulcer that hadn't given me trouble in nearly ten years. To make it a well-rounded unpleasant experience, I did a fair amount of research into child abuse and found myself in absolute, sick-making awe of the unspeakable brutality that we as a race will allow children to suffer — but the story demanded that I be locked into a certain emotional state throughout the writing, and I never question that. It's just the way I Go About It. Be thankful you don't have to live with me.

All right, then; I've been jumping from point to point like an electron without traversing the space between for long enough; now that you know the most important thing I do to prepare for writing a story, it's time we got down to business.

Shifting gears and going into Jack-Webb mode, I'm going to give you Just the Facts on some things:

1) The act of physically writing the first draft of *Indifference* took a scant two-and-a-half months. It had to be written quickly not only because the story demanded it, but also because the threads of the plot depended on *momentum* to keep everything from unraveling — and to not give you, the reader, too much time to spot the footprints in the snow, lest

you figure out where things were going before we got there.

On a personal note, it had to be written quickly because there was no way I could sustain that level of emotional intensity on a daily basis and not wind up a basket case or dead. No romance here, folks, just the good old ugly truth.

2) I did not write an outline for this novel. I *never* outline. It's too much like following a road map. Whenever I sit down to begin a story, unless it emerges full-blown from the depths of my brain like Athena from Zeus's forehead, I'm careful to never overthink where I'm going. I usually only "plan" the events of a story to the half-way point, and ninety-nine per-cent of the time, when I reach the half-way point, things have already started to dictate to me where they're going. I rarely know how something is going to end when I start writing. I like it like that.

Yes, I did plan out certain sequences for *Indifference* in my head far in advance of actually writing them, and a few times I even wrote down some notes on a slip of paper and taped it near the corner of my monitor's screen — "Nurse #1's Statement, the Doctor's, then Nurse #2, then Newspaper Article" — just to make sure the order remained consistent, but at no time during the three months and five days between Word One and Final Draft did I ever create an outline. I had been living with this story in my head for so long (the better part of five years) that I knew almost every detail of it before I sat down in front of my keyboard.

3) Not to negate anything said previously, but there were 2 occasions where things took over and I was powerless to stop them (and believe me, I tried for a while before the story reminded me that it and not my ego was the important thing here).

I will detail these two happy occasions later on, so hang in there.

4) When I began writing, I was convinced that there was *no way* this story would go more than fifty of sixty thousand words — my short story bias showing there. Imagine my shock and the stunned silence which followed when I did the final word count and saw *120,000* words pop up on my screen. *Indifference* is the longest thing I've written. (Hope-fully, it didn't *seem* 120,000 words long to you.)

5) *Indifference* was written in sequence. I am not one of those writers who can jump from point "B" to "Q" and then back to "C" while writing a novel. Everything plays out in sequence in my head, so that is the way I have to write it.

I also never stopped in the middle of a sequence. I can't. I'm always afraid that if I do, I'll come back to it later and found that I've lost not only the momentum, but the rhythm of the section, as well. Not stopping was particularly difficult in several instances, because, as it turned out, *Indifference* emerged as a series of set pieces. If one were to break it down by scenes, I think the novel in its entirety has something like only thirteen scenes.

These are just a few little tidbits I felt compelled to share with you before moving into the next section, which, as promised, presents one of the stories from which *Indifference* sprang.

I say "one of" instead of "the story" because *Indifference* was the result of combining two unpublished pieces — one a short story, the other a novella.

I had originally intended to include the novella, "Progeny," with this bonus material, but upon re-reading the piece I realized that much of it is redundant; there are scenes in the novella which were used word for word in *Indifference*, and I cannot in good conscious subject you to reading a piece that smacks of *deja vu* all over again. It seems a waste of time, mental energy, and paper.

What I will do, however, is give you a synopsis of "Progeny" so you'll have some idea of what it was like and hopefully understand why I chose not to include it here.

Keep in mind that neither Ian, *matryoshka* dolls, Rael, Bill Emerson, or the Children of Chiaroscuro appeared in the piece.

Breaking it down incident by incident, here's the way "Progeny" unfolded:

1) The story opens with the scene in the movie theater. Robert is watching the movie, he's hearing the litany on his head (*"They're dead . . . they're dead . . ."*), and he gets the nosebleed.

2) He stumbles into the lobby and finds his sister waiting there. Lynn chews him out in much the same way she did in

the novel, and insists that he come home and stay with her on this night.

3) The story breaks here, going into the first of several flashbacks which detail — as did the first chapter of the book — the argument Denise and Robert had, and his fleeing to the park to pout and think about the importance of his career. Unlike the novel, Robert sees dim, fuzzy images from the movie screen instead of the parade of ghost-women. One of those images looks like a dead baby trying to claw its way out of a grave, he panics, and runs back to the house to find Denise lying on the floor.

4) Back in present time, Robert is trying to sleep in the guest room at Lynn's house. He rolls over and sees himself and Denise reflected in the mirror. He rises, goes to the window, looks out, and sees a figure standing in the trees. Something about it looks familiar — looks, in fact, like one of the fuzzy images from the movie — but he cannot make it out, so he returns to bed and falls into a fitful sleep. He dreams of babies crawling out of graves.

5) The flashback sequences continue with Robert and Dr. Steinman. Robert signs the donor consent forms, and is allowed to see his wife and child after they have had their organs removed. Denise and the baby come alive. He holds hid daughter and kisses his wife, all the while wondering in the back of his head why the lights seem to be flickering. He also cannot shake the sense that he's being watched.

6) The funeral scene, which unfolds more or less as it does in the novel. Everyone leaves, and Robert shovels the dirt over the coffins of his wife and child.

7) Flashback: Steinman pulling open the curtain and seeing Robert kissing his dead wife, holding his dead child. The good doctor moves to subdue Robert as Robert starts to totally Lose It.

8) Present: Robert is climbing into the car with Lynn and Danny. He realizes that he left his gloves back at the grave site. He excuses himself and walks back to retrieve them. The sky is flickering, and he hears an odd but persistent sound, somewhere between a click and a rattle. He reaches the grave, bends down for his gloves, and his child's hand reached up through the soil of its grave to grab his wrist. Denise crawls out of her grave, and Robert finds himself being pulled down into the soil with them. The last thing he sees before the dirt

swallows him is a movie screen that has taken the place of
the horizon; beyond the screen, he sees an audience watching
the movie. He sees himself sitting in the audience, his nose
starting to bleed.

END

At the time, I really liked it. (Screwed again.)

Looking it over, I saw that what I had was the basis for
something longer and much better, but as it stood it was only
a series of rather intense scenes with no real direction, and
an ending which usurped the story's tenuous ground rules
for the sake of a cheap and obvious shock ending.

Yeech.

At the top of my game, I can be pretty good; but I wrote
this story before it was ready to be written, and the result was
an ambitious mess with a solid idea hidden amongst the
detritus and a few good scenes scattered throughout.

It would have been a grand waste of time and resources to
include it. You're not missing anything; trust me on this.

What I *have* chosen to include here is a short story entitled
"In a Hand Or Face." Some of you might recognize the spine
of this piece from its appearance in the DAW anthology *The
Fortune Teller.*What appeared in that anthology is a *severely*
watered-down version of what I had originally written. Now,
it would be the whiner's way out to point a finger at *The
Fortune Teller's* editor and say, "He gutted my story, it's his
fault!" But that would be a disservice to the anthology and
its contributors.

Yes, the editor asked for — and in some cases *demanded* —
changes that I not only didn't really agree with, but sometimes
absolutely despised. But I made every change he asked for,
even when they seemed to me to be, well . . . silly and obvious.

I'm not slamming said editor. I realize now that he saw the
story in a much different light than did I, and — despite the
great effort on both our parts — we found ourselves in a
"Never the twain shall meet" situation. What appeared in *The
Fortune Teller* was a solid, if somewhat two-and-a-half dimen-
sional tale entitled "The Child Screams and Looks Back at
You." On a scale of 1 - 10 I would give that version of the
story a 6 or 7. It is not at all a bad story, but it's a far cry

from what I originally envisioned when I wrote it; the published version contains a little more than 45% of the material I originally wrote.

I am as much to blame for this as the editor. At any point in the editing/rewriting process I could have said, "Nope, that's it, sorry, I can't do that, I'm withdrawing the story," and emerged with my story intact, all smug and self-righteous in the knowledge that my integrity had not been compromised, cha-cha-cha.

But I didn't.

The sale of this story meant five hundred dollars which I *desperately* needed at the time, so I swallowed my pride, put my perceived integrity in moth balls, and made every change that was asked for. The editor accepted the story after five — count 'em — rewrites (the most I have ever done for any piece), and soon thereafter I had the check in hand and could pay the rent and buy food.

Sometimes, folks, you gotta do this in order to pay the bills. It sucks, but that's the way it goes.

Moving on.

"The Child Screams . . ." was well-received; every review I read of *The Fortune Teller* singled it out as one of the best in the collection, and Ellen Datlow even included it among the Honorable Mentions in that year's edition of *The Year's Best Fantasy and Horror.*

Okay, maybe I'm being a little rough on the revised story, maybe it's a lot better than I give it credit for, but that's secondary to where I'm going with this.

The story which follows (though none of its characters or situations appear in the novel) contains much more of the "seed" for *The Indifference of Heaven* than did "Progeny."

I still think this is the better version, but at the same time I'm glad that the editor made me distill it, often times cutting out entire sections and — in one notable case — completely removing an element I felt was central to the story.

I'll clarify all of this for you on the other side, after you've read this piece.

Here goes:

In a Hand or Face

A weary remnant of the young woman she once was, Fran McLachlan stood in the center of the midway holding her five-year-old son's hand and trying not to think about the way her life had gone wrong.

"Mommy," Eric said, "what's wrong?"

Fran was glad that the massive bruises on his cheek and jaw looked far less discolored and painful today. If only she could say the same for her own abrasions — but, after all, wasn't that why God created makeup and Tylenol?

"Mommy?"

"Wha — ? Oh, I'm sorry, hon. What did you say?"

"Did that lady say something bad to you?"

"No, hon, she didn't."

"Then how come you look so sad?" He clutched his balloon-doll as if his very life depended on it.

Oh, Christ! How could she answer that question honestly *now*, after what Madame Ariadne had shown her? How could she tell her son — the only good thing she had — that she was thinking about abandoning him on a fairgrounds nearly a hundred miles from home because of a palm-reading?

You didn't give her a definite answer, she thought. *The group's not going to head back to the shelter for another hour — you can* at least *make this time count. You can make sure he has so much fun that nothing will ever taint the memory for him, ever.*

God, Eric, do you know how much I love you?

"Hey, you," she said, tugging on his hand and smiling.

"Hey, *you!*" he replied, grinning.

"We'll have to . . . to be leaving soon, so what say until then we do whatever you want?"

"Really?"

"Uh-huh. You pick."

"Then I wanna go on the merry-go-round."

This surprised her. "Why? We've been on it three times today."

"'Cause you laughed when the tiger started bouncing and it wasn't a pretend-laugh like all the other ladies. I liked it."

Oh for the love of God, kiddo — why'd you have to go and say something like that?

Fran kissed her son's cheek and told herself she. Would. Not. Start. Crying.

"Okay," she whispered. "The merry-go-round and then . . . then m-maybe we'll meet your new friend and get some hot dogs."

"Hot dogs!" shouted Eric, dragging her down the midway, his balloon-doll thrust in front of him as if it were flying.

For a moment there, Fran could've sworn that her son's face actually *shone* with happiness.

And not pretend-happiness, either.

*I*t began three hours before. Fran and Eric were having lunch at a long picnic table with several other women from the Cedar Hill Women's Shelter and their children, the kids occupying themselves by pointing out all the sights to one another while the mothers took the time to regroup and count the money they had (or, in most cases, *didn't* have) left.

"You look a lot better today, Fran," said one of the women. "So does Eric."

"Yeah," Fran said. "We're both feeling better."

"Have you thought about, well . . . about Ted?"

Fran shook her head. "No — I mean, yes, I have, but Eric hasn't mentioned him and I'd appreciate it if none of you would bring up his father today, okay? I don't want anything to spoil the day for him."

Eric and most of the other children wandered over to watch a group of balloon-toting clowns breeze by. One of the clowns stopped to make balloon-dolls for several of the children. Fran saw this and smiled. "Just . . . *look* at them will you?

Everything's still *new* to them. Even with what's happened to
them, they still laugh and giggle and . . . I don't know . . .
hope, I guess. Remember when you were that young? How
nothing bad ever followed you to the next morning? Moment
to moment, with a new excitement each time; that's what I
think 'childhood innocence' is. Maybe something bad happened *this morning*, but *now* . . . now's fun, you've got a ball
to bounce or a model plane to fly or a doll to pretend with,
and the day's full of mystery and wonder and things to look
forward to and . . . and —"

You're babbling. Shut up.

They scattered shortly thereafter, instructed to meet back
at the south entrance at six p.m.

Fran and Eric rode the merry-go-round for the third time
that day, but from the way Eric acted you'd have sworn this
was the first time he'd ever been on it. Fran envied him his
joy, but was at the same time aware of how precious it was,
and knew by the wide smile on his face and the gleeful
shimmer of his eyes that she'd made the right decision to
leave Ted and take Eric to the shelter where he wouldn't have
to worry about Daddy coming at him with the belt or his
fists, or be forced to cower upstairs in his room while Daddy
thrashed Mommy into a whimpering, broken, swollen zombie who shuffled around, whispering, never looking up, afraid
of the violence the next five minutes might or might not
bring.

Since they'd moved to the shelter two weeks ago, Eric —
who before had been a good fifteen pounds underweight,
nearly skeletal — had begun eating again and laughing again
and was able to sleep soundly for the first time in his short
life. God, how she cursed herself for having waited so long,
for having kept Eric in such a brutal, hateful, terrifying
environment!

At first it was just a couple of slaps every now and then,
and Ted was always sorry afterward, so Fran allowed herself
to believe that he really *was* going to get better about things,
that he was going to get some counseling, but then he went
on graveyard shift at the plant, sleeping during the day,
refusing to see a counselor on the weekends, and as Eric grew

older Ted's violent outbursts grew not only in number but in brutality – a couple of slaps turned into a bunch of slaps, a bunch of slaps turned into fists to the chest, stomach, and face, which evolved into slamming her against walls and choking her, sometimes knocking her down to the floor where, until the night she'd sneaked out of the house with Eric, he'd begun to give her a couple of kicks to the side –

– she was, for a moment, so numb with the weight of her thoughts that she didn't even realize the merry-go-round had stopped, then she noticed that Eric was standing outside the circular gate of the ride talking to a little girl who looked to be around seven or eight.

"Eric!" she called to him. "You stay right there."

Better watch it, you, she thought. *That's how kids wind up with their pictures on the sides of milk cartons. "I only turned away for a minute," says the mother/father.*

She quickly exited through the gate, sprinting to where Eric and the little girl – who looked vaguely familiar to Fran – were still standing.

"Hey, you," she said, taking Eric's hand in hers.

"Hey, *you!*" he replied, giggling.

The little girl seemed to hear someone calling her, said a quick good-bye to Eric, then turned and ran – but not before shoving a piece of paper into Eric's hand.

"Who's your friend?"

"I dunno," said Eric. "She was telling me 'bout her hand." He offered the piece of paper to Fran.

It was some kind of special fair pass. On the front were the words: **Good For Two Free Readings!** The back read:

Each line, be it in a hand or face, masks another; lines hidden
within lines, a
secret Hand beneath the surface of the one with which you touch
the world
and those you love. It is only in the secret lines on the hidden
hand that your
true destiny can be mapped, and only one who possesses Certain
Sight can
make an accurate reading. If you're content with mere showmen,
then please
take your business to any of the fortune-teller tents – but if you
want the truth,
see Madame Ariadne.

"So, kiddo – wanna get your palm read?"

"Wha's that?"

Fran turned over Eric's hand, sticking the tip of her finger into the middle of his palm. "A lady looks at your hand and tells you what's gonna happen to you."

"Aw," he said, grinning. "I saw that on a TV show. It was *neat."*

"Does that mean 'yes'?" She couldn't resist tickling his palm.

"Stop!"

She did. "Wanna go?"

"Sure. It'll be like on TV."

The interior of Madame Ariadne's tent was not what Fran expected – no crystal ball or beaded curtains, no candles or spicy incense or stuffed ram's head or shelves overflowing with philtres and potions; if anything, the interior more resembled the white sterilized rooms where a veterinarian might examine a family pet: white rolled-tile floor, white partition walls, chairs, and a table upon which sat – most surprising of all – a computer. Next to the computer was something Fran assumed was a flatbed scanner.

"This is Weird City, kiddo."

"Like on *X-Files!"*

"That doesn't make me feel any better."

Eric laughed, then a door opened in one of the back partitions and Madame Ariadne entered. If things didn't feel off-kilter enough, Madame Ariadne — instead of being a weathered, sinister Maria Ouspenskaya clone — looked to be no older than thirty-three, her cheeks flushed as if she'd just finished a good aerobic workout; judging from the light grey cotton warmup suit she wore, that was probably the case.

"Well, *hi,*" she said, brushing a thick strand of strawberry-blonde hair from her eyes and kneeling down to face Eric. "My name's Ariadne. What's yours?"

"Eric."

"Ah, that's a good name."

"Uh-huh."

She offered her hand. "Well, it's a pleasure to meet you, Eric."

Eric looked at Fran, who gestured *Go on.*

He shook it. "Hi."

It happened so quickly that Fran almost missed it; as soon as Eric's hand was enfolded in her grip, Madame Ariadne visibly flinched — not in such a way as to cause Eric any alarm, but to the eyes of an adult it was clear that she'd felt something that startled — maybe even frightened — her.

Fran cautioned herself to be careful, that this could be part of an act — scare the parent with some crap about "bad vibrations," then con them into a more complicated and expensive reading.

"We have a pass for two *free* readings," said Fran.

"I know," said Ariadne, smiling at Eric and releasing his hand. "This isn't a scam operation, Fran. The pass says free and free it shall be."

"How did you know — ?"

"So, Eric," said the fortune-teller, "how would you like to go first?"

"'Kay."

She led him over to the table, then took her place behind the computer and typed in a few commands, activating the scanner. "Eric, I want you to take your — are you left-handed?"

"Uh-huh."

"I thought so. Take your left hand and press it down on the glass right there."

"On the box?"

"Mmm-hmm. Don't worry, it won't hurt. It's just going to take a picture of your hand."

"Promise?"

Ariadne's smile was spring itself. "Promise."

Eric pressed his palm onto the scanner. Ariadne took a plastic cover device and placed it on top of Eric's hand, which now was completely hidden from sight.

"Arm's in a box," he said to Fran, grinning.

"Oh, boy."

"Hey, Eric," said Ariadne cheerfully, "did you know that each part of your hand was given to you by an angel?"

"*Nuh-uh!*"

"Uh-huh. As a reward for their love and friendship, God allowed each angel to add one small part to the hand of every human being; thumbs, lines, bumps, every part of your hand's a gift from an angel." She winked at him. "I read that in a book when I was a little girl. I don't know if it's true, but I think it's kinda neat, don't you?"

"Uh-huh."

There was a slight hum, a slow roll of blue light from under the cover, and it was over.

By now Fran was standing behind Ariadne, staring at the computer screen as a holographic copy of Eric's hand — composed mostly of grid lines — appeared on the monitor.

Ariadne playfully poked Eric with her elbow. "Now watch this — it's so *cool!*" She hit a key and a dark blue line rolled down from the top of the screen, passing over the grid-hand and changing it to a three-dimensional, flesh-colored hand that looked so real Fran almost expected it to reach out and tweak her nose (a favorite past-time of Eric's).

Eric squealed with delight. "Izzat mine? Izzat *my hand?*"

"It sure is," said Ariadne. "And it's a good, strong hand, with strong lines. See that line right there? That means you're a good boy, and this line means you've got lots of imagination — I'll bet you like to make things, don't you? Like models, and draw, and build things with clay."

"Oh, yeah!"

"I knew it! The lines never lie. This line right here — ah, this one's very special, because it means that you're going to grow up" — she gave Fran a quick, secretive look — "to be someone really special — even more special than you are right now. Oh, you've got a good life ahead of you, Eric. You should be so happy!"

"Oh, boy!"

This went on for a few more moments, until the little girl from the merry-go-round came out of the same door from which Ariadne had entered and said to Eric, "You want to come and watch a video with me? I got *The Great Mouse Detective.*"

"Mouse Detective!" shouted Eric. He turned to Fran. "Can I, Mommy? Can I go watch *Mouse Detective?*"

Fran was once again struck by the notion that she knew this little girl from somewhere. "I don't . . . I don't know, hon —"

"That's one of my daughters, Sarah," said Ariadne. "I've got a little play room set up for her right back there. Toys, books, a TV/VCR unit, and — God! — *tons* of Disney videos — I swear she'll bankrupt me with those things. I'll have them leave the door open so you can keep an eye on them.

"He'll not be out of your sight for one second, Fran. I swear it."

Fran looked down at Eric. "You really want to watch the movie?"

"Yeah!"

"Okay, then. But be polite."

The only things faster than light is the speed at which some children rush to watch a Disney video — a principle that Eric and Sarah proved a second later: *Whoosh-Bang!* — Disney rules.

Fran stood in silence for a moment, watching the two children through the door as they took their seats in front of the television.

"That's quite a collection of bruises on his face, Fran" said the fortune-teller. "Ted must've really clobbered him."

A breath in, a breath out; one, two, three; then Fran whirled toward Ariadne and said: "How the hell did you know my name?"

"The same way I know that you've been at the Cedar Hill Women's Shelter for the last fifteen days. The same way I know that both you and Eric were in Licking Memorial's ER *sixteen* days ago because the two of you 'fell while taking in the groceries.'

"The same way I know that Ted spotted you at the free clinic five days ago and followed you back to the shelter."

"He *what?*"

"You heard me. He — don't get panicky, he didn't follow the group here today. He's on swing until the first of next week, but you have to believe me when I tell you that he *is* going to be waiting for you outside the shelter sometime in the next eight days, resplendent in his remorse."

"You can't possibly know that."

"Do you think I'm trying to scare you? You're damned right I am."

"How did you — ?"

Ariadne hit a key, and Eric's hand disappeared, replaced by scrolling records: Fran's birth certificate; the date of her high school graduation; a copy of her marriage license; Eric's birth certificate (complete with foot- and hand-prints made at the hospital); her student loan application for college tuition (check returned, full amount, student withdrew from school before deadline, no monies owed); copies of police reports (three domestic calls, no charges filed); and several hospital records detailing treatments given to one Francine Alicia McLachlan and Eric Carl McLachlan, some together, most separate — including at least two doctors' handwritten notations, nearly indecipherable except for "abuse?" and "possible mistreatment."

"So?" snapped Fran, trying to keep the anxiety from her voice. "You or someone who works with you is a hacker, so what? Anyone with a computer could get this information these days."

"True enough," said Ariadne. "But would they also know that you once came very close to killing Ted while he was asleep?"

Fran blanched, shocked into silence.

"December 22, two years ago," said Ariadne. "He'd lost his temper and started pounding on you and Eric came running downstairs and put himself between you and Ted — something he does quite a bit, doesn't he? — and Ted pushed him down. Eric fell against a coffee table and the corner missed his left eye by less than half-an-inch. Five stitches in the ER took care of the gash, and in the cab on the way home Eric said he wanted to go away because Daddy scared him. Ted was already asleep when you got home, so you put Eric to bed, waited until he was asleep, then you went to the downstairs hall closet and took out Ted's .357 Magnum, put in one bullet, then wrapped the muzzle in an old towel to muffle the sound of the shot —"

"Stop it!"

"You never told anyone about that, did you, Fran?"

". . . no . . . I mean, I don't *think* I . . ."

"So I couldn't have hacked that information from any computer, could I?"

". . . no . . ."

Ariadne placed a warm, tender hand against Fran's cheek. "Listen to me very carefully. I don't want to frighten you, but I have to. Eric's in danger."

Fran's legs suddenly felt like rubber, and she just barely made it into the chair facing the computer. ". . . someone . . ." she whispered. "I . . . I must have told someone about . . . about wanting to kill Ted, and you . . . you . . ."

Ariadne placed a finger against Fran's lips, silencing her, and in a soft voice, the whisper of leaves caught in the wind brushing across an autumn sidewalk, spoke of other things that *only* Fran knew, intimate details of solitary experiences, hopes, desires, petty jealousies and silly girlhood fantasies extending back through nearly three decades, and when she'd finished (by describing in detail Fran's first childhood memory of getting her arm caught in the toilet when she was ten months old because she wanted to see where the water went after you flushed), Fran — confused, frightened, and feeling so godawful helpless — was certain of one thing:

Madame Ariadne had . . . *powers* of some kind, incomprehensible, unknowable, incredible.

"What . . . what *are* you?"

Ariadne leaned over Fran's shoulder and typed a command. "First you need to see something."

The screen blinked, display Eric's hand once again.

"Both you and Eric have Conic hands. See the shape of his fingers? Just like yours — they're very smooth and taper from the base, gradually lessening toward the rounded tip. The Conic Hand is the Hand of Imagination. Just from the shape of Eric's hand any fortune-teller would know that he's very sensitive, often highly emotional — but not emotionally unstable. He's like you in that way, isn't he?"

Fran nodded. "He's pretty anxious a lot of the time but he tries to hide it because he doesn't want to upset me."

"Not surprising." The image of Eric's hand turned slightly to the left, displaying the height of the mounts on the surface of the palm. "See this rise here at the base of the middle finger? This is called the 'Mount of Saturn' — also known as 'The Mount Which Brings Sadness.' If you've got a Conic hand with a pronounced Mount of Saturn, you constantly worry about the safety of the ones you love, even above your own well-being — which would explain why Eric always tries to get between you and Ted when —"

"— he wants to protect me," whispered Fran.

"Of course he does; he loves you very, very much."

"I know."

"Good."

Eric's hand turned toward them, palm facing outward.

"Why do you use a computer and scanner?" asked Fran. "I mean, most fortune-tellers —"

"— would whip out the candles and crystal balls and hold your hand in theirs as they made the reading, yeah, yeah, yeah — believe me, I know this is a bit weird. I use this because . . . because the naked eye — even mine — cannot clearly see the lines within the lines, the —"

"— hidden hand within the hand?"

"Yes. This equipment was designed specifically to reveal those hidden lines, the secret hand."

Fran looked at the image on the screen. "Okay. . . ?"

"Can you recognize any of the lines?"

Fran leaned in, squinting. "I can see that his life line is really long." Her mood brightened. "He'll have a long life."

Ariadne shook her head. "A long life line doesn't necessarily mean a person will live to be very old. I mean, sure, in places where it weakens or breaks you can expect some health problems, but a lot of people have life lines that are incredibly short — some fade entirely — and they still live to piss on their enemies' graves. No, we're interested in one of the Fate Lines, Saturn — right here, staring at the base of the wrist and going straight up to intersect with its sister mount." She altered the image so that it now displayed only a flat red outline of Eric's hand, with the Fate Line of Saturn enhanced in bright blue, the Mount of Saturn in bright green —

— and at the point where the two intersected, a cluster of small markings in jaundiced yellow.

"What are those?" asked Fran.

Ariadne magnified the cluster.

Fran puzzled at the sight. "They look . . . almost like stars."

"They are. On the Mount of Jupiter or Apollo, they mean great success and wealth. On Mercury they mean a glorious, happy marriage. . . ."

Fran faced Ariadne. "What aren't you telling me?"

The fortune-teller looked back at the children happily watching their video and singing along with the voice of Vincent Price, then pulled in a deep breath and released it in a series of staggered bursts.

"Jesus," said Fran. "If you want my attention, you got it."

"Have you talked to your husband since moving to the shelter?"

"What's that got to do with — ?"

"Have you?"

"Once — okay, twice. The psychologist says it's good for us to call our husbands or boyfriends, let them know we're all right — if they care — and to get things off our chests. The shelter gets part of its funding from Catholic Services, so they're kind of big on aiming for reconciliation if it's possible."

"Do you think there's any chance you and Ted will get back together?"

Fran shrugged. "I don't know. Maybe. If he gets his ass into counseling and does something about his temper, if he admits that there're emotional problems he's been carrying around and stops treating me like — okay, okay, please don't look at me like that.

"Maybe. *Maybe* we'll get back together."

Ariadne took Fran's hand in hers, examining it. "You still love him?"

". . . yeah . . ."

"Sounds like you wish you didn't."

"Sometimes I do wish that, but —" She pulled her hand away. "Why do you need to know?"

Ariadne pointed at the screen. "When a Conic hand has a direct intersecting of the Line and Mount of Saturn, and when that intersection is marked by stars, it has only one meaning, and it's never, *never* wrong: death by violence."

Deep within Fran McLachlan's core, at the center of her interior world where all hopes, regrets, dreams, emotions, experiences, and sensations coalesced into something beyond articulation, a crack spread across the base, threatening to bring it all crashing down.

Very quietly, words carefully measured, heart triphammering against her chest, she managed to get it out: "Say it."

"Ted's going to kill Eric. I knew it the moment I held his hand."

". . . no . . . no . . . he w-w-wouldn't do something like . . . like that . . ."

"On purpose, no, probably not. But you know what happens when he loses his temper —"

"— he doesn't . . . he doesn't *think*, he just —"

"— he just lashes out at what- or whomever happens to be in his path, which is you and Eric —"

"— don't know how many times I've told him that he should just stay in his room when Daddy gets that way, but he won't, he doesn't like it when Ted hits me —"

Ariadne cupped Fran's face in her hands. "Fran? Look at me. Look at — there you go. Take a deep breath, hold it, hold it, now let it out. Good. Do you trust me?"

"I . . . I d-don't know —"

"Yes, you do."

Fran looked into the face of the woman before her, and saw there nothing but concern, kindness, and deep, abiding compassion. "Yeah, I guess I do."

"Then you believe what I'm telling you?"

"Oh, God, I . . . I don't know. . . ."

The fortune-teller looked over her shoulder and called, "Sarah? Honey, would you come here for a minute?"

"Aw, they're just getting to the part with the clock!"

"You've seen it before. Just come here for a second, okay?"

"'Kay."

She appeared a few seconds later.

"Sarah, I'd like you to meet Eric's mother."

The little girl held out her hand. "Pleased to meet you, ma'am."

Fran saw the little girl's hand, saw the scar that ran from between her index and middle finger all the way down to her wrist (from when her father had gone at her with a pair of scissors), then looked up into her eyes and thought, *Please, don't let them be two different colors,* but they were — the left gray, the right soft blue — and she tried to get her mouth to form words but everything was clogged in the bottom of her throat.

"You okay, ma'am?" asked Sarah.

"I'm . . . I'm fine," Fran managed to say, shaking her hand. "Do you like Bobby Sherman records, Sarah?"

The little girl's face brightened. "Oh, yes! My favorite song is —"

"'Julie, Julie,'" said Fran.

"How'd you know?"

"Lucky guess."

Ariadne touched her daughter's face. "Sorry that I interrupted your movie. Just for that, I'm buying pizza tonight."

"Pizza! Oh, boy!" And Sarah surpassed the speed of light once again to bring the news to Eric.

"Don't bother trying to tell yourself that you didn't see her," said Ariadne. "In her way, she's as real as you or I."

Fran was shaking. "That w-was *Connie Jacks!* She w-was my best friend when I was a little girl. Her father used t-to hit her all the time, knock her around, but she never told anyone but me. She died when I was seven. Everyone thought that she'd fallen down the stairs and hit her head on the r-r-radiator, but I always thought that —"

"— he did," said Ariadne. "He beat her to death. If it's any consolation, he blew his brains out about ten years ago. Guilt usually catches up with you, eventually."

Fran looked at Ariadne — having now decided that the woman couldn't be human — and said: *"What are you?"*

"I am a Hallower: a half-human descendant of the *Grigori,* who were among the Fallen Angels. In retaliation for God's not having shared all Knowledge with them, the Fallen Angels stole the Book of Forbidden Wisdom and came down to Earth and gave countless Secrets to Man. Most of the *Grigori* coupled with human women during their time on Earth, and my race was the issue of that coupling. I am a direct descendant of the Fallen Angel Kokabel. He gave mankind the Forbidden Knowledge of Time and Science and assisted the *Grigori* Penemue in giving children the Knowledge of the lonely, bitter, and painful." She lifted her left hand, palm facing outward. "He also tainted the Mark of the Archangel Iofiel, who holds dominion over the planet Saturn." She placed the tip of her right index finger at the base of her left middle finger. "It's because of Kokabel that the Mount of Saturn brings such deep sadness with it.

"That's why I've chosen to do what I do. In a hand or face, Fran, the mark of my ancestor's sin can be found; I am the only being who can read the signs, and I will spend eternity trying to ease what sadness and pain I can.

"Maybe you won't ever reconcile with Ted, I can't say — but what I *do* know is that there are six stars on Eric's hand — one for each year that he will live, and the stars are in the Patriarchal Configuration — meaning the danger will come from Eric's father. Maybe he'll do it after you guys get back together, maybe he'll do it after your divorce when it's his turn to have Eric for the weekend — hell, who knows? He might come by Eric's school and take him, he might snatch him from your backyard when you get your own place — it's secondary to the fact that somehow *he will kill Eric* and you can't prevent it. But I can.

"Which is why you have to leave him with me. Take Eric with you, and he won't live to see his seventh birthday."

Fran laughed; she couldn't help it; it's how she fought back panic. Rising from the chair, she felt lightheaded. "You know, you really . . . really don't give a person a chance to cath her breath."

"There's not much time. What can I do to convince you? — and don't ask me to sprout wings or perform some tacky parlor trick, though I can do either as a last resort."

Fran glared at her. "Tell me how Connie Jacks can still be alive, how she can still be a little girl after all this time."

Ariadne rubbed her eyes. "I suppose the simplest explanation is to say that she's a ghost who doesn't *know* she's a ghost."

"Buy you said she was as real as —"

"— and she is. She can bruise, throw a temper tantrum, break a bone, muddy her good shoes, get a stomach-ache . . . sometime in the next eight months she's going to need to have her appendix removed and in a year or so she's going to have to get braces on her front teeth and she's *not* going to be happy about it.

"When a child — *any* child — perishes at someone else's hand, their body dies, yes, but their *promise* lives on. What they *should have* grow up to be doesn't cease to exist because the child is dead, it simply wanders alone on a different, more abstract plane that ours. Because I am what I am, I have the ability to . . . *guide* that potential into a new corporeality. Do you understand?"

"You can . . . you can bring them back to life?"

"Not in the way you're thinking, no hocus-pocus or *Frankenstein* stuff. I give their displaced potential a new home — flesh — so that it can take up at the point where everything was snuffed. That girl in there, Sarah, is the girl Connie Jacks *should have* lived to become. The only thing different is her name and her memories, because as far as she knows *I'm* her mother. She has no memory of being beaten to death, of whimpering in lonely agony for someone to come help her because it never happened to her. To Sarah, the world is a new and wondrous place, filled with fairs and pizzas and mouse detectives, and she'll never have to be afraid."

Fran tried to catch her breath. "I still don't understand how —"

Ariadne put a finger to her lips. "Shhh, not so loud — I don't want them to hear you.

"There are two kinds of time, Fran: *chronos* and *kairos.* Kairos is not measurable. In kairos, you simply *are,* from the moment of your birth on. You *are,* wholly and positively. Kairos is especially strong in children, because they haven't learned to understand, let alone accept, concepts such as time and age and death. In children, kairos can break through chronos: when they're playing safely, drawing a picture for Mommy or Daddy, taking the first taste of the first ice-cream cone of summer, when they sing along to songs in a Disney cartoon, there is only kairos. As long as a child thinks it's immortal, it is.

"Think of every living child as being the burning bush that Moses saw; surrounded by the flames of chronos, but untouched by the fire. In chronos you're nothing more than a set of records, fingerprints, your social-security number, you're always watching the clock, aware of time passing — but in kairos, you are *Francine.*

"Children don't know about chronos, and in my care, that's how it remains.

"Sarah's not my only child, Fran. I've got hundreds more just like her, too many of whom died at the hands of a parent who was supposed to love them, care for them, protect them from harm. Some died at the hands of family friends, or suffered unspeakable deaths inflicted on them by people who stole them away for their twisted pleasures. I have *babies,* some who lived less than a month because they were starved or beaten or dumped in trash cans or left out in the cold to freeze to death or locked in cars on summer days to slowly suffocate — but that can't touch them now because in my care they live only in kairos. Chronos isn't part of them any longer.

"I will save as many living children as I can from having to die at abusive, neglectful, violent hands." She entered a series of commands, and the flesh-colored, holographic copy of Eric's hand was restored to the screen. The image magnified to focus on the stars, then focused deeper, to a series of markings beneath the stars.

"Look closely, Fran. Do you see them?"

"They look like . . . like squares."

"Those are the mark of kairos. They're called the 'Walls of Redress.' They're very faint on Eric's hand, but you can see that there are six of them, one for each of the stars, and that if they were more solid, each would hold a star inside of it. The Walls of Redress are the promise of protection. No matter what danger is marked on the hand, if there is a square near or around it, the person can escape the danger if the signs are read in time."

"Why are they so faint?"

"Because the part of the world in which they might or might not exist in still in flux; they can fully form in kairos or they can fade away in chronos. It depends on the decision you make."

Fran's eyes began to tear. ". . . *ohgod* . . ."

Ariadne grabbed Fran's shoulders. "It's all been arranged. When you leave here, take him around the fair once more, do whatever you want, but make certain that the last thing you do is ride the merry-go-round, and that you get off the ride before he does — who'll notice? A tired mother walking a few steps ahead of her kid when the ride's done?"

"Who will — ?"

"Sarah will be there with some of her brothers or sisters and they'll bring him back to me."

"But . . . *Christ!* . . . h-h-how can I . . . wh-what would I s-say to — ?"

"There are over six thousand people here today. Countless children disappear each year on fairgrounds, at carnivals or amusement parks. He won't be living among only children like Sarah, there are hundreds of other children just like Eric in my care, children I got to *before* violence claimed them."

Fran gulped in air, trying to staunch her sobs. "I . . . I'll . . . can I . . . come with you?"

Slowly, sadly, Ariadne shook her head.

Something inside Fran crumpled. *"Why?"*

"Because the place we're going is only for Hallowers and the children in their care." A small, melancholy grin. "Think of it as the ultimate kids' clubhouse: No Grownups Allowed."

"Will I ever . . . ever see him again? I don't know if . . . if I could live without —"

"Yes. It won't be soon, but you'll see him again. He'll — and I know this isn't much comfort — but he'll write to you. A letter a week, a videotaped message four times a year; that's my rule. Don't worry if you move because his letters will arrive wherever you are every Friday, even if it's a national holiday." A short, wind-chime laugh. "We sort of have our own private delivery service."

She touched Fran's cheek, lovingly. "I promise you, Fran, *I swear* he won't forget about you, he won't feel angry for your leaving him with me. He'll miss you, because he loves you so much, but it will get easier as time goes on. He'll never lose his love for you, and he'll grow up to be everything you hoped and more. You will have your son back, one day, and there will be no love lost.

"Don't say anything right now. You've got a little while, so go on, take your son to the fair and make him laugh, make him smile, and be certain that you miss nothing — not a word, not a look, a touch, a whisper, nose-tweak, or kiss. The next few hours will have to last you for a good while. Waste no moment.

"Go on. I'll know your decision soon enough."

Fran called for Eric, then wiped her eyes and stared at Ariadne. "I don't really believe in God, you know?"

Ariadne shrugged. "Not a prerequisite for the service. The belief you're talking about only has to work one way, anyhow."

"Good-bye, Ariadne."

"So long, Fran. Catch you on the flip side."

As they were leaving the tent, Eric turned back to Madame Ariadne and flashed his palm. "I got a angel hand."

The fortune-teller smiled. "You are a strange and goofy kid, Eric McLachlan."

"Yes, I am!"

They stopped to play a few games (Eric won a small toy

fire truck at the ring-toss booth), watched some clowns parade around, shared a soft pretzel, and then, suddenly, feeling as if she were a weary remnant of the young woman she once was, Fran McLachlan stood in the center of the midway holding her five-year-old son's hand and trying not to think about the way her life had gone wrong.

"Mommy," said Eric, "what's wrong? Did that lady say something bad to you?"

She told him no, and asked him what he wanted to do, and he chose the merry-go-round.

This time both of them rode on the tiger, and Eric's laughter, in his mother's ears, during those final moments of the ride, was the voice of forgiveness itself.

"Can I go again?" he asked as Fran climbed down.

"Sure, honey. Of course you can." The attendant was walking by at that moment, so Fran gave him the last ticket.

"You have fun," she said to Eric.

A happy bounce. "'Kay. You . . . you stand out there and watch me, okay?"

". . . okay . . ."

Steady.

"I'll wave at you when I go by."

Hang on.

"Have you had a . . . a good time today, honey?"

"*Yeah!* This was the best fun ever!"

Oh shit, don't let him see it.

"I'm g-glad." She leaned in and kissed his cheek. "I love you, Eric."

"Love you, too — better get off now, Mommy, so they can start the ride."

Not daring to look at her son's face, Fran McLachlan turned around and left, catching a peripheral glimpse of Sarah getting onto the ride with a two younger children whose hands she was holding: the protective big sister.

Fran looked down at her hand and wondered what secrets were hidden there in the lines within the lines, the hand beneath the hand.

Walking away from the merry-go-round, she was startled when a sudden, strong breeze whipped past, pulling the balloon-doll from her grip and sending it upward, soaring, free, rising on the wind toward a place where chronos had no place, where the children were safe and never wept or knew fear.

Good-bye, she thought. *Be happy.*

And was surprised to feel a smile on her face.

Not the greatest story I've ever written, but one in which I think the head and the heart where in the right place, and hopefully you'll forgive it its clunks because of that.

Obviously the two elements that carried over into *Indifference* were the Hallowers (my invention) and the concepts of *chronos* and *kairos.* (I later brought those concepts into play, albeit peripherally, in the science fiction novel *Time Was: Isaac Asimov's I-Bots,* which I co-wrote with the redoubtable Steve Perry. It was only during the writing of *Indifference* that I decided to resurrect t and grapple with them in depth.)

The whole Hallower element was cut from the revised version of the story, as were several other elements that were deemed "too secondary" and therefore cluttered the narrative. (Again, I'm not going to wail on the editor; I could have said no but I didn't, so I've no one to blame but myself.)

Chronos and *kairos* remained in the revised version, but were presented with much less emphasis.

So, how did *this* story, and not "Progeny," spark *Indifference?*

Madame Ariadne.

I had used her once before, in a story entitled "The Friendless Bodies of Unburied Men." She was still a fortune teller in that story, but her nature wasn't nearly as compassionate; in fact, she was one *scary* bitch. I had planned to do a series of stories featuring her, each time making major changes in her character, until the last story, which would reveal that she was not one, but several incarnations of the same spirit, each one embodying and emphasizing a different aspect of her psyche.

Again, this was a concept — like "Progeny" — that was not fully realized, and I abandoned the idea of an Ariadne series because I think readers have better things to do with their time than see how a particular storyteller is going to write his way out of a corner.

Still, the idea of a person re-inventing him/herself over and over – not just behaviorally, but physically, as well – appealed to me. As did the idea of *where*, exactly, Ariadne took these children.

At the time I wrote this story, I had only the vaguest notion of where these children were hidden away. I knew it was probably someplace underground, and it would be a kingdom of sorts, but that was all.

More so than any other idea I've had, I knew this one was going to have to simmer for a while, because when it came time to write it down, I had to get it *right*.

So, I took those elements – *chronos, kairos*, the re-invention of the self, the Hallowers, and this hidden kingdom of discarded children – and filed them away in the back of my head. I knew, somehow, that all of these elements were going to be connected, *had* to be connected, in fact, because I could not think of one without all of the others revealing themselves to be hidden within.

Hence, the image of the *matryoshka* doll. Disparate elements of the same device.

I wrote out the fictional history of the Hallowers in great detail, without consulting any of the reference literature I had collected on angels over the years. Once this was done, I found their mythology to be a bit inconsistent in places. So the question became: how do I make the Hallowers fit into the known mythology of angels?

I read through several books on the subject, the gnostic *Gospel of Mary*, the *Apocrypha of John*, Doresse's *The Secret Books of the Egyptian Gnostics*, a couple of different translations of the *Kabbalah, The Canonical Prayerbook of the Mandaeans, The Zohar*, countless pieces on Native American Mysticism, Jewish Mysticism, a rare, uncensored version of the *King James Bible* (not as easy to find as you might think, by the way), and Gustav Davidson's invaluable *Dictionary of Angels*.

Throughout my reading, I found that – despite the radical differences in their belief/worship systems – almost all of the religions of the world which incorporate angels into their

Fear in a Handful of Dust

theology shared certain core beliefs about these "divine beings" that almost always, without fail, fell into a "So-and-so
begat so-and-so, who begat so-and-so, who begat begat begat."
(If you ever do any in-depth research into this subject, you'll
find – as I did – that, damn, the Angels are a horny bunch.)

I found these various religions also almost always made
mention of a sacred, secret book/text/scroll/what-have-you
which contained "forbidden" knowledge.

That text – The Book of Forbidden Knowledge – became
the anchor in my mythology for the Hallowers. Incorporat-
ing elements from several different histories of angels, I ended
up with a 120-page linear "family tree" of angels, all of it –
I'll say it again – *all of it* drawn from actual theological texts
through the ages.

Once this was done, I re-read this linear history . . . and
found it to be a cluttered mess.

And I hadn't even begun to work in the Hallowers yet.

To lessen your suffering here, I'll cut to the chase: I stream-
lined this 120-page history into a 55-page history, using *The
Book of Tobit* as my base (a work external to the Hebrew
cannon, apocryphal in Protestant Scripture, and canonical in
Catholism, the latter in which I was raised in but no longer
subscribe to). Once that was done, I incorporated my own
Hallower history into the timeline, cut out every bit of excess
that I could and still have the mythology be consistent and
clear, and – bingo! – I had the central mythology of the novel.
(With a few doses of thinly-disguised Greek mythology sprinkled throughout.)

Then I realized that there was no way I could just shove it
down readers' throats in one big chunk, so I broke up the
narrative as much as I could, and gave it to Rael.

Ah, yes, *Rael.*

I mentioned earlier that writing *Indifference* yielded two very
happy surprises; Rael was one of them.

I had originally intended for him to appear only twice in
the story, once at the beginning, and once at the end. But
from the moment he made his second appearance (at the
funeral) I realized that he wasn't content to be a mere supporting player. I had not planned for him to show up at

Denise's funeral, but there he was, an uninvited guest, with several tricks up his sleeve. He was a smartass, a trickster, a clown, a con-artist, a figure of tragedy, and a loud-mouthed pain the ass.

I liked him — I didn't *want* to, but I did.

I tried to get him to shut up and go away, but he refused, and the result was that *Indifference* wound up having not two cental characters (Robert and Denise), but three. Looking over the novel now, I'm quite proud of the way the relationship between Robert and Rael develops. They end up as friends, and that was not in the original game plan, folks; but there are times — rare and precious in a writer's life — when a character walks into your narrative and simply takes over. I won't bore you with my own theories as to *why* this happens, just know that it does, and it's often wonderful, as it was with Rael. He remains, methinks, one of the best characters I've ever created. In fact, there are times now when I can't believe that *I* actually came up with him.

Ah, sweet mysteries of life . . .

Another thing that Rael did for the narrative was instill it with a hefty dose of the oral tradition of storytelling — something that I think is sadly lacking in all genres today. Jonathan Carroll is a master at this, as is Stephen King (check out the dazzling *tour de force* "The Ballad of the Flexible Bullet" and you'll see what I mean); Peter Straub, Kate Wilhelm, Harlan Ellison, Russell Banks, Dan Simmons, J.N. Williamson, Chet Williamson, and Elizabeth Massie complete this too-small list of contemporary (read: still-living) writers who, with their love for the oral tradition of storytelling, create a bridge between the days when tribes would gather in the center of the village to hear a tale spun by the campfire and the modern written word, be it on an actual page or in the coding of an E-book. (Other writers I would include on that list — who sadly are no longer with us — are Kobo Abe, Carson McCullers, Elswyth Thane, Booth Tarkington, and Robert Nathan — who remains, in my opinion, the father of Magic Realism.)

The other happy surprise was that — again, quite unexpectedly, hence the use of the word "surprise" — *Indifference* allowed me to write a sequel to one of my short stories, "Drowning With Others."

I have killed many of my characters, and I have left many more emotionally scarred for life or inescapably alone and lonely. Just my way of sharing my cheery view of life. But when I finished "Drowning With Others," it was the only time in my career that I felt *bad* over the fate of a character.

(If you'd like to read "Drowning," check out the antholgies *Tombs* or *Imagination Fully Dialted, Volume 1*; it's even included in my first collection, *Things Left Behind.*)

Anyhoo . . . I felt terrible about the way Joseph Connor ended up. It always haunted me.

Then I realized that, in order for Robert to understand just how serious the threat of *chronos* was to the children of Chiaroscuro, someone had to die, and that someone had to be Ian.

I didn't want to kill Ian, I liked him a lot, but it had to be done.

The problem was, how to make Robert aware of it.

Then I thought of the ending of "Drowning With Others," and knew I'd found a way to save Joseph Connor from the fate I'd saddled him with so many years ago.

For the sake of continuity, I had Bill Emerson (a character who is based, both physically and in the way he behaves, on the immensely likable Ed Gorman) recap the major points of "Drowning" in the form of Joseph's statement and his recorded history; this way, you wouldn't be losing anything if you hadn't read the story . . . but if you had read "Drowning," and if you'd remembered it, then this element would be (hopefully, as it was for me) a little extra icing on the cake.

I couldn't save Ian, but I did manage to save Joe, and both of these elements, as it turned out, were necessary to bring *Indifference* to its conclusion.

Rest easy, I'm nearly finished.

It might interest you to know that all medical conditions described in Denise's files are real; rare, yes, but real nonetheless. Alan Clark provided me with a medical textbook which described and illustrated these conditions in graphic, sick-making detail. If you'll go back and look at the figures on the cover, you'll see them. Alan's renderings are based on photographs of actual cases.

Let's see, a few other pieces of trivia, for those of you who might be interested:

The legend of the First Children was borrowed from Greek Mythology.

The legend of the Three Sorcerers was based on a story from the *Popol Vuh*.

The title of the novel was taken from a song by Warren Zevon.

The Hundred Years War actually lasted 116 years.

Panama hats are made in Ecuador.

Those last two have nothing to do with the novel, but seeing as how I've got a brain full of utterly useless information I felt compelled to inflict it on someone.

I want to thank you for buying this deluxe edition of *The Indifference of Heaven.* It took me several years to find my voice as a short story writer; with *Indifference,* I finally found my voice as a novelist. I hope it's one you'll want to hear again.

4

Get It Right; "This Is Where I Came In"; and a Prayer for the Coming Revolution

Now to put my own work fully on the chopping block.
Axes ready?
Good.

*T*he title of this section (as well as the subtitle of the book itself) is: *Horror as a Way of Life.*

I did not say horror *fiction* as a way of life, because the writing's only half of the equation; the other half is learning how to find a healthy and non-destructive way to embrace both the concept and the reality of horror in everyday life so that it can be used to enrich your fiction and, hopefully, in some way, the lives of those who read it. So it only stands to reason that I should relay some real-life horrors that have bled over into my fiction, why I allowed them to do so, and what the final results of this bloodletting were.

The late John Gardner (*The Sunlight Dialogues, Nickel Mountain, Freddy's Book*) once said: "You should write each story as if you are trying to prevent someone from committing suicide." I completely agree with that.

But how can that be applied to, of all things, *horror* fiction?

Because it's been my experience that if someone who is about to surrender themselves to the Big Bad Dark can find something, someone, *anything* that lets them know they are not alone in how they feel, then there is always hope they will not go gentle into that not-so-good night, be it the night of depression of something worse and far more permanent and irreversible. Like a lot of people, I may not embrace it, but I have to have hope in my life, and I find that hope, more often than not, by stumbling around in the shadows.

So what follows is a crash course of how I do it, and how I try to get it right.

As I said earlier, I have only lifted experiences whole-cloth from my own life for use in stories 4 times; the first was the "Union Dues" disaster.

The second time — and one that worked out far better — was for my short story "Iphigenia," which can found in my collection *Graveyard People: The Collected Cedar Hill Stories, Volume 1.*

The bare bones of that story are this: A teenaged boy whose younger sister was trampled to death at a rock concert is goaded into attending another concert by his girlfriend. Once in line at the stadium, the horror of his previous experience begins manifesting itself once again, resulting in several new deaths . . . and one resurrection.

Okay, "Iphigenia" came about like this:

In the winter of 1978, the state of Ohio was hit with the worst blizzard it had experienced in over one hundred years. It wasn't *supposed* to be a blizzard, no: weather reporters had been warning us for a few days in late November that a collision of fronts would be dumping 3–5 inches of snow on us over a 48-hour-or-so period. They said it would be slow in starting but heavy and steady for a little while. It would be starting sometime late Wednesday night/early Thursday morning.

Well, ask any certified meteorologist just how exact a science it is today and odds are they'll throw out terms like Döppler and storm-track capabilities and espouse the price-lessness of satellites and digital imaging and neighborhood storm-watch centers. . . .

All of which is great. Terrific. Makes them tingle.

(In all honesty, meteorologists have some damn fine technology to help them with their forecasts today, and I, for one, might chuckle when I hear local stations one-upping each other with their Dual-Döppler Radar and what-have-you, but, since it enables them to track the movements of a storm with such precision they can tell you almost the exact minute it will be hitting and then leaving your area, I let them have their fun, which I think is darned baroque of me, don't you?)

But in 1978, forecasts were still referred to as *predictions* — not just by the general population, but often by local weather reporters. Which is to say, there was a helluva lot more guesswork involved back then. Also, a lot of today's technology didn't exist in 1978, and what there was of it was mostly the sole domain of NASA or the National Weather Advisory.

I know, I know — enough of this stroll down Meteorological Memory Lane.

I subject you to this so you'll understand there was, for all intents and purposes, no effing way that weather reporters in Ohio in November of 1978 could have tracked the third, slow-moving, warm-air low-front that came up in the middle of two already-colliding fronts and caused the whole damn party to simple *stall* over the middle of Ohio, which is what did, dumping not 3, not 5, not 7, but *42* inches of snow and freezing rain in just over 36 hours. Add to that wind gusts of the 25-miles-per-hour variety and, by the time it was over most of Ohio was under Martial Law, there were snowdrifts twelve-to-fifteen feet high, several people froze to death because they couldn't get out of their homes and the power was out and the phone lines were down, people were rationing food because there was no way they could get to the stores to buy groceries, which wouldn't have made any difference since most of the shelves had been emptied late in the evening the night the blizzard first began to hit . . .

You get the idea.

It was a mess; is some cases, a deadly mess. It took the state months to recover from all the damage, and by the time Martial Law was lifted and people were able to get out their houses and go buy food again, most of central Ohio had been trapped inside their houses for the better part of two weeks.

But for a moment, come with me now back to the good old halcyon gory days — uh, er, *glory* days — of Stadium Seating.

For those of you under 35 who regularly attend rock concerts, I should explain that Stadium Seating was a method employed by concert agencies and promoters to ensure that the groups under their wing would be guaranteed to sell at least 75% of their large stadium/coliseum gigs. With few variations, it worked like this: You offered assigned seating at various rates, but you also offered, at a significantly lower rate, Floor Seats.

Yes, they were exactly what they sound like; folding chairs set in pointlessly organized rows (they never stayed that way, never) on the floor of the stadium, no assigned numbers, first-come, first-serve, get in early if you want to be close enough to count the guitarist's nose hairs or catch a flying drum stick.

As would be proven not too long after the night which inspired this story, Stadium Seating was a disaster waiting to happen.

Just ask anyone who was at The Who's infamous Cincinnati concert.

Okay, then: A Wednesday night in November, 1978. Myself and four of my friends were piling into a car in Newark, Ohio, to head over to the Fairgrounds Coliseum in Columbus to see Emerson, Lake & Palmer (who were then on the last leg of their ill-fated *Works* tour). We'd already seen them once before on this same tour, and they blew the roof off the arena in Cleveland, so we had no doubt that the fairground would be left in ruins, as well.

We had no idea how close to the truth that would turn out to be.

In addition to the five of us, my then-8-year-old sister, Gayle Ann, was coming along. Gayle had learned to love ELP because they were practically the only band I listened to that year, and she was also at the tail end of her "I-Wanna-Go-With-My-Big-Brother-'Cause-I-Think-He's-Fun" phase, a time I dearly miss the older I get. (Between the ages of 5 and 9, Gayle Ann was almost always with me wherever I went, and even though I acted like it was a Big Pain, I secretly loved it because I'd never had someone look up to me before, and screw the jibes my friends threw my way.)

It began to snow much earlier than had been predicted; we were probably less than halfway to Columbus when the storm began, slowly but steadily, as had been predicted. There was a little freezing rain, so driving was tricky in some spots, but we always made it a point to leave at least two hours before a concert was scheduled to begin, just to Be Safe.

We get to the fairgrounds, we park, bundle up, check to make sure everyone has their tickets, then climb out and get in line.

It's still snowing at this point, but not as much as before.

Temperature was probably around twenty-seven, twenty-eight degrees and dropping.

I was holding Gayle's hand, even though she didn't want me to because she said it made her look like a little kid. I acquiesce and let go, but tell her to make damn sure she stands close to me, which she does.

The line starts getting longer and deeper.

7:15 p.m. arrives, and the doors haven't opened yet. The concert is supposed to start at 8.

People start grumbling.

Then word comes down that two of ELP's equipment trucks haven't arrived yet because of road conditions. (They'd played in Kentucky the previous night.)

The crowd gets a little less irritable when it hears this and, for a little while, as the snow comes down and the temperature continues to drop, the long, long, *long* line breaks up into a series of microcosmic parties. Several people make hot-chocolate-and-donut runs, so even though we're all starting to get really cold, it's kind of fun.

8 p.m. comes and goes and eventually turns into 9:30.

By now, the snow is really starting to come down, along with freezing rain, and a lot of us can't feel our feet anymore. It's too late to say the hell with it and just head back to Newark because the crowd has gotten too big and too deep and too irritable.

*W*e were trapped.

By now, Gayle isn't quite so reluctant to let me hold her

hand; she even lets me pick her up and let her sit on my shoulders; when I get tired, one of my friends holds her on his shoulders, and so on. (I should add here that Gayle, like her counterpart in "Iphigenia," was — and still is — very small and delicate for her age; she was 8 at this time, yes, but looked 6, maybe even 5.)

9:30 turned into 10:15.

Little fights have started to break out up and down the line. Through the skirling snow — heavier now than it's yet been — we can see the whirling visibar lights of several police cars. Gayle is crying because she's so cold. She wants to go home and so do I, but the crowd is now starting to push forward. I fall at one point and someone steps on my back, but I manage to get up.

I don't know if any of you have ever had the experience of being stuck dead-center in a crowd that's going to move no matter what, but if you have then you know this mass of humanity becomes a single and terrible entity; there are physical forces at work within the mass that you absolutely cannot fight against, regardless of how strong you might be. The crowd surges forward and you either go with it or are crushed; it surges back, and you respond in kind or die. It's scary as hell and reminds you, in no uncertain terms, that there are primal circumstances where the individual doesn't matter a damn, only the whole.

This was one of those times.

The crowd surged back and forth, usually *en masse* (except for one terrible moment that's coming), fights continue to break out — these much more violent — as beer bottles are smashed and a few trash-can fires (set by sympathetic Fairgrounds workers in an effort to keep us warm) are overturned, scattering flaming debris into the cold, high winds. More than once I had to cover Gayle to prevent her from being burned by a piece of flaming paper that was whipped in our direction.

10:15 turns into 10:30. Goddamn concert's supposed to be almost over by now, we're supposed to be in there screaming for ELP's quintessential encore, "Fanfare for the Common Man," and smiling as another kick-ass concert reaches its crescendo and we look forward to raving about it at school tomorrow.

Not happening.

At this point, part of the crowd toward the front starts slamming themselves into the doors; even back where we were — some 75 yards away — we can hear the metal starting to buckle from the force of the bodies.

It's getting really seriously absolutely goddamn terrifying, because now we can see police decked out in riot gear assembling along the line, and more than a few of them are armed with tear-gas launchers.

I pick up Gayle Ann and cradle her head against my shoulder. She's shaking and cold and crying and hungry and so scared.

It wasn't supposed to be this way. This was supposed to be fun.

Then it happened.

At 10:37 the doors were finally opened.

And the crowd turned into a human meat-grinder.

The people up front who'd been throwing their weight into the doors were in the process of surging back for one more push when the doors came open; someone toward the end of the crowd saw that the doors were opening and screamed, "They're opening the doors!" and the back half of the crowd began to surge forward.

*A*nd right smack in the middle of these two colliding human fronts stood me, my friends, and my small-for-her-age sister — whom I'd just set down only a few seconds before because I'd gotten the godmother of cramps in my arm; all I needed was just two or three seconds, that was all, just long enough to shake the cramp out, then I'd pick her back up and carry her through this mess.

I never got the chance.

The force of the forward-moving crowd hit the force of the backward-moving crowd in front and people — I swear to God — started to shoot up like finished Pop-Tarts from a toaster. I lurched down to grab Gayle Ann and someone kicked me in the back of the head. I lost my grip on her and, the next thing I know, I'm stumbling to my feet just in time to see my little sister's arm get sucked into the crowd like a log in quicksand. I screamed and tried to run for her, but there were people colliding all around me. I could no longer see any of the guys we'd come here with. All I could hear was the blood howling though my ears and some nearby screams of panic, all I could think of was my little sister, who I pretended was a Big Pain but who I loved more than anything, being swept along in this mass of fucking mindless monsters. I imagined her terror. I imagined her cries. I began to push forward, slamming my elbow into a few ribs along the way, screaming her name.

A tear-gas grenade went off (by accident, as it turned out), and an already-panicked crowd went, as the saying goes, Medieval.

I was getting body-slammed all over hell's half-acre. I might have hit a few people myself, truth be told. This was a fucking nightmare.

*A*nd then, for just a second, there was a little clearing, an eye in the storm, and I stumbled into it, my shoulders hunched and my head down —

— and saw one of my sister's shoes lying there.

I knew it was hers because I'd bought those shoes for her two days before. It had taken us three hours to find a pair she liked.

I remember bending low and picking up that shoe. I remember noticing that one of the straps was torn.

Then I looked inside, at the pristine-white lining, and saw a single smear of blood.

To this day, I can't say for sure what I said or did during the next several minutes. I know that my heart tried squirting through my ribs about a million times; I know I was hit by several panicked people; I know I helped several people up from the ground and was helped up a couple of times myself; I know I hit a few people in my rabid panic.

It took me perhaps seven minutes to get from where I'd

been standing to the Coliseum entrance. I was numb. I still clutched Gayle's shoe in my hands. I gave some faceless person my ticket and staggered through the gate —

— and saw my sister.

One of my friends back then was a fellow named Dan Butler who was a fullback on the Newark High School football team. He'd spotted Gayle about ten seconds after I lost her, and had cut his thumb on the zipper of her jacket when he'd scooped her up (the blood on her lost shoe was his), hunkered down, and charged through the crowd like a bull elephant.

I was so relived that I broke down weeping. (It occurs to me that I cry a lot. Note to self: start watching more Adam Sandler movies. Then again. . . .)

I don't know that I've ever had a sweeter hug from my sister than the one she gave me a few seconds later.

I held onto her for dear life the rest of the evening.

ELP started the concert with a snarling version of the "Peter Gunn" theme, then stopped after the applause to ask if everyone was all right. I remember the way Keith Emerson apologized for the "unpardonable delay," then said, "We're not going to go on until you take a moment and check yourselves, then ask your neighbor if they need any medical attention."

The band waited while the audience checked to make sure everyone was all right. A few people had to be sent out for medical attention but, overall, there were no genuinely serious injuries.

And so, the concert went on. ELP started playing at 11:10 and — despite protests from Fairground officials and neighbors in the area — played their entire 3-hour set.

"You waited bloody long enough out there to hear us," said Greg Lake, "so you're getting the whole show. If anyone doesn't like it, they can piss off!"

For all I know, ELP might have played the worst set of the tour that night, but for me, with my little sister alive and well and laughing and dancing, it was the best effing concert I'd ever heard. It took us over two hours to drive back to Newark afterward — and don't think my mother wasn't, to put it lightly, beside herself when we came through the door at 4 in the morning. I was grounded for two weeks — which, as luck would have, ran concurrent with the time we were all trapped in the house during Martial Law.

More than once since that night, I've asked myself the inevitable "What If?"

Specifically: What if Dan Butler hadn't come with us that night?

He'd decided to come along at the last minute; another friend of mine, Sam Shaw, had gotten sick that morning and couldn't make it. Dan had happened to stop by the house because he needed to pick up something that my mother had borrowed from his — a cookbook or something like that — about the same time I got off the phone with Sam. When he heard there was an extra ticket, he asked if he could come along. I said sure, why not.

I'm fully convinced that if he hadn't been there that night, I wouldn't have a sister today, nor the wonderful niece and nephew, Kylie and Eric, she's brought into this world.

More than once I had puke-inducing nightmares about What might have happened If.

So, after many, many years of getting the necessary distance in order to view it through the fiction writer's lens, I finally wrote "Iphigenia" and set that particular What-If? nightmare to rest.

The two immediate problems I faced when trying to use this event in a story were, 1) Which parts to use and how; face it, I don't remember a lot of the details about that endless goddamn walk through the corridors to the Coliseum's entrance, mostly what I have are a bunch of aches and impressions, so there would be no whole-cloth lifting of that event; I decided to use as many of the "What-If?" scenarios my brain and dredged up over the years as I could, but to filter them through my remembered impressions and current sensibilities; which brought me to, 2) exactly how to portray the riot itself and its effect on Danny. I'd learned from "Union Dues" that putting myself into the story, no matter what disguise I used to convince myself I wasn't getting in my own way, would stymie the piece before it took its first step —

— and then I suddenly had my opening; it would involve
Danny being interrupted in mid-step:
"He was checking the seat numbers on the tickets when he
heard Mrs. Williamson scream.

'Danny! Watch out!'

He looked down in time to see seven-month-old Julie crawl
into his path, her body so low to the ground it would be easy
to step on her fragile skull and crush it all over the sidewalk.
He pulled back in mid-stride and fell back-first onto the
pavement, cursing both the pain and the memory of his sister
— which found him as soon as the cement knocked the air
from his lungs. After a moment he managed to push himself
up on his elbows to see little Julie — sitting up now — look
at him and giggle, a thin trickle of saliva dribbling off her
chin. She looked so cute, so safe.

Safe. With someone to watch over her. Protect her. Trusting
was easy when you were that young. Trusting was fun.

So little Julie was giggling."

Satisfied that I'd nailed the setup and tone with this opening, I set about the task of tackling what happens once Danny
and everyone arrives at the concert. I knew that some rules
were going to be broken, out of necessity, because the portrayal of the riot itself would be easy — it was everything
leading up to it that was giving me headaches.

What I basically had once Danny and the others arrived
was this: four teenagers standing in a long and massive line
that isn't moving and where nothing much is happening.

Not the stuff of great suspense, that.

Still, the core of the story's action was going to happen
before all hell broke loose, but how to create a palpable sense
of tension with almost no physical movement going on?

The most obvious solution was to employ the use of a
deliberate run-on sentence (see the line reprinted from
Ketchum's "Gone" in Part Two), but the problem there was
that a run-on should only be used when things are immediate,
when things happen very quickly, events are piling up one
on top of the other faster than a character can deal with or
fully comprehend them, and when you want to create an

overwhelming sense of confusion and panic; a run-on might serve the story well once the violence began, but as a lead-in to the violence, it was useless; it would grafting feverish action onto a sequence where it didn't belong, and would detract from what was to come.

The next solution was to portray everything in short, staccato sentences: "They moved forward. A little. Stopped. Moved a little more. Someone in the back shouted. Someone else shouted back. The narrative came to a screeching halt."

Close, but still not right. The terse, disjointed brand of sentence (of which Richard Christian Matheson remains the undisputed master), while creating definite agitation, would ultimately work against the scene because each period would be the equivalent of Danny taking a breath to steady himself, and the idea here was to create a sense of *constant and building tension*; forward momentum was vital, and there could be nothing to give the subconscious impression that Danny was being granted even a momentary reprieve – which is what each period would have done.

Scratch the short ones. Definitely.

Which left me with only one option, and that was to somehow strike a balance between the run-on and the staccato.

Below is a sample of my solution, see if you agree with the choice I made:

". . . Danny looked around him as he squeezed Laura's hand tighter, trying not to give into panic, a panic he felt pushing its way up from his balls into his throat, but there was at least the feel of Laura's hand, a good feeling, a safe feeling, even here, even now . . . pushing against them, someone was pushing against them from behind . . . he turned to get a look, maybe say something to them, tell them not to be so impatient, everybody paid their money and they were going to get in . . . but only more faces, more bodies, more red-pin-prick-black eyes that glanced around, behind, ahead, all of them meeting his own at one pint, never staying for long, and he thought for a second . . . a *fraction* of a second, that he saw a small, fragile figure making its way through the crowd, trying to get somewhere in particular, trying to get to *someone* in particular, but in a blink and a noisy shifting of the crowd it was gone, lost in the swirling mass of voices, eyes, and flesh . . .

. . . he took some deep breaths and looked down at his feet, trying to stay calm, they hadn't been here all that long, there was no reason for him to feel so panicky, so why did he . . . his shoe, there was something wrong with his shoe . . . he bent over just a little and glared down, watching as a shadow of some kind shifted under his feet . . . no, not a shadow, it was a . . . a . . . a *leg* . . . no, not a leg, just part of a bug that he'd scraped off, only . . . wait . . . only it seemed to be moving, seemed to be trying to pull itself out from under his weight, a small, twiglike hairy leg squirming from under his shoe . . . he froze as he stared, thinking for a moment that he could hear the clatter of its hard- shell body, could see its mandibles starting to jut out from under . . .

. . . Laura leaned in and kissed him on the cheek, whispering something about later on tonight, after the concert, Mom and Dad weren't home and she was all alone did he wanna come over, soft promises of flesh and tongues and bodies . . . bodies pressing, bodies sweating, groaning, pumping steadily . . . he looked at her and smiled, kissed her, but felt nothing, only the sour liquid in his stomach churning around, churning and bubbling as the crowd shifted once again, and Danny looked around, feeling the sourness spread into his mouth, drying his saliva, gluing his tongue down, unable to speak now, almost unable to breath, but then Laura kissed him again with her wet and wonderful tongue and he was all right, moist again, able to swallow, then he noticed that Jim and Theresa were nowhere to be seen . . .

. . . the figure again, he saw the figure again, so tiny, so frightened, and he almost moved to reach for it, but then Laura grabbed his arm and said, "You're not going anywhere without me, not in this crowd," so he pulled

her along beside him, positive he'd seen . . . seen someone wandering around the crowd, a frightened gleam in
their gaze, maybe tears streaming down their cheeks, but
no one saw because she was so small, no one heard
because her voice was too weak and they were too busy
trying to push other people out of the way, trying to get
as close to the doors as possible, that's what counted,
getting ahead so you could get inside, get a good seat,
toke it up, party down, drink and chug Big Time . . .

. . . "Christ, slow down, will you," said Laura, demanding that he give her a break, just wait a minute . . . Danny
slowed and stood still, his eyes darting around . . . Laura
moved closer to him, putting her arms around his waist
. . . he took another deep breath and put a protective
arm around her shoulder and said, "Are you all right?"
and she said, "I'm fine, how about you, lover?" and he
laughed, laughed and held her close because she'd never
called him "lover" before and he liked it, liked it very
much as he stretched his arms out to relax them and
went to step closer to Laura . . .

. . . someone pushed from behind and he lost his
balance, fell forward, rammed his foot out to try and
break his fall but in the second before his foot connected
with the pavement a child crawled out in front of him,
a small child, a baby crawling, and he tried to cry out
but someone else pushed and he felt his foot connect
with the fragile skull, felt the baby's head pop like a
melon below his foot, and his stomach heaved then but
nothing came up as he looked down and saw the feelers
worming around, saw the baby's arms flailing out as it
kicked and wriggled in its death spasms, so he pulled
back and lifted his foot, not wanting to see what he'd
done but having to look . . ."

The use of the ellipses accomplished two things; it created
a sense of forward momentum in a scene where there was not
a lot of physical movement, and it enabled me to structure
the entire sequence (which lasts for several pages) around the
agitation of the staccato with the immediacy of the run-on.

In the years since this story first saw print, I have re-read it every now and then to assure myself that I made the right choice. I think I did — in fact, I think I made the *only* choice that would have worked for the story as I wrote it. If someone else had written this story, they would have found another way to tell it, I'm sure. But in the end, "Iphigenia" was me telling a particular story in the best way I could.

Which became a real challenge when it came to the next incident I lifted whole-cloth and dropped into a story: the rape scene in "Some Touch of Pity."

If you've not read it, "Pity" is about a werewolf — not someone who gets bitten by same and then becomes one, but someone who, through an act of horrible violence, outwardly changes into a wolf in reaction to the violence. As the years pile up, he finds that he can tap into this violence and change into a werewolf at will.

The central event by which he defines his life — and which he relives on an almost hourly basis — is his sexual assault at the age of eight by three drunken teenagers (friends of the family) who, in order to prove their nerve to one another before they ship out for Vietnam, gang-rape him during a camping trip.

Now, bear something in mind: everything is bigger to a child, not only physically, but per4ceptually and emotionally, as well; a dollar found becomes a discovered pirate's treasure; a heap of dirty clothes in the corner turns into a nasty, fanged beastie after the lights have been turned out. Everything is amplified when you're a kid. I know it was when I was eight.

Let's get this out of the way so we can move on. When I was eight years old I was sent on a camping trip with four other kids, and three teenagers (friends of the family), two of whom would be shipping out to Vietnam in a week or so. After everyone crawled into their sleeping bags or tents and fell asleep, the Holy Trinity of Really Wonderful Guys got roaring drunk and began playing a game of "Dare" that got louder, more violent, and progressively more outrageous and twisted. The oldest of them, while talking about what he'd heard was going on in Vietnam, said that a guy had to be willing to do anything in order to survive. Anything? another one asked. What followed was a bunch of eat-this-bug or drink-a-cup-of-my-spit or stick-your-finger-up-my-ass, and then one of them came up with the bright idea of a gang-bang; stinking drunk and out of control — and with no girls around to fit the bill — they decided to end their game of "Dare" with me; after all, I was the smallest, and the weakest, and the most easily terrified into silence.

So I was pulled from my sleeping bag and dragged deeper into the woods and forced to pretend my mouth and ass were pincushions while they pretended their dicks were the pins.

Don't dig camping to this day, oddly enough.

Anyone who's ever read "Pity" remembers the rape scene. I agonized over that thing for weeks for several reasons, not the least of which was I didn't want any element of that scene to come off as sensationalistic or titillating — what my buddy Ray Garton calls ". . . whacking material for pedophiles." It's not just the rape scene in "Pity" but the whole open wound of the narrative that it was hard to approach. But an invitation came along to write a story for Marty Greenberg's *Werewolves* anthology, I needed the money from a sale, and I was right smack in the middle of finally seeking out counseling about several unpleasant incidents from my life that I had never really dealt with.

I was about a fourth of the way into writing "Pity" when I began to face the facts about what had happened to me when I was eight. No, there was no "breakthrough" or anything so melodramatic, I had never blocked it from my mind, I remembered every detail — every last lousy, stinking, god-damned detail — but had trained myself to keep it all tucked away in a filing cabinet in the background where I wouldn't bother it and it wouldn't bother me.

Well, that method of self-therapy had just about run its course at the time I got the *Werewolves* assignment, and the events of that night were pretty much in the forefront of my mind all the time.

I was not, as they say, a happy camper.

The story kept stalling on me. My central character was coming off as more of a literary construct than a fully-dimensional human being and every situation I put him into seemed either too convenient or too contrived; nothing was going well, I had no central conflict, only a jumble of ideas and vague notions about what I wanted to do somewhere along the line, the deadline was fast approaching, I wasn't sleeping worth shit, my mood was in the toilet, my wife (now ex-wife, all my fault), Leslie, was beside herself with concern and frustration, I wasn't getting anything done around the house like I was supposed to, and all because I'd allowed myself to buy into the pop-psychology bullshit about "the healing process" and was remembering the specifics about an event I'd really rather not give a second thought to, thanks very much.

So I finally gave up. I would stop writing the story, I would write about what happened to me and how I felt about it, I'd get it the fuck out of my system, and then I could move on to something constructive.

I write about the assault. It's nasty, it makes me mad, sick, and sad all over again, and once it's finished it doesn't appear to have served any purpose because I sure as shit didn't feel any better and the story deadline wasn't any further away.

I went on auto-pilot. I started the story with the narrator, in wolf form, battling a large dog. He kills the dog. He feels bad about it. He changes back into human form. Crawls to his car. Gets inside —

— only there's this little boy sitting in the car, waiting on him; the little boy's all scraped up and cut up and bleeding and naked and crying and the first thing the narrator says to him is "Get away from me" but this kid, he won't stop crying or saying "I'm sorry, I'm sorry, please don't be mad at me" over and over and all it's doing is making the narrator more pissed off and the more pissed off he gets the more the little kid apologizes and I don't know where this shit is coming from, I got no idea who this little fucker is, I hadn't planned on any little snot-nose to be in the car, it's as big a surprise to me as it is to the narrator, who's really screaming at kid now, but the kid just keeps saying how sorry he is and I'm thinking about having the narrator wolf-out on his ass just to get him out of the story —

— but as soon as I move to do that I realize that I can't.

I can't because the kid is the ghost of the narrator as a little boy.

Which, I suddenly realize, means he's the ghost of *me* as a little boy.

Which meant the narrator was me.

Which meant that I was doing another "Union Dues."

Which meant I. Was. Screwed.

Lots of stomping, yelling at Leslie over nothing, secret drinking, taking too many sedatives to calm myself down; a regular happy camper jamboree at the Braunbeck house.

I go back, apply ass to seat, hands to keyboard, and start again.

The dog. The fight. The feeling bad about it. Crawling back to the car. Getting inside. This time he's thinking about blowing his head off with a silver bullet he has in his gun. He closes the door. Takes out the gun, turns around —

— and fuck me with a fiddlestick, that little kid's *sitting there again.*

I started worrying about serious Bin time at that point. So I could either go with it and hope that another "Union Dues" disaster didn't happen, or I could give up writing and become a cesspool cleaner.

Until then, I'd done a fairly decent job at keeping my work separate from what I was going through, but then it occurred to me that something in this character was utterly ruined because I myself had felt for most of my life that I was nothing more than damaged goods in a flashy package . . . so I went with it. I decided there was no way in hell I'd ever be able to shape this into a saleable story, but for some reason the memories of the assault and this goddamn werewolf story kept trying to join together, so who the hell was I stop it? Luckily, my little camping excursion was not only accepted but embraced by my central character — who wasn't as much like me as I'd first thought — and as a result of his embracing of the incident, the rape scene emerged as a vital, necessary, and justified element of the story. In this case, that type of line-crossing indulgence worked out for the best; I wound up with what I think is a pretty solid story, and the power what had happened to me as a kid had less hold on me because I'd finally seen it in black and white, put it into a fictional context, and thus, in my own silly way, given it some value.

Call Oprah. Ring the happy bells. Let the healing begin. (Insert rim-shot here.)

I think don't think there *is* such a beast as "healing," ultimately; things scab over, scars can be removed, blood mopped up and wounds cauterized, but the painful memories remain; oh, sure, they eventually lose their hold over you and your life, but that doesn't help win back the friends you've lost as a result nor does it erase the cruelties and hurts you inflict on those you love, and it sure as hell doesn't get back any of the time you've lost trying to come to grips with them. The half-assed optimist would say that you "learn" from such things; well guess what I learned from what happened? I learned, A) I don't like camping; B) Never dare a drunken teenager to do *anything*; C) It does you no good to whine about it; and, D) That for every perceived horror that's been inflicted on you, there's half a dozen other people out there whose experiences make what you've gone through look like a carousel ride in summer. To this day, every so often — usually when I'm under a great deal of stress or am incredibly tired — my ass still bleeds from the torn tissue in there, tissue that, according to the surgeons I've consulted, can never be fully repaired; so every now and then, like some misguided form of stigmata, I'll start to leak and will have to beat a hasty retreat for a new pair of pants and underwear and usually I'll have to bum a tampon off one of my female friends to staunch things until it stops.

So let's not talk about "the healing process" — at l east, not as you would have me try and apply it to myself. You confront it, get the upper hand, and get on with life as best you can.

The strangest thing is, of all the stories I've written, "Pity" is the one which gets the most positive reaction. Go fig. I've lost count of how many people have approached me at conventions (when I attend them) and tell me how much "Pity" meant to them, because they or someone they know have/has experienced a similar violation in their lives and, for them, that story puts into words a lot of what they themselves have felt. It's one of the angriest, darkest, most violent stories I've ever written, and there are folks out there who find a great deal of hope and comfort in it.

So I guess, in its way, this goes to illustrate how, sometimes, horror can perform the duty of which John Gardner spoke.

And that word — duty — leads me into the final example of lifting an event whole-cloth from real life and creating a worthwhile story from it. Bear with me a bit longer; I'm nearly out of your hair, promise.

A little over a year ago I had to make the decision and then give the order to take my mother — who was suffering from final-stage emphysema — off life-support. It was not an easy decision to make, despite her obvious suffering. She had been going downhill steadily since my dad's death nine months previous. My sister and I were burnt beyond belief; Dad had died, then our grandmother (Mom's mother, who for a while shared the same nursing home wing with her daughter), and now Mom.

She had been in a coma for nearly a week and her doctor saw no chance of her coming out of it. Gayle and I had Mom's living will, but there was no way Gayle could bring herself to make the decision on her own, and she sure as hell didn't have it in her to give the order. Not to imply that she was weak, far from it, but she had two kids to take care of, a job to hold down, a husband, and had been the one to drive Dad back and forth to and from Columbus five times a week for his radiation treatments. She was exhausted.

I was in the middle of my divorce, and it was not friendly. I admit here that it was my fault, I betrayed Leslie; after all the love and faith and support she'd given me, I threw it back in her face. I will never forgive myself for having hurt her as I did. She remains the single finest human being it has ever been my privilege to have known, and I mourn every day for the loss of her from my life.

I wasn't as exhausted as my sister, but I could see the neighborhood. Neither one of us had had a chance to catch our breath or get our bearings since Dad's death, and now here we were, about to kill our mother.

Please don't hand me any of that soft-peddling rigmarole about how it "was the right thing to do" or how it was "for the best" or all the rest of it; yeah, I know it was the right thing to do, I know it was for the best, she was sick and was never going to get better, she'd never be able to breathe without the aid of a machine, never be able to get out bed for the rest of her life.

Well, at least she was in a coma, so we didn't have to face that.

My mother, Mary Virginia Braunbeck, spent the majority of her childhood as a ward of the county, growing up in a childrens' home (what used to be called an orphanage) with dozens of other children whose families could not or would not take care of them. She was abused there, both physically and emotionally. But she survived. She never made it past high school. She worked hard all her life at a variety of jobs – cashier, maid, cable-assembly worker – and, as far as I could tell, never really had a happy day in her life. Whatever mechanism it is that people possessed that enabled them to be happy had been whipped out of her long before I came along. She was second only to Dad as the saddest person I ever knew.

And after all that, after a life of hard work and little reward and being humiliated by snotty clerks in grocery stores because she used food stamps and occasionally had to put items back because she couldn't afford them, after holding her husband's hand and those of both her children through some pretty rotten times, her life boiled down to long evenings alone in a house where there was no longer a Frank for her to talk to, so she contented herself with calling me or Gayle all the time to see if we'd come over and watch *Touched By An Angel* and *Jeopardy* with her. She had the house to herself for all of six months before she took the last bad turn, went into the nursing home and then the ICU where she was hooked up to machines to help her breathe, and slipped into a coma.

Gayle and I made the decision together to remove Mom from life-support. When it came time to give the order, I was the one who would give it.

Gayle and I called all friends and family to let them know what we were going to do. I contacted the parish and asked for a priest to come and give Mom Last Rights. He arrived around 1:30 p.m.; Gayle and I had decided that I would give the order to take her off support at 3:30 — the time when Mom usually got off work during the years she'd been working. She'd always joked that she'd probably "die right at quitting time," so we hoped she'd appreciate the humor of the scheduling.

The priest arrived around 2; Gayle and I said hello, shook his head, then went back to Mom's room. The doors were closed, the curtains pulled. The priest blessed us, made the Sign of the Cross, and began giving the Last Rights —

— and that's when Mom woke up.

I'm going to spare you the details of the next three hours (for reasons that will become clear very soon); Mom died, we left her body behind as we were supposed to do, made the arrangements for her funeral, and buried her on an unseasonably windy and cold day in April, the day that would have been Leslie's and my fourteenth wedding anniversary.

I came back after the funeral and, in the middle of the night, sat up in bed, wide-awake and panicked because from somewhere in the back of my mind a little voice had whispered, "I hate to bother you with this right now, but . . . don't you have a story due in a couple of days?"

Shit, shit, shit.

I climbed out of bed and went straight to the computer, opened a new file, and began typing.

I had no idea what the hell I was going to write about.

Sure, I'd had some idea for a story a couple of weeks back, before things took another bad turn, but in the ensuing days I'd lost all contact with whatever that idea was. I had a big zero, a goose egg, zilch, blank slate — *nothing.*

The thing is, I needed to work right then as badly as I'd ever needed anything. Getting some kind of story down would seem like something constructive, something life-affirming, and I needed there to be something life-affirming right there in front of my face, something that wasn't all sickness and sadness and pain and regret — I'd had a fucking bellyful of that, enough to last me a lifetime, thanks so much — and I wasn't about to rise from the chair until I had at the very least the first lines of a story.

I sat there and stared at that screen for two hours. Didn't move, didn't type a word, didn't even get on-line and do the meandering surfing of the brain-dead. I just stat here, looking at a bright screen and thinking about nothing.

I didn't know it at the time, but I was in the early stages of the single worst psychological and emotional meltdown I would ever experience, one that would culminate in massive and humiliating public breakdown that would land me in the Bin, doped to the gills and under a suicide watch, Stephen King's *From A Buick 8* the only thing to remind why it was I thought I had the right to go on breathing air and taking up space.

Somewhere in the early minutes of Hour Three of the stare-down between me and the computer screen, I put my hands on the keys and typed these words:

"Mom woke up just as the priest was giving her Last Rights."

Uh-huh.

Another frothy, light, carefree and gay chuckle-fest from Yours Truly, Mr. Happy-Go-Lucky.

I deleted the line, stared at the screen a little while longer, then typed the same line again.

"Mom woke up just as the priest was giving her Last Rights."

This routine of writing that line, erasing it, staring at the screen, then writing it again would go on for a while — at least another hour — before I finally got wise and did something about it.

When that at last did happen, when it occurred to me that my repeatedly writing this was starting to feel a bit like that scene in *The Shining* where Shelley Duvall takes a gander at the book Jack Nicholson's been working on and finds that he's written "All work and no play makes Jack a dull boy" over and over and over, I admitted to myself that I had no goddamn idea, but I needed to write, so what the hell — I'd write about what happened after Mom woke up. I was fresh out of original ideas, so I'd steal something from real life and hope I'd get away with it.

As soon as I started to write the second line, the writer in me elbowed his way to the front and said, "Whoa there, slick. Are you sure first person is the way to go, all things considered?"

I admitted that maybe it wasn't the best choice.

So I tried doing it in third. Third person made it far too detached and cold. So I switched to third-person present-tense and that was even worse; aside from seeming too cold and detached, it now had the added bonus of sounding pretentious (I almost always find present tense to be self-consciously literary, as if the writer is trying to draw your attention to the writing and not the story), so I went back to regular old third person.

Not doing the trick.

I was really tired by this time but knew there was no way I'd be able to sleep (severe sleeplessness was one of the things that led to the meltdown later), so I thought, what the hell? Let's go for second person — better yet, let's go for second-person present-tense because God knows you can't ever be *too* pretentious or self-conscious.

I didn't care.

Except it turned out that second-person present-tense allowed me to somehow make the events of the story (I now thought of it as just that: the story) much more immediate while giving myself a thin but necessary scrim behind which to hide from the bald, ugly facts of what had happened; it allowed me to write the events as they happened, but also gave me the distance to view them only in a fictional context.

I had never before written a story in either second person or present tense, let alone a combination of the two; by taking this swan-dive into a narrative voice I never would have considered under normal circumstances, I was able to both write an actual (and hopefully worthwhile) story, and give myself a little perspective on what had happened.

I cannot judge this story, even now. I think it's pretty okay. I don't think Mom would have liked it, but she wouldn't have said so because she wouldn't have wanted to hurt my feelings. The editor, William Simmons, accepted it, and it appeared in a nifty anthology called *Vivisections,* and people seem to respond to it, but, still . . . I don't know.

I only know that I miss my parents, goddammit, and I miss my ex-wife's friendship and affection, and all I really have to offer this world when day is done are these little stories that I tell; so hopefully I did my job with this one and will continue to do so with the next one and the one after and the one after that.

So, after all the brouhaha of persons first or second or third, I give you the story I wrote over the course of that night and most of the next day. Mom wouldn't have cared for it, but this was and is my last gift to her, my way of thanking her for all she did for, and meant, to me.

See what you think:

Duty

"There are some mistakes too monstrous for remorse."

— Edwin Arlington Robinson

*M*om woke up just as the priest was giving her Last Rites.

(Is this part of the penance? you asked of the Guests. *Isn't it all?* was their reply. Smug fucks.)

For six days she'd lain unconscious in the ICU at Cedar Hill Memorial Hospital, kept alive by the ventilator which sat by her bed clicking, puffing, humming, buzzing, measuring her blood, inspiratory, and baseline pressure, waveform readouts showing the fluxes of tracheal and esophageal pressure, proximal pressure at 60 to + 140 cmH2O, 1 cmH2O/25 mV, output flow at 300 to 200 LPM, 1 LPM/ 10 mV, the whole impressive shebang running smoothly at maximum system pressure of 175 cmH2O, the ribbed tube rammed securely down her throat into her lungs, ensuring that she continued to breathe at the acceptable rates of 250 milliseconds minimum expiratory time, 5 seconds maximum inspiratory time. Details. Specifics. Minutia. Like the Drain-Swirl of the Black Flecks. Like the title of a bad 50's horror movie, the kind you used to watch with Dad on Friday nights when you were a child and there was no sibling to compete for his attention. All of this comes to you as you stand there studying the details, the specifics, the minutia. Things to look at and memorize because you can no longer look at the pale, pinched, collapsed ruins of the face and body lying motionless on the bed. A glowing number changes, a monitor beeps softly to register the new data, the pump presses down, expanding the lungs, raising the chest, and all is right in god's techno-savvy world. Except.

(Except, say the Guests; *ah, there's the rub, as Willy S. once wrote, right, pal? 'Except.' What a word that is, so much disaster and heartache and ruination and disappointment and pain and all of it always follows one little two-syllable word. Very dramatic, don't you think? Yes, we thought you'd agree, so what say we get back to things and see what follows that word of all words that you seem incapable of getting past right now so, as usual, we have to do it for you. Be a Good Boy and say it with us, now.)*

Except that she never should have been here in the first place. Her DNR order had ceased to be in effect at the hospital when she was transferred to the nursing home, but some stupid nurse over there panicked and called an ambulance when Mom went into respiratory arrest, so she was brought back here and immediately placed on life-support; the last thing she'd wanted was to be hooked up to some goddamn machine at the end of her life – she'd told you and your sister that often enough when her emphysema had entered the advanced stage, this a full year before the double pneumonia now snarling inside her – and the two of you had promised you wouldn't let that happen. But it has happened. You wonder if she blames you. But doesn't she realize it isn't your fault? Someone should have called you, should have made sure that the DNR order was attached to her chart at the nursing home, should have been paying attention to the fucking records when her name was entered into the computer and her information came up in the ER, but all of this is for lawyers to deal with later. Right now a duty needs to be performed. You and your sister have already tracked down Mom's doctor and told him what you want; you have shown him the living will and he has nodded his head solemnly, he has picked up the phone and called the ICU; you and your sister have shown the living will to the nurse in charge, have called various friends and family to tell them what you are about to do, and have contacted Father Bill at St. Francis. The two of you have agreed to wait until everyone is present before giving the order. That's everything so far, right? Well, no, but that's *most* of it. Even now as you stand here witnessing these events, you're already replaying their beginning in your mind, as if by doing so and focusing on the details, the specifics, the minutia, you might find a way to alter the outcome which hasn't even been determined yet. To whit: Father Bill was the first to arrive, all soft words and sympathy — "This must be terrible for the two of you, so soon after your father's and grandmother's deaths." — as he donned the garments and uncorked the vial of holy water and found his place in his book of blessings. "In the name of the Father, the Son, and the Holy Spirit: 'O God, great and omnipotent judge of the living and the dead, we are to appear before you after this short life to render an account of our works. Give us the grace to prepare for our last hour by —'"

And that's when Mom woke up.

She blinked a few times, then looked up, saw Lisbeth, and smiled as best she could with that tube in her mouth and throat.

Father Bill continued: "— a devout and holy life, and protect us against a sudden and unprovided death.'"

(Bummer, say the Guests. *Hadn't planned on this turn of events, had you, pal?)*

Mom's eyes grew wide and she began to shake; at first you thought she was having some kind of seizure, but she tore her hand from Lisbeth's and began to shake it in the air: No. Stop this. Stop it now.

"'Let us remember our frailty and mortality,'" continued Father Bill, "'that we may always live in the ways of your commandments. Teach us to watch and pray, that when your summons comes for our departure —'"

Mom started shaking her head and making wet, querulous, awful sounds as her hand shook more violently, the index finger trying to uncurl from its arthritic brethren to point at someone or something; her head jerked to the side, then back again, her eyes staring into those of your sister.

(The Guests again: She'll cave. She will. Sis always does wherever Mom's concerned. Next stop, Cave City. And you know it.)

"'" — from this world, we may go forth to meet you, experience a merciful judgment, and rejoice in everlasting happiness. We ask this through Christ our Lord. Amen.'"

Father Bill then placed his hand on Mom's forehead — or *tried* to, rather. She was having none of it. "It's all right, Mary," he whispered. "It's all right, Frank and your mother are waiting for you, there's no need to be scared. God's love will ease your fear and carry you home."

He whispered something to her that you couldn't understand, then with a nod to you and your sister, made his way out.

You didn't want to turn around and look back into the room because you knew what you'd see, but eventually Father Bill disappeared from view and you had no choice.

There. All up to date now, yes? Yes. The outcome was determined even as you were trying to alter it by your observation at the time. And you didn't notice until it was too late. What's wrong with this picture? Too many black flecks, dancing.

Okay, so what now?

Duty.

You turn back into the room and there's Lisbeth, looking at you with a surprised smile and a "Maybe-Everything-Will-Be-Okay" gleam in her eyes. She's holding Mom's hand and trying to look happy while all the while silently asking: Should I be happy or not? She's back with us, we didn't think that would happen but here she is. Maybe this is a sign, her coming awake when she did. Maybe. Maybe?

(Cave City – this stop, Cave City.)
You shake your head. The gleam fades from her eyes for a moment, appears again as if she's thought of an argument against this, then leaves completely. She knows what you shaking your head means.

And so does Mom.

She's looking right at you, and you know what this look means. Oh, the lids are droopier than they've ever been, and the eyes are both dull and bloodshot, but the look is a classic: How can you do something like this?

How often in your forty-one years have you seen that look from her? Or, for that matter, from everyone else in your life? *Yes, Mom, look at me. I'm no longer your son – I'm what became of him. Forty-one, divorced, living alone* (well, sort of, but you wouldn't understand, *no one* would understand about the Guests), *no real friends, and here I am about to kill you – because that's what you're really thinking, isn't it, Mom? "My son is going to kill me." Because you know if it were just Lisbeth, she couldn't do it. You could always talk Lisbeth out of anything, but me? I inherited your stubborn streak, and you hate that. Does that also mean you hate me right now? Or maybe you always have, who knows?*

"I'm glad to see you," Lisbeth whispers to Mom, squeezing her hand and kissing her cheek. But Mom is still shaking, still trying to point a finger, still objecting.

"There's a lot of people who want to see you," says Lisbeth. "We called everybody. You're going to be real popular today."

You pull in a breath and cross over to the bed. "Hi, Mom," you say, but it doesn't sound like your voice, does it? When did you start speaking with someone else's voice? Odd – Lisbeth and Mom seem to recognize it. "I thought you were gonna stay asleep on us."

She continues to shake her head, and you notice for the first time how wide her eyes are. *('Deer in the headlights' is the simile you're looking for,* say the Guests.) For the first time you let yourself acknowledge that she's scared. She knows what's going on and she doesn't want it to happen but one look in your eyes and she knows she's toast, that maybe she'd have a chance if it was only Lisbeth but with *you* . . . oh, yeah: toast. Browned on both sides.

Tears form in her eyes as her mouth works to form words but she can't speak, not with that tube, so what emerges is a series of squeaks and whistles and deeply wet groans, a vaudeville of language but it's all she's got, that and her shaking head and pointing finger and tears.

You reach out and grab her shaking hand, squeezing it gently. "I love you, Mom," you say, and this time the voice sounds a little more like your own; an echo, yes, distant and thin, but yours nonetheless. "I'm so sorry you've been so sick for so long. But the doctor's told us that you . . . you can't breathe on your own anymore. You have to be hooked up like this, it's the only way you can breathe, you see?"

Her eyelids twitch as a single tear slips out from the corner of her left eye and slides a slow, glistening trail down her temple into her ear. You pull a tissue from your pocket and wipe the tear away before it drips into her ear canal. That's always irritated you whenever you've been on your back and crying so it must be twice as awful for her because she can't raise that arm, what with all the IV needles decorating it like a seamstress's pincushion. So you wipe away the tear just like a Good Boy should do for his Mom.

"Please don't cry," you say, hating the hint of desperation that's suddenly there in the echo of your voice, but Mom's wrinkling her brow and every last line in her face, the short ones, the long ones, the deep and not-so deep ones, all of them become so much more pronounced, each one looking more painful than the one next to it, or over it, or crisscrossing it: the map of a face, the topography of a life: *This is from the night when your spleen burst and we had to sit the emergency room, your dad and me, wondering whether or not you'd make it out of surgery or if we were going to lose our little boy; this one here, under my right eye, is from all those nights I spent squinting over grocery store coupons when your dad was on strike at the plant, we had to watch every penny so the coupons were a big help but, Lord, there were so many of them, and maybe I wouldn't have this line if I'd admitted to myself that I needed glasses, but even if I had admitted it we couldn't afford them, not with the strike and all, so I squinted* . . . and there are no rest-stops on this particular map, are there? No, not a one that you can find.

"You'll wear yourself out," you say, squeezing her hand a little tighter. "You don't . . . you d-don't want to do that because everyone is coming over to see you."

Her private vaudeville of language continues, and every squeak is wrapped up in sandy, sputtering, wet rawness that makes your stomach tighten and your throat constrict. Her hand in yours is cold and leathery but she's trying to squeeze back, to let you know *Please don't do this, please don't do this, I know I'm sick and I know it's hard on you kids but I don't want to die, not yet, I don't want to die not yet not yet not yet please don't do this pleasepleaseplease.*

You let go of her hand as a nurse comes into the room and asks if she can speak to you or your sister. You nod at Lisbeth and walk out into the hall, but not before bending down and kissing Mom on the cheek; it still tastes of the tear you wiped away earlier, and the saltiness is unexpected; it tastes of flavor, of something being prepared, Christmas dinner where Mom always used just a little too much salt in her stuffing, but you loved that smell, didn't you? The way it wafted up the stairs and tickled your nose to wake you: *It's Christmas, come on down, sleepy-head, and see all the goodies Dad and me have got for you!*

"I'll be right back," you whisper to the tear's trail, hoping Mom hears it, as well.

Outside, the nurse pulls closed the glass door separating Mom's room from the rest of the ICU. "Is there anything more you'd like us to do?"

"I think she might need a sedative of some kind. She's really scared and —"

"— doctor already wrote the order for a sedative and morphine, as well. I can give it to her any time you say."

You nod your head and chew on your lower lip for a moment.

(Handling things just like the Good Boy we all know you are, say the Guests. You can't tell if they're making fun of you or not, so before you get too caught up in this moment you tell them to fuck off and simply jump to the outcome without benefit of observation.)

"I don't want her knocked out, understand? She'll want to say g-good . . . good-bye to everyone and I want her to be conscious."

"It won't knock her out, I promise."

"Then please give it to her now."

The nurse nods her head and looks at you – she has very pretty grey eyes, doesn't she? They look just like your ex-wife's – but here you are observing the moment while it rides right on by, and have to ask the nurse to repeat what she's just said.

"Is there anything we can do for you or your sister?"

"No, thank you. I just want Mom to feel . . . I mean, she's been so sick for so long and we – Lisbeth and I, we . . ."

The nurse puts a hand on your forearm. Her fingers are soft and warm, the first time a woman's fingers have touched there in – what? – a year-and-a-half? Two years? Who remembers?

(We do, say the Guests. *We remember everything, pal. That's why you invited us here.)*

"Is everything the way you want it?" asks this nurse of the warm soft fingers on your arm.

What you want to say is: *No, everything is not the way I want it, so if you'll pardon me, then, I think I'll just go over here and scream for lost things, throw back my head and open my mouth and just scream. For a smile I haven't seen in years, or the chime that's missing from a laugh, or the noise not made by a child now ten years in its grave, for the toys my ex-wife and me don't have to pick up; I'll scream for all the school pictures that aren't decorating a mantel, then maybe for songs no one but me remembers of cares about, songs from dead singers that make me smile or cry when I hear an echo of their choruses from a passing radio accidentally tuned into an Oldies station, and finally I'll scream for my only living parent whom I am about to kill. Yes, that sounds good. Sounds splendid, in fact. So if you'll just excuse me for a moment, I'll go take care of this. Sound okay? Good. If you need me I'll be right over there. Can't miss me. I'll be the one screaming.*

That's what you want to say (as you observe in the moment that hasn't quite gotten away from you yet), but what actually comes out of your mouth is: "Yes, thank you, everything is fine . . . as fine as it can be under these circumstances, I guess."

Nurse of the warm fingers lingers for just a moment longer, maybe longer than is necessary or even professional, and the sad smile on her face is echoed by the one in her eyes.

You both release a breath at the same time. She blinks, squeezes your arm, and with a soft swish of shoes against the polished tile, heads off for the syringe.

(Were you just flirting? the Guests inquire. *Oh, pal, what stones you've got. Mom lying in there choking to death on the ruined slop of her insides and you're making time with Florence Nightingale. Show of hands: spit or swallow?)*

"Shut the fuck up!" you growl through clenched teeth. An older gentleman passing by you snaps his head in your direction, his offense at your language all over his face.

"Sorry," you mumble. "I wasn't talking to you, I was —"

But he's gone, turned into another room a few yards down.

(A flirt and a charmer. What self-respecting nurse wouldn't want some of this action?)

Shaking your head, you go back in to Lisbeth and Mom.

"She's *scared,*" Lisbeth whispers. You wonder why she bothers. Fer chrissakes she's standing right there next to Mom, holding the woman's hand, and Mom might be hard of hearing but she isn't deaf and she may not have been the ideal parent but her life's going to be over — repeat that, turn up the volume, OVER — in less than two hours and the woman deserved to not be spoken of in Third Person.

"I know you're scared, Mom," you say, taking your place by the bed. "But this is what you wanted."

The shaking of the head again.

You reach into your pocket and remove the copy of her living will, unfold it, and hold it up for her to see. "You made us promise you that if this time ever came, we'd go through with it. Even if you said 'no,' we'd go through with it."

Lisbeth snaps your name and you give her the Glare. The Glare has served you well over the years, hasn't it? The Glare scares even the Guests sometimes. Burns right through a person, makes it damn near impossible to maintain eye contact with you. You know this, and you use it to your advantage whenever you want to be left alone, which is most of the time, so many have known the terror of the Glare.

Lisbeth looks away almost at once. You feel terrible for having looked at her this way, but dealing with that is for later.

(You got that right, pal. We'll just add that to the list, shall we?)

You grab Mom's hand away from Lisbeth and hold it tight. You look at your sister — who's still not returning your gaze — then directly into Mom's eyes. You have looked into her eyes this intensely maybe three times in your entire life. "Listen to me, Mom. You will *never* be able to function without this machine, do you understand me?"

A slow nod. Another tear.

"Even if we were to call this off right now and leave you hooked up to this thing, you're not going to last another week. You're on borrowed time, Mom. You should have been dead six days ago."

Once again Lisbeth says your name, this time spitting it out as if it's some rancid chunk of food.

"You're here with us now," you continue, "and you're awake, and you're getting the chance to do something Dad didn't get to do. You're getting a chance to say good-bye to all the people who love you. They're all coming, and they're all going to stay right here with you until you fall asleep for the last time. The nurse is going to give you a shot so you'll be comfortable, and all you have to do is just let us say good-bye and tell you that we love you and then you can rest. You're tired, Mom. You've been tired for so long —" Your voice cracks on these last two words, and you have to turn your head away for a moment to get a grip on yourself.

(Aw, say the Guests, look at this. Widdle baby cwying faw his mommy. Little late to feel sad about this now, isn't it, pal?)

You ignore them and turn back. "— and you need to rest. You've earned it."

Her hand squeezes yours.

"I have no idea how scary this must be for you, but we're going to be right here, however long this takes. But I'm — *we're* — going to keep our promise to you, Lisbeth and me. Because this is what you wanted. But there's something you need to do for me, Mom. You need to let me know you understand. Can you do that? Can you squeeze my hand and let me know that you understand so I don't have to go through the rest of my life feeling like I've killed you?"

She looks in your eyes.

And for some reason you remember something from twenty years ago: you were still living at home and had picked up the phone one day, just to make a call, but Mom was talking to someone so you started to hang up when you clearly heard her say the words: "I love you."

Phone in hand, staring.

Dad was raking leaves in the back yard.

You lifted the receiver to your ear and listened. Details. Specifics. Minutia. Three years this had been going on. They laughed. At your dad. At you. But not Lisbeth, not the light of everyone's lives, not her.

You hung up loudly and waited. It didn't take long. Mom at the door to your room, her eyes wide and frightened by the headlights.

"How much did you hear?"

"Enough," you said.

Her face took on many forms in a very few seconds; sadness, shame, anger, indifference, confusion and, finally, resignation. "Go ahead and tell him. I don't care." Bullshit bravado, that.

"I figured out that much from what I heard. So you really think I'm useless?"

Shock, for just a moment. Then: "Sometimes."

You nodded your head. "It would kill Dad if he knew."

"I'm not going to tell him."

"Neither am I."

She'd smiled at you, then, and for a moment you thought it was a smile of love and appreciation, but it was in her eyes, wasn't it?

You were now in it with her. If Dad ever found out, she could deflect part of his hurt and anger and anguish by saying, "Your son's known about it almost the whole time." And that *would* kill Dad.

There are times you wonder whether or not it *did* help kill him, just as much as the diabetes and high blood pressure and prostate cancer. Had he somehow found out? Then just let his heart break along with everything else so he could die alone in the toilet of his room at the nursing home? That's where they found him — dead in the crapper.

You never found out what happened to the other guy, never asked his name, never kept an eye out for a strange car or truck parked near the house.

Dad's gone. Grandma, too. Now it waa Mom's turn; not because you want it this, because it has to be this way.

"Please squeeze my hand," you whisper, and the begging in your voice disgusts even you.

Mom looks at you the same way she had after that phone call twenty years ago.

"Please?"

Mom does not blink, does not try to speak, does not shake her head.

After a moment you look at your sister. "She squeezed my hand," you say. Softly.

Lisbeth releases a breath, her shoulders slumping, then smiles and weeps at the same time. The relief she feels is palpable even from where you're standing.

(She bought it, pal. Very nice, very smooth.)

You look back down at Mom. She will not look at you.

"I love you, Mom." And you do. That's the terrible part. If she's going to hate you for this, so be it. It's what she wanted, and you promised.

(That you did, pal.)

You were her son. You were a Good Boy. And it was your duty.

The first of the friends and family begin to arrive, and you're relieved to step back from the bed and give the rest of them the chance to say good-bye.

The warm-fingered nurse comes back in, smiles at you, then gives Mom the shot. "This will help you relax, Mary. You'll feel better here in just a minute, I promise."

Mom smiles at her, a smile full of gratitude and affection. Part of you wishes she'd look at you like that, just once, just for a moment, but the rest of you

(And us, pal. Don't forget us, we'll take it personally!)

knows damn well that you've already gotten the last direct look from her that you'll ever know, and there you were in the moment, observing the event while not being a part of it so now all you've got is the impression of something that may or may not be a memory of an experience you weren't really a part of in the first place.

(Let's hear it for our Fearless leader, folks! Nothing gets by him, nosiree!)

The room fills quickly; aunts, uncles, Mom's co-workers from the cable assembly plant, friends of the family you haven't seen in years, and a few people you've never seen before. You winder if one of them is Him. You wish you could figure out which one He might be so you could follow him out to the parking lot and slit his throat with your car keys, then pull back his neck and expose the wet tissue and shit right down his throat.

(Now, now, say the Guests. *Is that any way to think at a deathbed?)*

Mom smiles at all of them, squeezes their hands, gestures for them to bend down so she can hug them and they can wipe away her tears. Warm Fingers comes back in and give Mom a shot of morphine, then stops beside you and whispers, "I have orders for two morphine shots. The second one is much stronger. I'll be at the desk, so when you want the second shot, just let me know." She touches your arm again, and this time there's a definite intimacy to her touch. You nod your head and place your hand on top of hers. For a moment her fingers entwine with yours, then she is gone.

A few moments later two technicians come in and ask for everyone except you and Lisbeth to clear the room. They wander into the hall. The first technician – a girl no older than Lisbeth, twenty-six, twenty-seven tops – closes the glass door and then pulls the curtain across it. The room becomes grey and shadowed; Death pausing to check his schedule: Here, is it? Ah, yes, I see. Okee-dokee; back in twenty minutes.

"Are you ready?" asks the technician.

You look at Lisbeth, then at Mom who still won't look at you, and say: "Yes."

She turns off the ventilator.

The sudden silence sings a sick-making sibilance of final things that cannot be taken back.

"Now, Mary," says the technician, "we have to take out the

tube now. Are you ready?"

Mom smiles around the tube and nods her head.

You look away for only a moment, hear the terrible sound of medical tape being peeled away, then decide this is something you have to see.

Mom's already wrenching upward from the force of the tube being pulled from her, her face collapsing forward, becoming a reddening gnarl of flesh as her body locks rigid and her tears stream down and her fingers shudder (somehow that is even more terrible to you than her face, the way only her fingers and not her hands shudder) and the veins bulge in her head and temples and her eyelids spasm —

— *make it stop*, you think. *OhGod I didn't think it would hurt this much, it's my fault, I'm so sorry, Mom, I'm not mad at you, I understand, I never hated you, never,*

please make it stop, please make it stop, please make it —

"Don't swallow, Mary," says the technician, her hands moving gracefully, one over the other, as she pulls and pulls and pulls.

It takes only ten seconds but it seems like ten minutes, and when it's done, when the tube has been pulled free Mom slams back against the bed with such force she actually bounces a little, and when she bounces a spray of thick black-flecked spit scatters across her face and down onto her chest and even onto your own hand even though you're standing a couple of feet away. Her face is covered in sweat but it's not quite so red now, and her chest is moving up and down as she pulls in breath and you feel the tears on your own face now, goddammit, and the snot running out of your nose but you don't move to wipe away any of it because look at her, she can't wipe the muck away so you won't, either, you'll stand here covered in your own fluids to show her that you understand, that you want to feel something of what she's going through now because this is the last thing you'll ever share, the last thing, the very, very, very last thing and you want to remember it, every specific, every detail, every minutia because you're a Good Boy and that's what a Good Boy does

(And noble, to boot. Look at all this fucking nobility. It makes you want to openly weep sensitive manly tears, it does.)

The ventilator is rolled into a corner, the tubes rolled into coils and deposited into the medical waste bin, Mom is wiped clean, and the technicians leave, opening wide the room to light and sound and the waiting throngs.

You move toward a corner and stand there, no longer trusting your legs.

Looking out of the glass, you see Warm Fingers and nod your head. She nods hers in return and runs to fetch the last syringe.

Bit by bit, Mom's eyes close — but not all the way. The light fades, the readouts become erratic, the last shot of morphine is administered . . . and then all of you wait.

No one in the room will look at you. At Lisbeth, yes, but not at you. You were the one to give the orders. You were the one who didn't get off at Cave City. You were the one with Mom's stubborn streak and the living will folded neatly in your pocket and the memory of the phone call and your ex-wife's tears when the police called about your little boy who you shouldn't have let ride his bike to the movies that day but, jeez, Dad, I'm almost ten and it's not that far and the screams in your ear of You Fucking Bastard How Many Times Have I Told You I Don't Want Him Riding That Bike Outside The Neighborhood and the fists against your face again and again and again and Dad whispering No Son of Mine Would Ever Put My Ass In A Nursing Home buy you're a Good Boy, aren't you?

(Well, say the Guests, *about that . . .)*

It takes Mom two hours and seventeen minutes to die. It is slow and painful to watch, but you never once look away.

When it is over and everyone begins to leave, you are the one who closes her eyes the rest of the way.

You wait until you are alone in the room with her, then lean down and kiss her. "I will miss you every day for the rest of my life," you say. "I loved you, Mom. I'm sorry for every bad thing I ever said to you. I'm sorry for all the times I forgot to do something for you, for all the times I could have called you but didn't, for every time you felt lonely and forgotten. Is that all right? Is it all right for me to say these things to you. It's just the two of us now, so I think it must be all right."

Then something small bursts inside you and you're crying again. "I'm sorry I wasn't a better son, a better man, a better husband and father. But Lisbeth and Eric, they gave you two wonderful grandchildren, didn't they? And they never let them ride their bikes too far from the house, you can count on that. They never get so busy with work that they just tell their kids it's okay, ride wherever you want, it'll be fine. They never do that. They never leave the bottle of prescription sleeping pills setting out open so that their Dad can sneak them into the toilet at the nursing home. They never will. They'll never disappoint you. Never.

"I have to go now, Mom, because there's a lot to do for your funeral. But I just wanted you to know that I always had the best intentions. In my heart, I always meant well. I love you. You should rest now, you've earned it."

You make sure no one is watching from outside, and you observe the moment as it passes; you can do this now, because the outcome is given. You move to one of he corners, and you take something, and then you leave.

Warm Fingers smiles sadly at you as you walk past the desk. She looks like she might cry herself. You wish she'd touch you again. Warm Fingers would forgive you all your trespasses and mistakes. Warm Fingers would understand.

*Y*ou park outside your house and see that all the lights are on. You look up at the windows and see the Guests moving around. One of them is playing the stereo. NIN. "Head Like A Hole." Too loud for this hour.

You smoke three cigarettes before going inside. The Guests don't like it when you smoke inside, and you are nothing if not a gracious host.

They're all waiting for you when you come inside. All of them have their props at the ready. None of them speak to you now. They never talk to you when you're here, only when you're gone, only when you're performing a duty like the one tonight.

One of them comes up to you, empty-handed. He's the new one. The one behind him, he arrived the day you buried

Dad. His is the face you wore the night you walked out of the nursing home knowing what Dad intended to do with those pills.

Lurking in a corner near the stereo is another guest. He showed up the night your ex-wife came over after little Andrew's funeral to slap you in the face yet again. You had been brewing water for tea and after she slapped you, you pushed her away and she fell against he stove and spilled the scalding water all over her arm. This Guest is holding the boiling kettle and wears the face you wore that night. Just like all of them. Wearing the faces you happened to have on when committing your trespasses.

The new Guest is still standing there, holding out his hand. You reach into your pocket and remove the coiled ventilator tube. He takes it with a smile and points to the chair. You remove your coat and sit down.

Other guests — the one who arrived after you had that brief affair with that temp before Andrew was born, for instance — bind your wrists and ankles to the chair.

The music changes. The James Gang. "Ashes, the Rain and I." The saddest song you've ever heard. It's important that you have sad music now.

One Guest has the pills. One the boiling water. One has the dart you stuck Johnny Sawyer with when you were six and you got mad because you thought Johnny was cheating.

There are pins. And burning cigarettes. And pieces of broken glass.

You wish you didn't remember what every last one of these items means, but you do, you remember so very, very clearly.

The phone rings. No one moves to answer it.

The answering machine picks up, gives its banal greeting, then a beep. A woman says your name. Her voice is soft and warm, just like her fingers. "This is Daphne. I'm the nurse who gave your mom the shots today. Listen, we're never supposed to do this — call patients' families personally like this — but, well . . . I just wanted to make sure you were all right. You didn't look good when you left and I was . . . oh, okay, I was worried. I hope you're not angry. I just thought that maybe you, y'know . . . needed to talk to someone. So I was wondering . . ."

Joe Walsh's voice drowns out the rest of the message. You almost smile. Maybe after all of this is over — a few weeks or however long it takes for you to heal this time — maybe you'll give her a call. Warm Fingers would be sympathetic. Warm Finger would listen. Warm Fingers would understand and squeeze your hand.

The new Guest stands in front of you, reaches out, and forces your mouth open. He has lubricated the ventilator tube with Vaseline. You remind yourself that it's important to swallow as the tube goes down. You just hope the Guest with the boiling water remembers his proper place in line.

You open wide your mouth and close your eyes. It is important for a Good Boy to remember things. Remembering, that's a duty, as well.

And you are nothing if not dutiful.

Nothing at all.

*T*here's actually a funny part to all of this.

Well, okay, maybe not fall-off-your-chair-guffawing funny, but kind of humorous; maybe not humorous so much as odd; maybe not so much odd as weird; and maybe not so much weird as it is, well . . . noteworthy.

Anyway . . .

The day I was released from the Bin I came back to the apartment where I was now living and sat down on the couch in front of the television. After a few minutes of getting acclimated to being pert of the real world again, I noticed that the VCR had been left on. I remembered that I'd been watching some movie before the crackup occurred, but I couldn't remember which one; so I turned on the television, grabbed the VCR remote, and fired up the movie.

I feel comfortable telling you this next part because it really happened, so it doesn't matter if you believe it or not.

The movie I'd been watching before trying to catch the oblivion express was John Frankenheimer's *Seconds*. I'd stopped watching it just before the final sequence where (spoiler ahead) Rock Hudson, strapped to gurney with a gag in his mouth, is being wheeled down the corridor to a room where he will be put to death so that his body can be used to fake someone else's death. The camera is planted directed over Hudson's head, and Hudson is thrashing around and screaming.

And screaming.

And screaming.

And screaming . . .

And I found myself smiling. Pulled out of my life once again by this movie, I was looking at the single most terrifying scene ever filmed, and I was smiling from ear to ear for the first time in many months because right there, right there in front of me, right there in front of me in glorious black and white was the perfect outward expression of everything that I was feeling and *had been* feeling for a long time.

Hudson kept on screaming.

I kept on smiling.

Screaming.

Smiling.

Screaming louder.

Smiling wider.

It was great. I was in tears, but it was great.

As soon as the movie was over, I turned off the television and VCR, went up to my room, popped *Quadrophenia* into my CD player, and listened to "The Rock."

Looking at a picture of my parents – the one I would use on the dedication page of *Graveyard People* – I turned up the volume just as the four themes began to merge into one, placed the photograph on my desk, rubbed my face, and thought: *This is where I came in.*

I have loved the darkness my entire life; from watching re-runs of *Zontar: The Thing from Venus* on Chiller Theater with my dad, to seeing *Christine* and *Cujo* with my mom, to all the novels and short stories that have kept me awake nights with the shivers and the jumps, I have loved the darkness and it, in its own way, has loved me in return.

That is why I have dedicated my life to horror fiction, and

have never once regretted it.

Well, okay, maybe sometimes, once in a great while, but never for long and not enough for it to really count against me.

It's the sentiment that counts, not the precision of the statement.

I can't speak for other writers, but I'm aiming for a small piece of immortality: the stories in my head will not allow anything less.

I try every month to read at least one novel or a couple of short stories in a genre that I've not read much before, if at all. High fantasy, sword & sorcery, historical fiction, romance fiction, children's books, mystery, suspense, erotica, even the dreaded *western*. And the more I read across the board, the more I see that all forms of genre fiction have a great deal in common; the more I see that all forms of genre fiction have a great deal in common, the more convinced I become that in order for genre fiction to prevail, a form of communion must take place — merging numerous forms of fiction into one — so that speculative fiction can take the next necessary step in its aesthetic evolution, but this communion cannot be forced, it has to come about naturally. Yes, I'm talking cross-genre fiction; storytelling unbound. The type of richly imaginative, wildly exciting, joyously unpredictable storytelling where you get everything from a straightforward character study to a hard-boiled mystery and even a ghost or two; not only ghosts, but cowboys, as well, if the writer feels they need to yippee-ki-yi-yea their way into a chapter or two. Time travel and high-tech intrigue, alternate universes and comedies of error; passionate romance and nerve-wracking terror — hell, throw in the kitchen sink and a robot domestic while we're at it. Go for broke — just don't go for the easy out. Read everything you can in as many different genres as possible. Don't feel that you as either writer or reader have to restrict your interest to "only cyberpunk" or "just the gaming-related fiction" or "SF, SF, and only, only, only SF!" And God please don't exclude the opinions, observations, or insights of those readers and authors who toil in fictional fields beyond the boundaries of yours.

This goes so much deeper than simply wanting all forms of speculative fiction to march to a different drummer; it's a fervent prayer that all of us will learn to foster a need and desire beyond all the needs and desires that have come before to catapult ourselves into the burning core of our imaginations and meet the whirling, winged, wondrous things that have been waiting for us to take that next step in our creative evolution. "Look at us," they'll whisper. "See what we are and know that you mustn't ever settle. Don't just be — *become!* And don't just become — *transcend!*" It's a prayer that we'll someday be able to get rid of all the misconceptions that insultingly oversimplify what the work is about because it will be impossible for anyone, no matter how hard they try, to put a label on our fiction.

Storytelling unbound, wherein we can do anything we want, anytime, and in any manner, knowing that there are truly no limits — and God, is that kind of knowledge power. We'll know, then, that a summer sky can be poured into a silver chalice and drunk down like Bacchus's headiest brew, that the touch of a lover's fingertips against the skin or the brushing of lips holds the answer to what love and life were supposed to be, every emotion revealing the sensual, smoldering, staggering beauty of the cosmos.

Storytelling unbound.

To live a thousand lives where every second is drenched in overpowering wonder, then turning yourself loose on an empty sheet of paper to see if you can possibility convey this amazement to others, rejecting rationality enough to have faith in the un-nameable *something* that drives you to want more out of your fiction than simply "a good read," that pushes you to push yourself and your work to new heights and maybe, just maybe, capture a piece of the Divine.

And you know where this revolution should start?

Down there in the darkness that I have loved all my life, that darkness in Literature's basement, with that drooling, scab-picking embarrassment of a bastard child called "horror" that no one wants to admit exists. No one's paying attention to it, not really, and those chains on the wall won't hold forever, so why not start now, while the shadows are there to protect us? By the time the lights come back on and the chains fall away, we'll be armed to the teeth with our stories and ideas and memories of drinking the sky from a silver chalice, and *then* just let 'em try to ignore us or lock us away once again.

Let 'em try.

My favorite poem is "I Saw A Man" by Stephen Crane. God, I get chills every time I read it or hear it read:

> *I saw a man pursuing the horizon;*
> *Round and round they sped.*
> *I was disturbed at this;*
> *I accosted the man.*
> *"It is futile," I said,*
> *"You can never —"*
> *"You lie!" he cried.*
> *And ran on.*

That should be the horror writer's battle cry against those who would tell him or her that their work must conform to specific genre boundaries and never, ever, ever dare venture beyond those boundaries because something that is too different isn't acceptable, even in speculative fiction.

"You lie!" we cry, and then on we go, chasing the horizon, freed from illusionary boundaries implied by popular misconceptions. Don't you want that from our fiction? To capture the horizon, to drink down the sky from a silver chalice, to know that, whenever you need it, a dream will call and raise its head in majesty?

Storytelling unbound.

But know this: You may be forced to live outside their city walls when your fiction "doesn't quite fit anywhere" because they'll be scared of you. "He must be mad," they'll say. "How else do you explain his producing this sort of stuff?" Then they'll go on coughing up safe, derivative fiction, occasionally looking down at the asphalt to make sure their feet are still on the ground while *you*, you'll be kissing the hem of Venus's gown and flying alongside Daedalus and solving crimes with Marlowe and dancing with Gatsby atop the Pyramid of the moon at a celestial ball given by the gods of ancient Mexico while vampires, ghosts, and robots gather round the base and sing otherworldly chants.

It's really nice outside those city walls, trust me. You don't have to write what they say you should write, you don't have to settle for reading the same old same old thing repackaged and rewritten for the umpteenth time. You can be, you can become, you can transcend! So come on, all ye Cyberpunks, ye Gamers and dreamers of darkness, ye techno-files, *X-Filers*, *Babylon* 5ers, and Trekkers true, come on all ye mystery mavens of the hard-boiled and cozy schools, ye romance writers and historical scribes with your sense and sensibilities refined, ye rusty-spurred cowpokes and poets of brilliant brevity, over there, ye comics connoisseurs and artists, with pencils and paintbrush and airbrush raised high, step outside, join us beyond the city gates; you'll see our campfires burning in the night as we gather round to spin our tales in the manner, *any* manner, we damn well choose. Join us. Our ranks are growing. You'll find no prejudice here by our fires, no one who'll say "It just doesn't fit." Bring your dreams, your angers, your sadnesses and passions as we begin our communion: all fictions merging into one.

And when you hear them calling to you from behind the city walls to come back, come back, come back here where everything is safe and in its place, remember the sacred words as you reach toward the horizon's hands:

"You lie!" we cry.

Storytelling unbound.

*S*neaking back into that theater where I'm sitting watching Rob Zombie's *House of a Thousand Corpses* ooze its way across the screen, we see that the credits are rolling and I am rising with a glassy look in my eyes. Everyone who saw this with me is wasting no time spewing their venom at Zombie, at the movie, and the state of horror in general . . . but mostly at the movie.

I should have hated this thing.

But I didn't.

Why did I think about Art while watching it?

Because it disturbed me on a very primal level, which is what art is supposed to do. Does it bother me that I'm grouping this movie and the concept of art in the same thought — and now in the same sentence?

Hell, yes.

But that's part of the game, isn't it — having to consider the merits of something on its own terms and not those you try grafting onto it through your own sensibilities.

I still can't put my finger on why I liked this movie, but I'll figure it out eventually.

Stay tuned.

*T*ime to make a semi-graceful exit, fellow revolutionaries. Take up those swords. Kick down those boundaries the next time you try to scare the shit out of me.

You know the battle-cry now, so —

— turn out those lights. Do it now.

You know you want to; like me, you have loved the darkness all your lives.

Ready? I thought so.

Onward. . . .

www.ingramcontent.com/pod-product-compliance
Lightning Source LLC
Chambersburg PA
CBHW030415100426
42812CB00028B/2965/J